Principles
of Classroom
Management

Principles of Classroom Management

A Hierarchical Approach

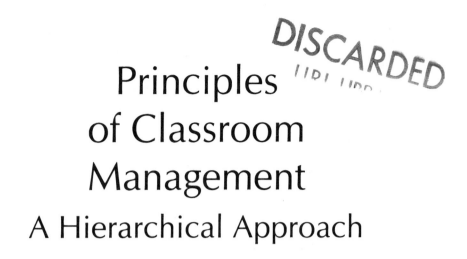

James Levin
Penn State University

James F. Nolan
Penn State University

Prentice Hall
Englewood Cliffs, NJ 07632

Library of Congress Cataloging-in-Publication Data

LEVIN, JAMES, (DATE)
    Principles of classroom management : a hierarchical approach /
James Levin, James F. Nolan.
      p.   cm.
    Includes bibliographical references and index.
    ISBN 0-13-691171-4
    1. Classroom management—United States—Problems, exercises, etc.
2. Teaching—Problems, exercises, etc. I. Nolan, James F., (date)
    II. Title.
LB3013.L47 1991
371.1'024--dc20

90-37550
CIP

Editorial/production supervision and
   interior design: Marianne Peters
Cover design: Miriam Recio
Prepress buyer: Debra Kesar
Manufacturing buyer: Mary Ann Gloriande

© 1991 by Prentice-Hall, Inc.
A Division of Simon & Schuster
Englewood Cliffs, New Jersey 07632

Printed in the United States of America
10 9 8 7 6 5 4 3 2 1

ISBN 0-13-691171-4

Prentice-Hall International (UK) Limited, *London*
Prentice-Hall of Australia Pty. Limited, *Sydney*
Prentice-Hall Canada Inc., *Toronto*
Prentice-Hall Hispanoamericana, S.A., *Mexico*
Prentice-Hall of India Private Limited, *New Delhi*
Prentice-Hall of Japan, Inc., *Tokyo*
Simon & Schuster Asia Pte. Ltd., *Singapore*
Editora Prentice-Hall do Brasil, Ltda., *Rio de Janeiro*

To
Sylvia and Herman Levin,
Jim and Mary Nolan,
Rocky and Andy—
for their support,
encouragement, and understanding

Contents

Appendix   **The Discipline Problem Analysis
Inventory (DPAI)**   **239**

Index   **245**

Preface

It was a warm sunny day in early June as I accepted my baccalaureate degree in engineering with a certificate to teach mathematics in the state's secondary public schools. The next day I was interviewed at the school administration building of a very large urban school district. Within a few days I was notified that, starting in September, I was to be a junior high school mathematics teacher.

The following week I met with the principal of the inner city school. The principal informed me that the school was the largest junior high in the city and one of the largest in the nation, with an enrollment of approximately 3,500 students. It served a blue collar community, with an ethnic background equally divided among whites, blacks, and hispanics. Classes were large, averaging approximately thirty-five students, but absenteeism was prevalent. The principal warned me that many of the students were low achievers and that the school had more than its share of discipline problems. He stressed that the school needed dedicated teachers and assigned me to teach four classes of eighth-grade general math and one class of ninth-grade algebra.

Over the summer I thought about what teaching would be like. How could I not do a good job? After all I graduated from the same urban district. I was tough and felt that I could handle teenagers. Also, my engineering degree provided me with the knowledge to relate mathematics to the students' lives; something I learned was necessary for effective teaching in my educational psychology class.

I arrived early the first day of classes and was met by the assistant principal. After welcoming me to the staff, she informed me that throughout the year she would observe my classes and work closely with me to help improve my teaching. With seating charts, a·list of rules, and a lesson plan that contained activities that I knew would capture my students' attention, I was ready to become a teacher.

As soon as school was in session, the vice principal visited at least one of my classes every week. The visits were always followed by an after-school conference, during which we discussed the observations that she made and plans for future classes. She was quite observant in noting both my and the students' behaviors in class, many of which I was unaware of. She continually stressed that teachers must not only be aware of their behavior, but how their behaviors effected students' behaviors.

One result of these conferences was that I began to watch other teachers, and particularly the vice principal, as they interacted with students. I noticed that she commanded the students' respect as no one else in the school.

As November arrived I was quite pleased with all my classes except my fifth period eighth-grade general math class. Students were constantly unprepared, out of their seats, calling out, and disturbing others. In other words, this class was out of control. I tried talking to them and reasoning with them. Then I began to scream, give detentions, and exclude students from class; but nothing seemed to work. This class began to ruin my day. It made me nervous, frustrated, and doubtful about my effectiveness as a teacher.

On numerous occasions the vice principal visited this class, noted how disruptive the students were, and continually asked how I planned on handling the situation. Finally around Thanksgiving, during one of our conferences, I reluctantly confessed to her that I needed help with my fifth period class. She said that she was waiting for me to realize that the class was not improving. Using her notes from past observations, we began to discuss my own and the students' behaviors in the class.

She pointed out that I began class when the bell rang no matter what the students were doing. After a few moments I would reprimand a few students and demand that they sit. This resulted in only a few additional minutes of quiet before the next disruption exploded. She also pointed out that I always reminded them, "I have material to cover, and I can't cover it if you don't stop fooling around!" She stressed that I was continually competing with my students and appeared to feel totally responsible for their learning. She asked if I was willing to begin to change my teaching behavior. I eagerly answered, "Yes!"

She suggested that I go to class prepared to teach as usual and when the bell rang start the lesson. She further suggested that as soon as the class interfered with my ability to teach, stop, and not saying a word, sit down at my desk. With a smile on my face, I told her that this would play right into the students' hands because this would allow them to engage in disruptive behavior during the entire class without any teacher reprimands. She reassured me by pointing out that what I had been doing wasn't working, so it was time for new approaches. She asked that I try it, and report back to her with the results.

The next day I employed these new techniques. I taught for only five minutes when the class became disruptive. As I had predicted, when I stopped teaching the students proceeded to walk around the room talking and kidding with each other for the rest of the forty-five minute period.

Upon hearing this, the vice principal asked me to please use the same strategy the next day. I did, and as on the previous day, within five to ten minutes I was sitting at my desk. However, by the end of class a significant change took place. A student came up to my desk and said, "Aren't you going to teach us any math?" I replied, "Yes. I'm ready to teach, but I can't when the class behaves the way it does." When I reported this event to her she was very pleased and told me that she felt the technique was beginning to have an effect. She requested that I continue to employ the same strategy.

The next day, I was able to teach for about twenty minutes before I had to sit down. But unlike the previous days, by the last ten minutes of class, the students were ending their conversations and most of the class was in their seats. When I observed this, I began to teach again. To my surprise, the next day I had to stop my teaching for only five minutes in the middle of the period.

Throughout the year, my fifth period class continued to be my most troublesome, but the class never returned to the way it was earlier in the year. Whenever their behavior reached a point that disrupted either my teaching or the students' learning, I stopped teaching and without my having to say a word, within minutes the disruption ceased.

This early experience in teaching taught me two important lessons. First, don't compete with your students or assume the full responsibility for their learning. Learning is a dual responsibility of both student and teacher. Second, if teachers want students' behaviors to change, they must first examine their own behavior and be willing to change any inappropriate or ineffective ones. These lessons have stayed with me throughout my teaching career and have assisted me in shaping my philosophy of classroom management. It is these two concepts that serve as the foundation of this book.

Throughout this book case studies have been used extensively to illustrate classroom management principles and techniques. Each of these cases is drawn from actual classroom experiences of the authors, who have combined experiences of over seventeen years of classroom teaching in rural, suburban, and urban schools and over eighteen years supervising hundreds of inservice and preservice teachers in hundreds of different classrooms. This book is a practical, eclectic approach to classroom management based upon both theory and practice.

ACKNOWLEDGMENTS

The authors wish to acknowledge the contributions of many people who have helped with the completion of this book: Dr. Andrea Commaker, Assistant Director of Penn State's Scholars Program, for her excellent critical feedback, editing, and encouragement throughout the development of the book; Dr. Benson Gever, psychologist, whose years of working with children provided significant contributions to the final chapter; and Dr. Robert Shrigley, Professor of Education, Penn State University, for introducing us to the systematic study of classroom management. Thanks also go to Patricia Simmett and Dawn Nelson for typing the manuscript and Sam Baldi, Andy Commaker, Jacque and Shannon Ewing, Joe Hall, Heidi and Sarah Levin, Earl Merritt, Rebekah Myers, David Petkosh, Mariah Rohrabaugh, and Amy Wade for their assistance with photographs.

We would also like to thank the following reviewers for their suggestions: Thomas J. Lasley, University of Dayton; Mark Pitts, Seattle Pacific University; and Eugene C. Schaffer, University of North Carolina—Charlotte.

As always, our thanks go to Rocky, Geoff, Daniel, Andy, Heidi, and Sarah for their understanding, interest, and encouragement. Finally, thanks to all the teachers, student teachers, and the many disruptive students who provided the real examples used throughout the text.

CHAPTER 1

The Basics

THE BASICS
Conceptualizing the Process of Teaching
Understanding Classroom Management Principles
Understanding the Hierarchical Approach

PRINCIPLES OF CLASSROOM MANAGEMENT

1. The single most important factor in determining the learning environment is teacher behavior. Intentionally or unintentionally, teachers' verbal and non-verbal behaviors influence student behaviors.
2. Teachers have the professional responsibility for assuming the role of instructional leader, which involves employing techniques that maximize student on-task behavior.
3. Teachers who have clearly developed ideas of: (a) the relationship between teaching and discipline; (b) the factors motivating students to behave as they do; (c) their personal expectations for student behavior; and (d) a systematic plan to manage misbehavior have classrooms characterized by a high percentage of on-task student behavior.
4. A preplanned hierarchy of management strategies increases the likelihood of appropriate student behavior.

INTRODUCTION

Many years ago we both had the opportunity to take a graduate class on classroom management. It was our first formalized instruction in this area. At that time not much research had been conducted on the subject of classroom management. Even with this limitation the instructor did an excellent job of organizing what was available into a systematic approach for managing disruptive behavior.

However, one persistent problem in this class comes to mind. Throughout students continually asked the instructor to define teaching and explain how teaching and classroom management were related. A satisfactory answer was never really given. This lack of specificity disturbed many students. Throughout the class questions about the relationship between teaching and classroom management continually arose: Should a teacher plan objectives for classroom management in her* lesson plan? How

---

* Gender pronouns, to foster equality without being cumbersome (for example, using *her/his* or *he/she* each time), will be alternated by chapter. Chapter One will have female pronouns; Chapter Two, male; Chapter Three, female; and so forth.

do various teaching strategies increase or reduce the likelihood of disruptive behavior? Should a student's grades be affected by misbehavior?

The lack of a definition of teaching not only plagued this class but also was a problem in several other education courses. Even today many books on management and many teachers who use various management techniques do so without having a clear definition of teaching. Classroom management is intricately related to teaching. They cannot exist independently of one another.

Therefore we begin by setting forth a definition of teaching and explaining how classroom management is part of the teaching process. The rest of this chapter presents a structural overview of the book. First, we present the principles of management that form the book's foundation. Second, an explanation of the hierarchical approach to management is provided. Last, the flowchart of the knowledge, skills, and techniques of the management hierarchy that results in successful classrooms—in which teachers are free to teach and students are free to learn—is illustrated.

DEFINING THE PROCESS OF TEACHING

Each year colleges and universities educate and graduate thousands of students who then enter the teaching profession. All of these future teachers have accumulated many credit hours of coursework in their chosen area of specialization, in professional knowledge, in methodology, and in practical experiences. With this background, they enter the classrooms of our schools and teach for an average of almost 20 years (National Education Association, 1987).

Even with all this education and experience, many teachers, including seasoned professionals as well as recent graduates, surprisingly are unable to provide an adequate operational definition of teaching. For instance, when pre- or in-service teachers are asked to define teaching, common responses include the delivery of knowledge, transferance of knowledge, giving information, or in many cases just blank stares. These definitions are grossly inadequate and provide little in the way of conceptualizing the extremely complicated process of teaching. Such descriptions give no clue to how such knowledge is transferred and what strategies are used to deliver it. They limit teaching to only the cognitive domain, thus failing to recognize the extraordinary level of competence needed for making hundreds of daily decisions in complex and dynamic classroom environments.

Teaching always has and will continue to emphasize the cognitive domain. However, when teaching is viewed as being concerned solely with cognitive development, teachers limit their effectiveness in managing students who exhibit disruptive behavior. Disruptive students often need growth and development not only in cognitive areas but also in the affective domain, such as cooperating with others, valuing others' viewpoints, volunteering, and developing motivation and interest. Teachers who understand the critical nature of the affective domain are in a much better position to work with disruptive students. These teachers do not get as frustrated or feel as if they are wasting their time when working with disruptive students because they understand that teaching is helping students mature not only cognitively but also affectively.

Some teachers argue that a formal definition of teaching is not necessary because they have been teaching for years and whatever they do seems to work. However, this approach is not adequate for those of us who consider teaching to be a more professionally sophisticated endeavor. Although experience is invaluable in many teaching situations, it is not the only means that should be used to develop and plan instruction. In addition, this "gut-reaction" approach is sorely limited when the old "proven methods" seem not to work and there is a need for modifying or developing new instructional or management strategies.

A formal definition of any profession is necessary to guide the activities of its practitioners. Teaching is no exception. When teaching is defined, teachers have a clearer perception of what behaviors constitute the practice of their profession.

Before we present a formal definition of teaching, we must consider an important underlying assumption concerning human behavior, which we deem essential for fully comprehending our definition of teaching. One of the major tenets of Adlerian psychology is that individuals make a conscious choice to behave in certain ways, either desirable or undesirable (Sweeney, 1981). Building on this principle, we believe that individuals cannot be forced to change their behavior. Therefore, individuals cannot be forced either to learn or to exhibit appropriate behavior. If this idea is accepted, it follows that teachers change student behavior only by *influencing* the change, not *forcing* it. This is the basis for our definition of teaching.

It is widely accepted that teachers influence change in student behavior by controlling and changing their own behavior. The teacher is continually involved in a process in which student behavior is monitored and compared with the teacher's idea of appropriate behavior for any given instructional activity. When actual student behavior differs from appropriate student behavior, the teacher attempts to influence a change in student behavior by changing her own behavior. The behavior the teacher decides to employ should be one that maximizes the likelihood that student behavior will change in the appropriate way. The probability of choosing the most effective behavior increases when teachers have a professional knowledge of instructional techniques, learning psychology, and child development and use it to guide the modification of their own behavior (Brophy, 1988).

Through lesson planning teachers can select strategies that have a good probability of affecting positive change in student behavior. (Ken Karp)

Therefore we define teaching as *the use of preplanned behaviors, founded in learning principles and child development theory and directed toward both instructional delivery and classroom mangement, which increase the probability of affecting a positive change in student behavior.* The significance of this definition in trying to change any student's behavior is threefold. First, teaching is concerned with teacher behavior, and this behavior is preplanned. Teaching is not a capricious activity. Second, the preplanned behaviors are determined by the teachers' professional knowledge. This knowledge guides them in selecting appropriate behaviors. It is the application of this specialized body of professional knowledge that makes teaching a profession. Third, there are many teaching behaviors that are well founded in professional knowledge. The teacher's challenge is to select those behaviors that increase the probability that a corresponding behavioral change will take place in the student. For this to occur, the teacher must not only know the students' initial behaviors but also have a clear picture of desired student behaviors for any given instructional activity. Because changes in teacher behavior produce changes in student behavior, the former is often termed "affecting behavior" and the sought-after student behavior is termed "target behavior" (Boyan and Copeland, 1978).

Case 1: Getting Students to Respond

Ms. Kelly believes that students must actively participate in class activities for learning to take place. She prides herself on her ability to design questions from all levels of the cognitive domain; she believes that students benefit and enjoy working with those questions that require analysis, synthesis, and evaluation. However, she is sorely disappointed because very few students have been volunteering to answer questions and those that have give very brief answers.

Observation of Ms. Kelly's class indicates a fairly regular pattern of behaviors during questioning. Standing in front of the class, she asks the first question: "Students we have been studying the westward movement of pioneers during the 1800s. Why do you think so many thousands of people picked up and moved thousands of miles to a strange land knowing that they would face incredible hardship and suffering during the long trip?" Two hands immediately shot up. Ms. Kelly immediately called on Judy. "Judy, why do you think they went?" "They wanted new opportunities," she answered. Ms. Kelly immediately replied "Great answer. Things where they lived must have been so bad that they decided that it was worth the hardships that they would face. In a new land they would have a new beginning, a chance to start over. Another thing might be that some of the pioneers might not have realized how difficult the trip would be. Do you think that the hardships continued even after the pioneers arrived in Oregon and California? Ted."

After discussion, Ms. Kelly realizes how her behaviors are affecting student behavior. Instead of increasing participation, they actually serve to hinder students from answering questions. After further discussions and readings about questioning strategies, she decides to change her questioning behavior. Ms. Kelly begins to ask questions from different locations throughout the room. She also waits between three to five seconds before calling on any student. After students answer, she again waits at least three seconds and then points out the salient parts of the response, rephrases another question using the student's response, and redirects this question back to the class.

As before, her behaviors affect student behavior. However, this time more students volunteer initially, responses are longer, and additional students are willing to expand on initial answers.

Case 1 illustrates the application of the definition of teaching to instructional delivery. Ms. Kelly was aware of the present student behavior and had a clear picture of what she wanted the behavior to be during questioning. To effect this change she modified her questioning behaviors. The behaviors she chose to employ were well founded in the educational literature on questioning methodology (see Chapter Five). Ms. Kelly performed as a professional. She analyzed her behaviors and how they affected

Asking questions from different locations in a classroom can increase student participation.

her students, and then, using her professional knowledge, modified her behavior to improve her practice of teaching.

The following case illustrates the relationship between teacher behavior and targeted student behavior in classroom management.

Case 2: Why Study? We Don't Get Enough Time for the Test Anyway!"

Mr. Fox has a rule that test papers will not be passed out until all students are quiet, in their seats, with all materials except a pencil under the desk. He explains this to the class before every test. Without fail he has to wait five to ten minutes before everyone in the class is ready. Typically, some students complain: "Why did they have less time just because a few other kids take their good old time?" Sometimes students would get visibly angry, explaining "This isn't fun," "This is stupid," or "Why study? We don't get enough time anyway!" Mr. Fox dreads test days.

In discussing this situation with another teacher, Mr. Fox is introduced to the concept of logical consequences, in other words, allowing students to experience a logically related consequence of their behavior. Employing this concept, Mr. Fox decides to change his pretest behavior. He announces to the class that he will pass out tests on an individual basis. "Once you are ready, you receive a test." He walks down the aisles giving students who are ready a test paper and passes by without comment those who are not. As a result of his changed behavior, student behavior changes, complaining stops, and more students are ready to take the test much more quickly.

As did Ms. Kelly, Mr. Fox changed his behavior to one that reflected a well-accepted educational practice. With this change came corresponding changes in student behavior.

How do teachers become aware of the methodology and theory on which to support their behaviors and from where do the methodology and theory come? The methodology and theory originally were generated by research, often conducted by educational psychologists in controlled laboratory settings. These findings were then applied to classroom situations, where they may or may not have been applied properly and may or may not have resulted in expected outcomes. Research about teaching moved into the modern era only within the last 25 years, when reliable, replicable studies began being conducted in actual classrooms with real teachers (Berliner, 1984).

Teaching research has accumulated rapidly and demonstrates that a set of teacher behaviors is present in many classrooms in which noteworthy gains in achievement are made by students. These behaviors are referred to as effective teaching or effective instruction. Teachers need to incorporate these effective teaching behaviors into their daily instruction. This may be accomplished by becoming thoroughly familiar with the professional literature that synthesizes and summarizes the research (Brophy, 1987; Good, 1987; Hosford, 1984; Office of the Superintendent of Public Instruction, 1986; Rosenshine, 1986; Smith, 1983; Wittrock, 1986). See also Chapter Five. A more experiential approach may be participation in many of the formalized workshops that use the research to develop effective teaching practices, such as Madeline Hunter's "Essential Elements of Instruction" and Phi Delta Kappa's "Teacher Expectations Student Achievement Program."

Although not as plentiful, research has also resulted in a body of knowledge concerning effective classroom management (Emmer et al., 1989; Evertson et al., 1989; Kounin, 1970; Redl and Wineman, 1952). As stressed throughout this book, effective classroom management is inseparable from effective instruction. Without effective instructional practices, teachers are unlikely to be able to maintain successfully appropriate student behavior. However, although effective instruction is absolutely necessary, it

Many teachers keep up to date on the latest teaching techniques by attending professional staff development workshops. (Laima Druskis)

is not in itself sufficient to guarantee that classrooms are free from disruptive behavior. Even the best teachers experience some disruptive behavior.

PRINCIPLES OF CLASSROOM MANAGEMENT

As with research on effective teaching, the research on classroom management has resulted in the formulation of well-accepted principles governing teacher behavior to prevent and control disruptive behavior. Some of these principles are quite specific to a particular philosophical underpinning (See Chapter Four), whereas others are philosophically generic. This book presents 37 generic principles of classroom management developed through years of experience, research, and study. Each of the remaining nine chapters emphasizes some of these principles and discusses in detail how they may be incorporated by the teacher into her effective management practices.

Following is an overview consisting of a summary of the contents of each chapter and its relevant principles followed by an explanation of its hierarchical approach to managing classroom behavior. Just as it is good classroom practice to provide the learner with an anticipatory set before in-depth instruction, this summary provides the reader with the scope, sequence, and structure of this textbook.

Chapter Two discusses the nature of the discipline problem. First, there is a review of the limitations of current definitions of what behaviors constitute a discipline problem. These limitations are rectified by offering a new operational definition of the term *discipline problem*. This definition is then used to classify which common classroom behaviors represent true discipline problems. Second, misbehavior is analyzed historically by frequency and type to determine what schools really are like today. Finally, research concerning the effect of disruptive behavior on both teachers and students is presented.

The related principles of classroom management are the following:

> A discipline problem exists whenever a behavior interferes with the teaching act, interferes with the rights of others to learn, is psychologically or physically unsafe, or destroys property.
>
> For effective teaching to take place, teachers must be competent in managing student misbehavior so as to maximize the time spent on learning.
>
> Teachers who manage their classrooms effectively enjoy teaching more and have greater confidence in their ability to affect student achievement.

Chapter Three provides multiple reasons why children misbehave by exploring the underlying complex causes of misbehavior. Societal changes have created an environment vastly different than that in which children of previous generations grew up. How these out-of-school changes have influenced children's attitudes and behaviors is examined first.

Children, like adults, have strong personal, social, and academic needs. At the same time, children undergo rapid cognitive and moral development. Typical behaviors associated with children's attempts to meet their needs and normal developmental behaviors are given. Behaviors that may appear when the home or school fails to recognize and respond to these needs and developmental changes are detailed.

It is emphasized that the teacher has little control over many of the changes that occur in society and in children. However, she does have total control over her instructional competence. Excellent instruction is a significant means to lessen the effects of uncontrollable factors as well as to prevent misbehavior from occurring.

The principles in Chapter Three are these:

> Teachers' awareness of the causes of misbehavior enables them to use positive control techniques rather than negative approaches stemming from erroneously viewing misbehavior as a personal affront.
>
> Basic human needs such as food, safety, belonging, and security are prerequisites for appropriate classroom behavior.
>
> Students' need for a sense of significance, competence, and power influences their behavior.

Societal changes beyond the schools' control exert much influence on student behavior.

Cognitive and moral developmental changes result in normal student behavior that often is disruptive in learning environments.

Instructional competence can ameliorate the effects of negative outside influences as well as prevent the misbehavior that occurs as a direct result of poor instruction.

Chapter Four describes three theoretical models of classroom management. Seven questions underlying one's beliefs about classroom management are presented. These questions are then used to analyze, compare, and contrast the three models. It is stressed that the teacher's underlying beliefs concerning how children learn and develop and who has the primary responsibility for controlling their behavior determine which model provides the best fit.

Different management strategies are presented as either compatible or incompatible with certain schools of thought. When teachers employ behaviors that are inconsistent with their beliefs about children, they feel emotionally uncomfortable and usually do not see the desired change in student behavior.

Similarly, teachers exert control through the use of five different social power bases. Each power base is placed along a continuum, which begins with those power bases most likely to engender students' control over their own behavior and proceeds to those bases that foster increasing teacher control over student behavior. The behaviors the teacher uses to manage the classroom that are congruent with the various power bases are discussed.

The principles of classroom management contained in Chapter Four are the following:

Theoretical approaches to classroom management are useful to teachers because they offer a basis whereby student and teacher behavior can be analyzed, understood, and controlled.

As social agents, teachers have access to a variety of power bases that can be used to influence student behavior.

The techniques a teacher employs to control student behavior should be consistent with the teacher's beliefs about how students learn and develop.

Chapter Five explores the effective instructional techniques used by the professional teacher. Effective teaching prevents most discipline problems from occurring. The components of effective teaching, based on recent research, are defined and explained. Students' positive perception of the teacher's instructional effectiveness increases the teacher's classroom authority, thus reducing the occurrence of misbehavior.

The two relevant principles are these:

Student learning and on-task behavior are maximized when teaching strategies are based on what educators know about student development, how people learn, and effective teaching.

Understanding and using the research on effective teaching enhances the teacher's instructional competence and helps to prevent classroom management problems.

Chapter Six details how to structure the environment to minimize disruptive behavior. Many classroom management problems arise because students are either unaware of or unclear about what types of behaviors are expected of them or why certain procedures must be followed in the classroom. This usually occurs when the teacher herself is unclear about how and why she wants her students to behave. Thus, developing meaningful classroom guidelines is extremely necessary.

The procedures for designing classroom guidelines are presented, with emphasis on the importance of having both a rationale and stated consequences for each rule. Techniques are given to communicate guidelines to students so that they understand and accept the guidelines. Besides setting long-term guidelines, a teacher must consider daily four ever-changing factors: student characteristics, teacher characteristics, learning activities, and environmental concerns. The components of each of these factors and their interactions make up a teacher's vulnerability quotient, that is, the likelihood of discipline problems arising. Techniques to ensure a low vulnerability quotient are then set forth.

Chapter Six's principles include the following:

When environmental conditions are appropriate for learning, the likelihood of disruptive behavior is minimized.

Students are more likely to follow classroom guidelines when the teacher models appropriate behavior and explains the guidelines' relationship to learning, mutual student and teacher respect, and protection and safety of property and individuals.

Clearly communicating guidelines to students and obtaining their commitment to them enhance appropriate classroom behavior.

Enforcing teacher expectations by using natural and logical consequences helps students learn that they are responsible for the consequences of their behavior and for controlling their own behavior.

The probability of classroom discipline problems occurring is reduced when teachers consider and modify, where necessary and possible, the interactions of student characteristics, teacher characteristics, environmental factors, and teaching and learning activities.

Chapters Seven and Eight explore the control of common misbehaviors by using a three-tiered hierarchical decision-making model of nonverbal and verbal behaviors called coping skills.

Research reviewed in Chapter Seven reveals that the majority of misbehaviors are verbal interruptions, off-task behavior, and disruptive physical movements. The frequency of these surface disruptions can be greatly reduced with proper planning, instructional strategies, environmental structure, and verbal and nonverbal teacher behaviors.

Chapter Seven covers the first tier of the decision-making hierarchy. It discusses the appropriate use and limitations of four nonverbal coping skills: planned ignoring, signal interference, proximity control, and touch control. Included is an intervention decision-making model that hierarchically orders nonverbal behaviors teachers can use to manage student behavior. The hierarchy begins with nonintrusive techniques that give students the greatest opportunity to control their own behaviors and proceeds to intrusive strategies in which the teacher assumes more responsibility for controlling student behavior.

Chapter Seven covers the following principles:

> Classroom management techniques need to be consistent with the goal of helping students become self-directing individuals.
>
> Use of a preplanned hierarchy of coping skills improves the teacher's ability to manage misbehavior.
>
> The hierarchy of coping skills is structured so that it starts with nonintrusive, nonverbal teacher behaviors, which give students the opportunity for self-control and cause little if any disruption to the teaching and learning process.

Chapter Eight discusses in detail the second and third tiers of the decision-making hierarchy, verbal intervention and application of logical consequences. Twelve verbal intervention techniques are presented along with nine guidelines for their appropriate use as well as their limitations. Once again these techniques are ordered along a continuum that ranges from nonintrusive student control to intrusive teacher control of behavior. The use of verbal intervention is founded on the assumption that teachers do have effective alternatives to angry, personal, sarcastic confrontations with students. Such alternatives typically defuse rather than escalate misbehavior.

The third tier of the decision-making hierarchy, application of logical consequences, is a powerful technique in controlling student behavior. The concept of logical consequence is explained in detail along with guidelines teachers use to develop effective logical consequences for a wide range of misbehavior.

These are the principles dealt with in Chapter Eight:

> When nonverbal teacher intervention does not result in appropriate student behavior, the teacher should employ verbal intervention to deal with the misbehavior.
>
> Some forms of verbal intervention defuse confrontation and reduce misbehavior, whereas other forms of verbal intervention actually escalate misbehavior and confrontation.

When verbal intervention does not lead to appropriate student behavior, the teacher needs to employ logical consequences to the student's misconduct.

Chapter Nine looks at classroom interventions for students with chronic problems. Most strategies used with chronic behavior problems involve referral outside the classroom. However, there are two effective field-tested in-classroom strategies: behavior contracting and anecdotal record keeping. The effective use of these two strategies assumes that the teacher's classroom behaviors have met the prerequisites discussed in previous chapters and reviewed here. The step-by-step implementation of these strategies is specifically explained along with a detailed discussion of the critical communication skills that can make the difference in successful management of chronic misbehavior. Lastly, teacher-controlled exclusion from the classroom, an interim step between in-classroom management and outside referral, is explained.

The guiding principles are the following:

When dealing with students who pose chronic discipline problems, teachers should employ strategies to resolve the problem within the classroom before seeking outside assistance.

When teachers employ effective communication skills in private conferences with students who have chronic discipline problems, such conferences are more likely to be productive in resolving the problem.

Techniques requiring students to recognize their inappropriate behaviors and their effect on themselves and others maximize the likelihood of improved behavior.

Techniques that require students to be accountable for controlling their own behavior on a daily basis maximize the likelihood of improved behavior.

Management techniques that call for gradual but consistent behavioral improvement by students who pose chronic discipline problems maximize the likelihood of long-term improvement.

The final chapter offers advice on seeking assistance. When in-classroom techniques have been exhausted and have not resulted in appropriate student behavior, it is necessary to seek outside sources of assistance. Teachers are offered guidelines to follow when deciding whether or not outside consultation is warranted. The concept of a success/failure ratio is explained along with a discussion of how this ratio contributes to persisting misbehavior.

Other students may need outside referral even though they do not display any chronic forms of misbehavior. These students exhibit certain signs that may be symptomatic of emotional stress or family dysfunction. Six such warning signs are discussed.

A referral process that stresses multidisciplinary team consultation is offered as an effective means of working with such students. The roles of the counselor, parents, administrator, and school psychologist as members of this team are presented along with the legal issues that must be considered when making outside referrals.

Parental support and cooperation with the school is critical when working with chronically misbehaving students. Specific guidelines that teachers can use to decide when parents need to be contacted are outlined. Techniques on how to conduct parent conferences to facilitate and enhance parental support and cooperation are discussed.

The classroom management principles in Chapter Ten are these:

> Professional teachers recognize that some chronic misbehavior problems are not responsive to treatment within the classroom or are beyond their expertise and necessitate specialized outside assistance.

> When outside assistance must be sought to manage a chronic misbehavior problem adequately and appropriately, the use of a multidisciplinary team is the most effective approach.

> Parental support and cooperation with the school is critical when attempting to manage a chronically misbehaving student. Careful planning and skilled conferencing techniques are essential in developing a positive home-school working relationship.

THE HIERARCHICAL APPROACH

Hierarchies, taxonomies, and *classifications* are all terms used to describe an orderly arrangement of objects, concepts, or strategies, which are systematically placed along a continuum of one or more properties. Placement along the continuum indicates the degree of relatedness of individual entries with respect to the properties on which the continuum is constructed. Hierarchies, taxonomies, and classification systems are used to organize information and guide the delivery of professional practice in many fields. Such organizational schemes allow vast amounts of isolated bits of data to become manageable, comprehensible bodies of related information and knowledge.

Some common examples of classification systems to organize scientific information are the periodic table of elements in chemistry, the taxonomy of the plant and animal kingdom in biology, and the electromagnetic spectrum in physics. In the social sciences there are the taxonomies of cognitive, affective, and psychomotor abilities in education and stages of cognitive and moral development in psychology, as well as many more.

Professional practices are also guided by the use of hierarchical approaches. Some examples are scientists, who use the scientific method to guide their inquiries; doctors, who diagnose and treat patients by using a step-by-step approach; and teachers, who question students by using hierarchical delivery strategies. The advantage of using a hierarchical approach is twofold: (1) it allows for the systematic implementation of the knowledge that informs the practice of a given profession and (2) it provides the practitioner with a variety of approaches rather than a limited few. Thus, such an approach increases the likelihood that successful outcomes will result. The hierarchical strategies are based on professional knowledge, and if early strategies are ineffective, there are numerous other strategies that can produce positive results.

Applying a hierarchical approach to classroom management allows teachers to employ knowledge effectively to understand, prevent, and manage student behavior.

Case 3: The Vice-Principal Wants to See Whom?

Ms. King decides one way to maintain discipline in her eighth-grade class is, from the beginning of the school year, to be firm and consistent with the enforcement of classroom rules and procedures. One of her rules is that students must raise their hands to be called on before answering questions. She explains this rule to the class: "By eighth grade I'm sure you all understand that everyone has an equal chance to participate. For this to happen everyone must raise her hand to be called on. I hope I will have to tell you this only once."

During the year's first question-and-answer session, Jill calls out the answer. Ms. King reminds her, "Jill you must raise your hand if you want to answer. I do not expect this to happen again." However, it isn't much longer until Jill calls out again. This time Ms. King says, "Jill please leave the room and stand in the hallway. When you feel that you can raise your hand come back and join us."

In a few minutes Jill returns to class and as before calls out an answer. This time Ms. King says, "Go to the office and speak with the vice-principal." Within minutes Jill is sent back to class. Later that day Ms. King receives a message in her mailbox requesting her to set up a meeting with the vice-principal to discuss the matter.

Needless to say Ms. King's approach to managing a common student behavior was a gross overreaction. Her approach not only led to an administrator-initiated meeting but also probably would result eventually in increased student misbehavior as students recognize the discrepancy between the minimal student behavior and maximum teacher response. Furthermore, the approach Ms. King decided to use left her with few if any alternatives in managing other students who called out answers in the future. Most likely neither parents, students, administrators, or other teachers would support Ms. King's approach because the technique of exclusion from class is usually reserved for use after many less intrusive strategies are attempted. In other words, classroom management is best accomplished when the teacher employs management strategies in a hierarchical order. The hierarchical approach is the foundation of this book.

Two hierarchies are presented in this book. The first is a broad, general overview of how classroom management should be viewed. This hierarchy is represented by the four parts in which the chapters are grouped. The first part, Chapters One through Four, is the knowledge base. The second part, Chapters Five and Six, is the prevention of management problems. The third part, Chapters Seven and Eight, is the management of common misbehavior problems. The fourth and final part, Chapters Nine and Ten, is managing chronic misbehavior problems.

The second hierarchy, the implementation of management strategies, is a decision-making model that uses specific techniques called coping skills. Entering the decision-making model, a teacher finds a variety of nonintrusive coping skills that provide the student with the opportunity to manage her own behavior while at the same time serve to curb the common forms of classroom misbehavior efficiently and effectively (Shrigley, 1985). As a teacher moves through the coping skills, the techniques become more and more intrusive, with the teacher playing an increasingly larger role in managing student behavior. The overall hierarchy of the book is shown in Figure 1-1. In addition, throughout the book each chapter begins with a flowchart depicting those parts of the hierarchy that have been covered in previous chapters and the specific parts of the hierarchy that are now to be discussed. This provides a systematic, step-by-step approach to building a comprehensive management system.

FIGURE 1   A Hierarchical Approach to Successful Classroom Management

PART 1: FOUNDATIONS (Chapters One–Four)

CONCEPTUALIZING THE PROCESS OF TEACHING
UNDERSTANDING CLASSROOM MANAGEMENT PRINCIPLES
UNDERSTANDING THE HIERARCHICAL APPROACH
DEFINING A DISCIPLINE PROBLEM
UNDERSTANDING THE EXTENT OF DISCIPLINE PROBLEMS
IN TODAY'S SCHOOLS
UNDERSTANDING HOW DISCIPLINE PROBLEMS AFFECT
TEACHING AND LEARNING
UNDERSTANDING SOCIETAL CHANGE AND ITS INFLUENCE
ON CHILDREN'S BEHAVIORS
RECOGNIZING STUDENT NEEDS
UNDERSTANDING DEVELOPMENTAL CHANGES
AND ACCOMPANYING BEHAVIORS

RECOGNIZING THE IMPORTANCE OF INSTRUCTIONAL COMPETENCE
UNDERSTANDING AND EMPLOYING DIFFERENT POWER BASES
OF TEACHERS
Referent
Expert
Legitimate
Reward/Coercive
UNDERSTANDING THEORIES OF CLASSROOM MANAGEMENT
Noninterventionist
Interactionalist
Interventionist

PART 2: PREVENTION (Chapters Five–Six)

DEVELOPING EFFECTIVE TEACHING STRATEGIES
Lesson Design
Student Motivation
Teacher Expectations
Classroom Questioning
Time-on-Task
Criterion-Referenced Evaluation
DESIGNING THE PHYSICAL ENVIRONMENT
ESTABLISHING CLASSROOM GUIDELINES
Determining Procedures
Determining Rules
Determining Consequences
natural
logical
contrived
Communicating Rules
Obtaining Commitments
Teaching Rules
LOWERING VULNERABILITY INDEX

PART 3: MANAGING COMMON MISBEHAVIOR PROBLEMS
(Chapters Seven–Eight)

USING PREVENTATIVE COPING SKILLS
USING PREPLANNED REMEDIAL NONVERBAL INTERVENTION
Planned Ignoring
Signal Interference
Proximity Control
Touch Control
USING PREPLANNED VERBAL INTERVENTION
Adjacent Reinforcement
Call on the Student

SUMMARY

This chapter discussed first a critical premise concerning successful classroom management that the reader should clearly understand before continuing. Teaching—which is defined as *the use of preplanned behaviors, founded in learning principles and child development theory and directed toward both instructional delivery and classroom management, which increases the probability of affecting a positive change in student behavior*—and classroom management are really the same process. Therefore, the teacher by deliberately changing her behavior can influence positive changes in students' behaviors.

Second, the principles and the hierarchical approach of management on which the entire book is based were explained. These serve as the foundation on which specific management techniques are developed throughout the rest of the book.

REFERENCES

BERLINER, D. (1984). The half-full glass: A review of research on teaching. In P. Hosford (Ed.), *Using What We Know About Teaching*. Alexandria, VA: Association for Supervision and Curriculum Development.

BOYAN, N. J., AND COPELAND, W. D. (1978). *Instructional Supervision Training Program.* Columbus, OH: Charles E. Merrill.

BROPHY, J. (1987). Synthesis of research on strategies for motivating students to learn. *Educational Leadership, 45,* 2, 40–49.

BROPHY, J. (1988). Research on teacher effects: Uses and abuses. *The Elementary School Journal, 89,* 1, 3–21.

EMMER, E. T., EVERTSON, C. M., SANFORD, J. P., CLEMENTS, B. S., AND WORSHAM, M. E. (1988). *Classroom Management for Secondary Teachers, 2nd ed.* Englewood Cliffs, N.J.: Prentice-Hall.

EVERTSON, C. M., EMMER, E. T., CLEMENTS, B. S., SANFORD, J. P., AND WORSHAM, M. E. (1989). *Classroom Management for Elementary Teachers, 2nd ed.* Englewood Cliffs, N.J.: Prentice-Hall.

GOOD, T. L. (1987). Two decades of research on teacher expectation: Findings and future directions. *Journal of Teacher Education,* July-August, pp. 32–47.

HOSFORD, P. L. (Ed). (1984). *Using What We Know About Teaching.* Alexandria, VA: Association for Supervision and Curriculum Development.

KOUNIN, J. S. (1970). *Discipline and Group Management in Classrooms.* New York: Holt, Rinehart Winston.

National Education Association. (1987). *Status of the American Public School Teacher 1985–86.* West Haven, CT.

Office of the Superintendent of Public Instruction, Professional Education Section. (1986). *What Recent Research Says About Effective Teaching.* Olympia, WA.

REDL, F., AND WINEMAN, D. (1952). *Controls from Within: Techniques for Treatment of the Aggressive Child.* New York: Free Press.

ROSENSHINE, B. V. (1986). Syntheses of research on explicit teaching. *Educational Leadership, 43,* 7, 60–69.

SHRIGLEY, R. L. (1985). Curbing student disruption in the classroom—Teachers need intervention skills. *National Association of Secondary School Principles' Bulletin, 69,* 479, 26–32.

SMITH, D. C. (Ed). (1983). *Essential Knowledge for Beginning Educators.* Washington, D.C.: American Association of Colleges for Teacher Education.

SWEENEY, T. J. (1981). *Alderian Counseling: Proven Concepts and Strategies, 2nd ed.* Muncie, IN: Accelerated Development, Inc.

WITTROCK, M. L. (Ed). (1986). *Handbook of Research on Teaching, 3rd ed.* New York: Macmillan.

EXERCISES

1. Many teachers define teaching as the delivery of knowledge or the giving of information. In your opinion are these definitions adequate? If so explain why. If not, what are the limitations?

2. What problems may arise when teachers base most of their decisions on "gut reactions"? Give specific examples.

3. In recent years there has been much discussion over whether or not teaching is a profession. In your opinion is teaching a profession? If yes, explain why. If no, why not and what must occur to make it a profession?

4. Review the definition of teaching presented in this chapter. Do you agree with the definition or should it be modified? If you agree, explain why. If not, what should be changed?

5. This chapter discusses how teacher behaviors (affecting) influence changes in student behavior (targeted). For each targeted behavior that follows, suggest an appropriate affecting behavior and explain

why such a behavior would increase the likelihood of causing a positive change in the student's behavior.

Situation	Targeted Behavior	Affecting Behavior
calling out answers	raising hand	
not volunteering	volunteering	
daydreaming	on-task	
forgets textbook	prepared for class	
short answers to questions	expanded answers	
few answer questions	more participation	
passing notes	on-task	
walking around room	in seat	
noisy during first five minutes of class	on-task from start of class	

6. Suggest some ways that a busy teacher can keep up with the latest research on effective teaching.

7. This book offers 37 principles of classroom management. Principles are usually quite broad statements. How can a teacher use these principles to guide her teaching practice and specific management techniques?

8. This book supports the use of a hierarchical approach to classroom management. Discuss the advantages as well as the disadvantages to such an approach.

CHAPTER 2

Nature of the Discipline Problem

THE BASICS

↓

NATURE OF THE DISCIPLINE PROBLEM
Defining a Discipline Problem
Understanding the Extent of Discipline Problems
in Today's Schools
Understanding How Discipline Problems Affect Teaching and Learning

PRINCIPLES OF CLASSROOM MANAGEMENT

5. A discipline problem exists whenever a behavior interferes with the teaching act, interferes with the rights of others to learn, is psychologically or physically unsafe, or destroys property.
6. For effective teaching to take place, teachers must be competent in managing student misbehavior to maximize the time spent on learning.
7. Teachers who manage their classrooms effectively enjoy teaching more and have greater confidence in their ability to affect student achievement.

INTRODUCTION

When educators, public officials, or parents with school-age children discuss schooling, inevitably the topic of classroom discipline arises. Discipline and classroom management are topics that have been widely discussed by both professionals and the general public for a considerable period of time.

In these discussions it is generally assumed that everyone knows what is meant by a discipline problem and that discipline poses major problems for educators. However, when we have asked pre- or in-service teachers at workshops "What is a discipline problem?" invariably there has been no consensus whatsoever. Thus, contrary to popular belief, there does not seem to be a professional operational definition of what behaviors constitute a discipline problem. So what would seem to be the obvious starting point for effective classroom management, that is, the definition of a discipline problem, has yet to be adequately formulated.

A second pervasive concern is the actual magnitude of discipline problems with which teachers must cope in today's schools. A common belief is that our schools are plagued by crime, violence, and frequent disruptive classroom behavior. In reality what are schools like today? Do today's schools differ greatly from those of 10 or 20 years ago? How does the lack of an agreed-upon definition of a discipline problem affect the gathering of statistics to assess the extent of disruptive behavior?

Finally there is the assumption of the importance of students behaving properly in a classroom. Again opinions of pre- and in-service teachers vary greatly on why this is so. What are the actual effects of misbehavior on students and their learning and on teachers and their teaching?

This chapter answers these questions by concentrating on three areas: (1) developing a working definition of what constitutes a behavior problem in a classroom; (2) accurately assessing the magnitude of the discipline problem in today's schools; and (3) determining the effect of misbehavior on both students and teachers.

DEFINING A DISCIPLINE PROBLEM

Teachers often describe students who have discipline problems as lazy, unmotivated, belligerent, aggressive, angry, or argumentative. These words at best are imprecise, are judgmental, and communicate only general patterns of a wide range of behaviors. Furthermore, students can be lazy or angry and yet not be a disruptive factor in a classroom. For a definition of a discipline problem to be useful to a teacher, it must clearly differentiate student behavior that requires corrective action from that which does not.

The amount of material that has been written on discipline and classroom management is staggering. There have been hundreds of books and articles on this subject for both the professional and the general public, the great majority appearing since the mid-1970s. These sources typically cover such areas as the types and frequency of behavior problems, the causes of student misbehavior, and the strategies that teachers can employ to improve classroom management. However, surprisingly, the most basic question, "What types of student behaviors constitute discipline problems?" has rarely been considered. Having a clear understanding of what behaviors constitute discipline problems is an absolute prerequisite for effective classroom management; without this understanding, it is impossible for teachers to design and communicate to students rational and meaningful classroom guidelines, to recognize misbehavior when it occurs, and to employ management strategies effectively and consistently.

In developing an operational term it is helpful to examine some of the few available definitions found in the literature. Kindsvatter (1978) defines discipline in terms of student behavior in the classroom, or "classroom decorum." He uses terms such as *behavior problems* and *misbehavior* but never gives meanings or examples for them. However, he does associate discipline with student behavior (which we will see does not always have to be the case).

Feldhusen (1978) uses the term *disruptive behavior*, which he defines as a violation of school expectations interfering with the orderly conduct of teaching. This definition is significant because it states that misbehavior is any student behavior that interferes with teaching. This definition attempts to provide teachers with a guideline to monitor student behavior. If a teacher follows this guideline, any behavior that keeps the teacher from teaching is identified as a disciplinary problem. On the other hand, if a behavior does not interrupt the teaching process, a disciplinary problem does not exist.

Under Feldhusen's definition the identification of discipline problems seems to be a relatively simple matter. Or is it? Let's test it by applying it to a number of common behaviors that students display in the classroom: (1) A student continually calls out while the teacher is explaining material; (2) a student quietly scratches his name into his desk; and (3) a student quietly passes notes to his neighbor. According to the present definition only the first student would be exhibiting a discipline problem because his calling out would directly interfere with the teacher's ability to teach. Unless a teacher was quite observant, the second and third behaviors could go unnoticed. Even if the teacher were aware of these behaviors, he could easily continue to teach. However, how many teachers would agree that scratching one's name on a desk and passing notes are behaviors that do not constitute discipline problems? Teachers realize inherently that such behaviors do constitute discipline problems and must be corrected. Therefore, this definition is inadequate.

Emmer et al. (1989) offer a more comprehensive definition: "Student behavior is disruptive when it seriously interferes with the activities of the teacher or of several students for more than a brief time" (p. 187). This statement adds that disruptive behavior is not only behavior that interferes with the teacher or teaching act but also behavior that interferes with students or the learning act. This is an important enhancement because it recognizes the right of every student to learn (Bauer, 1985), and most of the time in a classroom the need of the group must override the need of an individual student (Curwin and Mendler, 1980).

This definition, however, includes the terms *seriously, several,* and *brief time*. Although these terms are used to generalize to a wider range of situations, they allow room for disagreement and misinterpretation. First, what one teacher considers a brief time or a serious interference may not be true for another. Second, is it only when several students rather than one or two are disrupted that a discipline problem exists? If we apply this definition to the three types of behaviors listed previously, the student who calls out and possibly the note passer would be identified. However, the student who is defacing the desk would not be covered by the definition.

By far one of the most comprehensive definitions has been offered by Shrigley (1979), who states that any behavior that disrupts the teaching act or is psychologically or physically unsafe constitutes a disruptive behavior.

This definition includes behaviors that would not necessarily interfere with the teaching act but are definitely psychologically or physically unsafe and do require attention from the teacher, such as leaning on the back two legs of a chair, unsafe use of tools or laboratory equipment, threats to other students, and constant teasing and harassing of classmates. However the same problem is evident in this definition as in Feldhusen's in that the second and third behavioral examples would not be considered discipline problems because they do not interfere with teaching and are not unsafe.

A clear definition must be able to provide a teacher with a means whereby a definite and instantaneous decision can be made on whether or not any given behavior is a discipline problem. Once this identification has been made, the teacher must then decide if the behavior warrants intervention and what management strategies should be employed.

We propose the following definition, which recognizes that discipline problems are multifaceted. A discipline problem is behavior that (1) interferes with the teaching act; (2) interferes with the rights of others to learn; (3) is psychologically or physically unsafe; or (4) destroys property. This definition covers not only the student who calls out, defaces property, or disturbs other students but also other common behaviors that teachers are confronted with each day.

It also expands the responsibility for appropriate behavior to include

When teachers are unprepared to start class promptly, they interfere with learning. Thus, they become a discipline problem. (Carmine L. Galasso)

the teacher. It is usually assumed that discipline refers only to student behaviors, but this is not always the case.

Case 4: Can a Teacher Be a Discipline Problem?

When the bell rings, the students have their books out and are quietly waiting to begin class. Mr. Karis, the ninth-grade social studies teacher, finishes taking role and is asking a few questions to review the previous day's work when he notices that Tom is just starting to get his book out. Mr. Karis asks Tom why he isn't ready for class. Tom replies that he has a lot on his mind. This is followed in a strong tone by Mr. Karis reminding Tom that when the bell rings he is to be ready to start. Tom then replies in a tone that makes it very certain that he is annoyed, "Look, you don't know what my morning's been like!" Mr. Karis then reminds Tom that he "is not to be spoken to in that tone of voice." The rest of the class members are now either talking among themselves or deeply involved in the outcome of the confrontation rather than in social studies. By the time Tom decides it probably is not in his best interest to continue the escalating conflict, at least five minutes of class time has elapsed and no teaching or learning has taken place.

Our definition tells us that when a teacher inappropriately or ineffectively employs management strategies that result in interference with the learning of others, he in fact becomes the discipline problem. This is also true for inappropriate or ill-timed classroom procedures, public address announcements, and school policies that tend to disrupt the teaching and/or learning process.

Let's examine Case 1. Did Tom's late opening of his book interfere with teaching or his classmates' learning? Was it unsafe or did it destroy property? Wasn't it Mr. Karis's behavior that caused escalation of a minor problem that would have corrected itself? Using our definition, Mr. Karis was the discipline problem. It is doubtful that any teacher intervention was necessary at all. See Chapter Seven for a full discussion of when teacher intervention is appropriate.

Problem Student Behavior Outside the Definition

By now some readers have probably thought of many student behaviors with which teachers must cope that are not covered by our definition, for example, students who refuse to turn in homework, are not prepared for class, and are daydreaming, as well as the occasional student who gives the teacher "dirty looks." Careful analysis of these behaviors, in accordance with the definition, reveal that such behaviors are not discipline problems. More likely they are motivational problems.

Although in-depth coverage of motivational problems is beyond the scope of this book, as they generally do not interfere with other students' learning, it must be recognized that some strategies used to manage them disturb the learning of others or reduce the time spent on learning. Therefore when managing these behaviors, the basic guideline is to work with these students individually *after* involving the rest of the class in the day's learning activities. Thus, the teacher is protecting the class's right to learn and maximizing the time allocated for learning.

Even though the strategies presented later in the book are used to manage discipline problems, some of them can be used quite successfully for motivational problems, particularly the coping skills and anecdotal record keeping. Working with students who have motivational problems often involves long-term individualized intervention and/or referrals to sources outside the classroom. It cannot be stressed enough, however, that motivational problems must be properly addressed so that they will not develop into discipline problems. The following case illustrates how one teacher ensures that this does not occur.

Case 5: Solving a Motivational Problem

Mr. Hill teaches fourth grade. One of his students, Bill, rarely participates in class and often is the last one to begin classwork. One day the class is assigned math problems for seat work, and after a few minutes Mr. Hill notices that Bill has still not started. He calmly walks over to Bill, kneels down beside his desk, and asks Bill if he needs any help. This is enough to get Bill to begin his math problems. Mr. Hill waits until three problems are completed; he then tells Bill that since Bill did them so well, he should put them on the board. After the class finishes the problems, Mr. Hill begins to review the answers, making sure that he thanks Bill for his board work and reinforces the correct answers.

Mr. Hill recognized that Bill's behavior did not interfere with the teaching and learning act and so did not need immediate action. He employed effective strategies that protected the class's right to learn. Mr. Hill's technique was the beginning of a long-term effort to build up Bill's interest

Daydreaming students are not interfering with teaching or the rights of others to learn. Therefore, the teacher should first involve the rest of the class in the learning activity and then individually manage the daydreamer.

and confidence in mathematics and to have him become an active, participating member of the class. Many readers have witnessed similar situations in which the teacher unfortunately chose to deal with the student's behavior in ways that were quite disruptive to the entire class.

EXTENT OF THE PROBLEM

Discipline is one of the most serious problems facing public schools. This was the conclusion of all 21 annual Gallup Surveys of the Public's Attitudes Toward the Public Schools (Elam and Gallup, 1989). Teachers also seem to share the public's concern. In a survey of urban and suburban teachers in two schools in a mideastern metropolitan area, 60 percent felt that the public's alarm was warranted (Levin 1980b). In a nationwide sampling of teachers, 95 percent believed that efforts to improve school discipline should have a much higher priority (Harris, 1984). In the most recent national poll, 25 percent of those teachers surveyed felt that discipline was the biggest problem facing public schools (Elam, 1989). This is an increase of six percentage points since 1984.

   In attempting to assess the magnitude of the discipline problem in the past, Doyle (1978) pointed out that serious historical investigation of student behavior was lacking, and the studies that were available used data that were typically incomplete and in some cases unreliable. Doyle reviewed evidence from the few available sources and found that crime (violence and vandalism) was not a serious concern among school officials during the late 1800s to early 1900s.

In the early 1900s, many of the students prone to discipline problems did not attend school. (Library of Congress)

However, there is evidence that juvenile crime outside of school was a problem at that time. In the early 1900s, less than 50 percent of the school-age population was enrolled in school. Of this only 40 percent finished eighth grade, and approximately 10 percent graduated. Thus, students most likely to commit crimes were not in school (Hawes, 1971; Mennell, 1973; Schlossman, 1977). The growing concern over juvenile street crime initiated a movement for public education to improve the condition by bringing those youths responsible for street crime under the influence of the school (Doyle, 1978). Doyle therefore concluded that youth behavior is no worse today than it was in the past, but what was once a street problem is now a school problem, the result of more students attending school for longer periods of time.

Two of the most thorough sources of documentation on the misbehavior issue, particularly in the secondary schools, are the Report of the Subcommittee to Investigate Juvenile Delinquency to the Senate Committee on the Judiciary (Bayh, 1977) and the National Institute of Education's

(1977) Safe School Study Report to the Congress, *Safe Schools—Violent Schools*. These two reports spurred the almost unabated concern about school discipline by both professional educators and the general public.

After surveying personnel from more than 700 school systems around the country and meeting with over 100 representatives from education, government, and industry, Bayh's subcommittee concluded, ". . . there is abundant evidence that a significant and growing number of schools in urban, suburban and rural areas are confronting serious levels of violence and vandalism" (p. 8). *Safe Schools—Violent Schools* also noted that acts of violence and property destruction in schools steadily increased throughout the 1960s and early 1970s but by the late 1970s leveled off and in some cases decreased.

It is important to note that these studies made little attempt to provide a definition of discipline problems that differentiated between crime and common classroom disturbances. The lack of differentiation significantly contributed to the public's fervor brought about by these studies. Kindsvatter (1978) stated that the lack of specificity caused the term *discipline problem* to encompass all problems ranging from assault to talking out of turn. Wayson (1985) also pointed out the resultant confusion when the issues of violence and common misbehavior were tied together in both professional research and articles written for public consumption.

Recently, there have been concerted efforts to distinguish between crime (violence and vandalism) and common misbehavior (off-task and disruptive classroom behaviors). Such a distinction is essential because crime and routine classroom misbehavior are inherently different problems that require different solutions administered by different professionals both in and outside the school. Whereas teachers are responsible for controlling routine classroom misbehavior, crime often must come under the control of the school administration and outside law-enforcement agencies.

In view of this distinction now evident in much of the recent literature, what do the schools of the late 1980s and early 1990s look like? Data from the National Institute of Education reveal that by the early 1980s the number of incidents of crime in the schools had decreased (Moles, 1983). Teachers and principals also reported decreases in classroom misbehavior. In a 1983 National Education Association's Teachers' opinion poll, 45 percent of the teachers felt that student misbehavior interfered to a "great" or "moderate extent" with their teaching. This is a decrease of nine percentage points since the 1980 survey (National Education Association, 1983). A similar decrease in disruptive classroom behavior during a five-year period was reported by 66 percent of 900 secondary school principals nationwide (U.S. Department of Education, 1986).

Such improvement did not go unnoticed by the public. In the 1986 Gallup poll on the public's attitudes toward the public schools, the lack of discipline was listed for the first time in 15 years as the second most important problem facing public schools (Gallup, 1986). Replacing it as the most important problem was the use of drugs. This trend has continued through the most recent Gallup poll (Elam and Gallup, 1989).

By the mid-1980s, Wayson (1985) stated that "most schools never experience incidents of crime and those that do seldom experience them frequently or regularly" (p. 129), but disruptive behavior of ". . . the kinds that have characterized school children for generations . . . continue to pose frequent and perplexing problems for teachers" (p. 127). After a thorough examination of studies since the 1977 Senate and National Institute of Education reports, Baker (1985) concluded that there had been improvement, but ". . . the level of disruptive behavior in the classroom is a major problem for public education" (p. 486).

These conclusions are supported by numerous studies reporting that teachers and administrators consistently rank common classroom misbehaviors (excessive talking, failure to do assignments, disrespect, lateness) as the most serious and frequent disturbances, whereas they rank crime (vandalism, theft, assault) as the least serious disturbance to their teaching or the least frequently occurring (Elam, 1989; Huber, 1984; Levin, 1980a; Thomas, Goodall, and Brown, 1983; Weber and Sloan, 1986).

Today's schools, then, are perceived as experiencing less crime than in the 1970s. In addition, classroom behavior problems have also lessened, although the decline has been much smaller than incidents of crime. It must be stressed, however, that classroom misbehavior continues to be a major problem in public education. Therefore, every successful teacher must be competent in properly managing disruptive behavior in the classroom.

THE EFFECT OF CLASSROOM DISCIPLINE PROBLEMS ON TEACHING AND LEARNING

When classrooms are characterized by disruptive behavior, the teaching and learning environment is adversely affected. The amount of interference because of disruptive behavior is related to its type, frequency, and duration. In addition to the obvious effects on the teaching and learning environment, disruptive behavior also affects students' psychological safety, readiness to learn, and future behaviors.

In the course of the last decade, we have had the opportunity to interact with hundreds of college students preparing to become teachers as well as hundreds of in-service teachers and school administrators who want to improve their classroom management skills. One of the first questions we always ask is "Why do students have to behave in a classroom?" At first we were somewhat embarrassed to ask such a basic question because we felt there was a universally obvious answer. However, to our surprise, the answer was not so obvious to many who participated in these workshops. The answer, of course, involves the widely accepted learning principle that the more time spent on learning (time-on-task, or engaged time), the more learning will take place (Brophy, 1988). In other words disruptive off-task behavior takes away from learning.

Case 6: Discipline: A Costly Waste of Time

Mr. Kay is a seventh-grade social studies teacher who teaches five classes a day. He is content to allow students, on entering the room, to stand around and talk rather than preparing their materials for class. As a result it is usually five minutes after the bell rings before the students are ready and class begins.

Mr. Kay's class illustrates the tremendous amount of time that can be consumed over a school year by some very minor off-task behaviors. Over a period of a week, 25 minutes that could have been directed toward learning are not. Over the 40-week school year, 1,000 minutes are consumed by off-task behavior. This amounts to over 22 class periods, or approximately one-ninth of the school year, that could have been directed toward learning goals. If the calculations also considered that Mr. Kay taught 120 students per day, 2,640 "student class periods" were not spent on learning social studies.

It has been reported that some teachers spend as much as 30 percent to 80 percent of their time addressing discipline problems (Walsh, 1983). This highlights a previously mentioned basic fact of teaching: To be a successful teacher, one must be competent in managing student behavior to maximize the time spent on learning.

Case 7: The Ripple Effect

Rebecca is a well-mannered, attentive fifth-grade student. For the first time since starting school, she and her two best friends from her neighborhood are in the same class. Unlike Rebecca, her friends are not as attentive and are interested more in each other than in class activities. Their teacher often has to reprimand them for passing notes, talking to each other, and giggling excessively during class.

One day, Rebecca is tapped on the shoulder and is handed a

note from her friend across the room. She accepts the note and sends one back. Her friends quickly include her in their antics, and Rebecca willingly begins to participate. It takes the teacher a number of weeks to remove Rebecca from her friends' influence and reduce the off-task behaviors of the other two girls.

The off-task behaviors of Rebecca's friends also drew Rebecca off-task, which illustrates the fact that disruptive behavior can result in a "ripple effect." In other words, students learn misbehavior from observing misbehavior in other children (Baker, 1985). This observational learning is often accelerated when the onlooking student notices the attention that the disruptive student is getting from both the teacher and his classmates.

Not only does the initial misbehavior cause a ripple effect, but also both the methods the teacher uses to curb the misbehavior (Kounin, 1970) and the targeted student's resultant behavior cause a second ripple effect. Studies have shown that rough and threatening teacher behavior causes student anxieties, which lead to additional disruptive behaviors from onlooking students. However, students who see that disruptive students comply with the teacher's control technique rate their teacher as fairer and are themselves less distracted from their classwork than when they observe unruly students defying the teacher (Smith, 1969). This fact illustrates some of the complex dynamics that come into play with even minor classroom disruptions.

Common day-to-day off-task student behaviors such as talking and walking around exist in all classrooms to some degree. Although much less common, some classrooms and indeed some entire schools are plagued by threats, violence, and vandalism. A 1983 survey of middle school students found that their main concern was the bullying and disruptive behaviors of their classmates (National Association of Secondary School Principals, 1984). Other studies indicated that many students were afraid at school and avoided certain areas because of fear of other students (Menacker, Weldon, and Hurwitz, 1989; National Institute of Education, 1977). Obviously, when students are fearful for their own safety or the safety of their property, their ability to concentrate on their schoolwork is greatly reduced. Such fear creates a hostile learning environment, increases a feeling of mistrust in the school, and reduces students' confidence in their teachers' ability to control students (Wayne and Rubel, 1982). Some studies indicate that a student's ability to learn in the classroom is reduced by at least 25 percent because of fear of other students (Dade County Public Schools, 1976; Lalli and Savitz, 1976). When this fear reaches a high enough level, students actually decide not to attend school (Wayne and Rubel, 1982).

In conclusion, minor and major misbehavior reduces learning time for both the disruptive students and on-looking students. This equates to less learning. Although there is not a clear cause-and-effect relationship, there is a clear association between poor grades and all types of misbehavior (DiPrete, Muller, and Shaeffer, 1981).

Not only do classroom discipline problems have negative effects on students, but they also have very negative effects on teacher effectiveness and career longevity. We believe that the overwhelming majority of teachers choose to enter the profession because they enjoy working with children and are intrinsically motivated when they know that their efforts have contributed to the children's academic growth. Therefore, teachers are emotionally vulnerable to discipline problems. They put long hours of preparation into what they hope will be interesting, motivating, and meaningful lessons. When such efforts are met by disinterested off-task students, teachers begin to have attitudinal changes.

No matter how careful teachers are not to allow their personal feelings to play a role in their interactions with students, some of their personal feelings do influence their behavior. It has been well documented that there are observable differences between a teacher's interactions with males and females and with high-achieving and low-achieving students.

Similarly, teachers interact differently with disruptive students than they do with nondisruptive students (Walker, 1979). Such differential treatment is fueled by the negative feelings many teachers have toward disruptive students. This differential treatment unfortunately serves to escalate inappropriate student behavior. Even the most chronic disruptive student spends some time engaged in appropriate behavior. However, some teachers are so angry at certain students that they tend to overlook the appropriate behavior and focus only on the disruptive behavior. Therefore the teacher misses the few opportunities he has to begin to change disruptive behaviors to acceptable ones. The student soon learns that when he behaves appropriately, nothing happens, but when he misbehaves, he is the center of both the teacher's and students' attention. This process has been documented in studies, which concluded that teachers are much more likely to reprimand inappropriate behavior than to approve of appropriate behavior when interacting with disruptive students (Walker and Buckley, 1973, 1974).

Any teacher can attest to the fact that students easily realize when rules and expectations are not consistently enforced or obeyed by either the teacher or the students. Nonetheless, since teachers are so emotionally tied to the disruptive student, they often set and enforce standards for the disruptive student that are different from those for the rest of the class. Often these standards are so inflexible and unrealistic that they actually reduce the chance that the disruptive student will behave appropriately.

Since disruptive students have a history of inappropriate behaviors, they must be given the opportunity to relearn new behaviors. The relearning process is usually best accomplished in small manageable steps that enable the student to have a high probability of success. This process requires behavioral standards to be realistic and the same as those for the rest of the class. The teacher must recognize and reinforce what at first may be infrequent and short-lived appropriate behaviors. When behavioral standards are stricter for some students, the teacher risks losing the confidence and support of even the nondisruptive students while the disruptive student gains peer support.

As teachers begin to experience more discipline problems, their motivation to teach is often replaced by at best a "who cares" attitude. If conditions do not improve, this attitude may develop into a "get even" attitude. When a "get even" attitude overrides a teacher's motivation to assist students in learning, supportive and effective teacher behaviors that can possibly manage disruptive students are replaced by revengeful behaviors. Once a teacher operates from a basis of revenge, teaching effectiveness ceases and teacher-student power struggles become commonplace. Such power struggles often fuel and escalate disruptive behavior and place the teacher in a no-win situation (Dreikurs, 1964).

Discipline problems are significant contributors to job-related stress and doubts about career choice. Children who display disruptive behaviors are constant reminders to teachers that the classroom environment is not what they would like it to be. The time and energy needed to cope with some disruptive students can be physically draining and emotionally exhausting. Stress related to classroom management is one of the most influential factors in failure among novice teachers (Levin, 1980a; Vittetoe, 1977) and a major reason why they leave the profession (Canter, 1989).

Management problems are a major cause of job-related stress for teachers.

Teachers who are effective managers have greater job satisfaction. (Leslie Deeb)

Teachers who do weather their first few years of teaching report that students who continually misbehave are the primary cause of job-related stress (Feitler and Tokar, 1982). Finally when teachers look back on their career decisions, those who report that they would not choose the teaching profession if they had to do it over again were much more likely to have experienced discipline problems than teachers who would choose teaching again (National Institute of Education, 1980).

In contrast, teachers who manage their classrooms effectively report enjoying teaching more and having greater confidence in their ability to affect student achievement (Levin et al., 1985). Such enhanced feelings of efficacy lead to improvements in the teaching-learning process and job satisfaction, which ultimately result in gains in student achievement.

SUMMARY

This chapter has answered three questions that are critical for the understanding of discipline and classroom management. What is a discipline problem? What is the extent of the problem in today's schools? What is the effect of discipline problems?

First, after a discussion of the contemporary definitions of discipline and their shortcomings, an operational definition was provided: A discipline problem is any behavior that (1) interferes with the teaching act; (2) interferes with the rights of others to learn; (3) is psychological or physically unsafe; or (4) destroys property. An important aspect of this definition is that it expands the responsibility for appropriate behavior to include the teacher as well as the students.

Second, the common belief that today's schools are plagued by violence, crime, and disruptive classroom behavior was explored. It was pointed out that early studies were characterized by incomplete and in some cases unreliable data. Recent studies, which differentiate between crime and classroom misbehavior, characterize today's schools as having much less crime. Common classroom misbehaviors also lessened, but such behaviors continue to pose frequent and perplexing problems for teachers.

Finally it was shown that misbehavior reduces the time spent on learning. Disruptive behavior has other negative effects: misbehavior in onlooking students because of a ripple effect, fear, and a decrease in school attendance and academic achievement. Teachers are also adversely affected by misbehavior, including decreased teacher effectiveness, increased job-related stress, and decreased career longevity.

REFERENCES

BAKER, K. (1985). Research evidence of a school discipline problem. *Phi Delta Kappan, 66,* 7, 482–488.

BAUER, G. L. (1985). Restoring order to the public schools. *Phi Delta Kappan, 66,* 7, 488–490.

BAYH, B. (1977). *Challenge for the Third Century: Education in a Safe Environment—Final Report on the Nature and Prevention of School Violence and Vandalism.* Washington DC: U.S. Government Printing Office.

BROPHY, J. (1988). Research on teacher effects: Uses and abuses. *The Elementary School Journal, 89,* 1, 3–21.

CANTER, L. (1989). Assertive discipline—More than names on the board and marbles in a jar. *Phi Delta Kappan, 71,* 1, 57–61.

CURWIN, R. L., and MENDLER, A. N. (1980). *The Discipline Book: A Complete Guide to School and Classroom Management.* Reston, VA: Reston Publishing.

Dade County Public Schools. (1976). *Experiences of Teachers and Students with Disruptive Behavior in the Dade Public Schools.* Miami, FL.

DiPRETE, T., MULLER, C., and SHAEFFER, N. (1981). *Discipline and Order in American High Schools.* Washington, DC: National Center for Education Statistics.

DOYLE, W. (1978). Are students behaving worse than they used to behave? *Journal of Research and Development in Education, 11,* 4, 3–16.

DREIKURS, R. (1964). *Children the Challenge.* New York: Hawthorn.

ELAM, S. M. (1989). The second Gallup/Phi Delta Kappa poll of teachers' attitudes toward the public schools. *Phi Delta Kappan, 70,* 10, 785–798.

ELAM, S. M., and GALLUP, A. M. (1989). The 21st annual Gallup poll of the public's attitudes toward the public schools. *Phi Delta Kappan, 71,* 1, 41–54.

EMMER, E. T., EVERTSON, C. M., SANFORD, J. P., CLEMENTS, B. S., and WORSHAM, M. E. (1989). *Classroom Management for Secondary Teachers,* 2nd ed. Englewood Cliffs, NJ: Prentice-Hall.

Nature of the Discipline Problem **37**

FEITLER, F., and TOKAR, E. (1982). Getting a handle on teacher stress. *Educational Leadership, 39,* 1, 456–57.

FELDHUSEN, J. F. (1978). Behavior problems in secondary schools. *Journal of Research and Development in Education, 11,* 4, 17–28.

GALLUP, A. M. (1986). The 18th annual Gallup poll of the public's attitudes toward the public schools. *Phi Delta Kappan, 68,* 1, 43–59.

HARRIS, L. (1984). *Metropolitan Life Survey of the American Teacher.* New York.

HAWES, J. M. (1971). *Children in Urban Society: Juvenile Delinquency in Nineteenth Century America.* New York: Oxford University Press.

HUBER, J. D. (1984). Discipline in the middle school—Parent, teacher, and principal concerns. *National Association of Secondary School Principals Bulletin, 68,* 471, 74–79.

KINDSVATTER, R. (1978). A new view of the dynamics of discipline. *Phi Delta Kappan, 59,* 5, 322–365.

KOUNIN, J. (1970). *Discipline and Group Management in Classrooms.* New York: Holt, Rinehart & Winston.

LALLI, M., and SAVITZ, L. D. (1976). The fear of crime in the school enterprise and its consequences. *Education and Urban Society, 8.*

LEVIN, J. (1980a). Discipline and classroom management survey: Comparisons between a suburban and urban school. Unpublished report, Pennsylvania State University, University Park.

LEVIN, J. (1980b). Lay vs. teacher perceptions of school discipline. *Phi Delta Kappan, 61,* 5, 360.

LEVIN, J., HOFFMAN, N., BADIALI, B., and Neuhard, R. (1985). Critical experiences in student teaching: Effects on career choice and implications for program modification. Paper presented to the Annual Conference of the American Educational Research Association, Chicago.

MENACKER, J., WELDON, W., and HURWITZ, E. (1989). School order and safety as community issues. *Phi Delta Kappan, 71,* 1, 39.

MENNELL, R. M. (1973). *Thorns & Thistles: Juvenile Delinquents in the United States 1825–1940.* Hanover, NH: The University Press of New England.

MOLES, O. (1983). Trends in interpersonal crimes in schools. Paper presented at the Annual Meeting of the American Educational Research Association, Montreal.

National Association of Secondary School Principals. (1984). *The Mood of American Youth.* Reston, VA.

National Education Association. (1983). *Nationwide Teacher Opinion Poll 1983.* Washington, DC: NEA Research Memo.

National Institute of Education. (1977). *Safe Schools—Violent Schools.* Washington, DC: U.S. Department of Health, Education and Welfare.

National Institute of Education. (1980). *Teacher Opinion Poll.* Washington, DC.

SCHLOSSMAN, S. L. (1977). *Love and the American Delinquent: The Theory and Practice of "Progressive" Juvenile Justice, 1825–1920.* Chicago: University of Chicago Press.

SHRIGLEY, R. L. (1979). Strategies in classroom management. *The National Association of Secondary School Principals Bulletin, 63,* 428, 1–9.

SMITH, O. B. (1969). Discipline. In R. L. Engel, *Encyclopedia of Educational Research,* 4th ed.

THOMAS, G. T., GOODALL, R., and BROWN, L. (1983). Discipline in the classroom: Perceptions of middle grade teachers. *The Clearinghouse, 57,* 3, 139–142.

U.S. Department of Education. (1986). Discipline in public secondary schools. *Bulletin.* Washington, DC: Office of Educational Research and Improvement.

VITTETOE, J. O. (1977). Why first-year teachers fail. *Phi Delta Kappan, 58,* 5, 429.

WALKER, H. M. (1979). *The Acting-Out Child: Coping with Classroom Disruption.* Boston: Allyn & Bacon.

WALKER, H. M., and BUCKLEY, N. K. (1973). Teacher Attention to Appropriate and Inappropriate Classroom Behavior: An Individual Case Study. *Focus on Exceptional Children, 5,* 5–11.

WALKER, H. M., and BUCKLEY, N. K. (1974). *Token Reinforcement Techniques: Classroom Applications for the Hard to Teach Child.* Eugene, OR: E-B Press, Inc.

WALSH, D. (1983). Our schools come to order. *American Teacher.*

WAYNE, I., and RUBEL, R. J. (1982). Student fear in secondary schools. *Urban Review, 14,* 1, 197–237.

WAYSON, W. W. (1985). The politics of violence in school: Doublespeak and disruptions in public confidence. *Phi Delta Kappan, 67,* 2, 127–132.
WEBER, T. R., and SLOAN, C. A. (1986). How does high school discipline in 1984 compare to previous decades? *The Clearinghouse, 59,* 7, 326–329.

EXERCISES

1. Is it important that all teachers have a consistent definition of what types of student behaviors constitute discipline problems? Why or why not?
2. Do you agree with the definition of a discipline problem stated in this chapter? If so, why? If not, how would you modify it?
3. Give examples of teacher behaviors that would constitute a discipline problem.
4. Using the definition of a discipline problem stated in this chapter, categorize each of the following behaviors as a discipline problem or a nondiscipline problem and explain your reasoning:

Behavior	Discipline Problem	Nondiscipline Problem	Rationale
a. A student consistently tries to engage the teacher in conversation just as class is about to begin.			
b. A student continually comes to class one minute late.			
c. A teacher stands in the hallway talking to fellow teachers during the first three minutes of class.			

Behavior	Discipline Problem	Nondiscipline Problem	Rationale
d. A student does math homework during social studies class.			
e. A student interrupts a lecture to ask permission to go to the bathroom.			
f. A student often laughs at answers given by other students.			
g. A student doesn't wear safety goggles while welding in industrial arts class.			
h. A first-grader continually volunteers to answer questions but never has an answer when he is called on.			
i. A fourth-grader refuses to wear a jacket during recess.			
j. A seventh-grader constantly pulls the hair of the girl who sits in front of him.			

Behavior	Discipline Problem	Nondiscipline Problem	Rationale
k. An eighth-grade boy spends half of the time allotted for group work encouraging a girl to go out with his friend.			
l. A ninth-grade student consistently uses the last two minutes of class for hair combing.			
m. An unkempt student can't get involved in group work because all students refuse to sit near him.			
n. A student continually asks good questions, diverting the teacher from the planned lesson.			
o. A student eats a candy bar during class.			
p. A student flirts with the teacher by asking questions			

Behavior	Discipline Problem	Nondiscipline Problem	Rationale
about her clothes and personal life during class.			
q. A student consistently makes wisecracks that entertain the rest of the class.			

5. At this point in your reading, how would you handle each of the 17 behaviors listed? Why?

6. For each of the 17 behaviors, what types of teacher behaviors might escalate each student behavior?

7. Think back to your days as a student; to what extent would you say that discipline was a problem in your school? What type of discipline problems were most common?

8. Do you feel that the discipline problem in the schools has increased or decreased since you attended high school? On what evidence or information do you base your opinion?

9. Considering what a teacher's job entails and his relationship with students, why would he be prone to take discipline problems personally?

10. What are the dangers of personalizing student behavior? How might this affect the instructional effectiveness of a teacher?

11. How can teachers protect themselves from personalizing misbehavior?

12. Think back on your days as a student. Can you recall instances in which classroom discipline problems prevented you and others in the class from learning? How did you feel about the situation at the time?

13. When a student disrupts class and takes away the right of others to learn, does that student forfeit his right to learn? If you believe he does, what implications does that have for teacher behavior? If you believe he doesn't, what implications does that have for teacher behavior?

CHAPTER 3

Understanding Why Children Misbehave

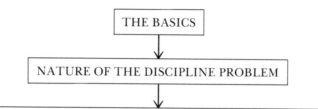

THE BASICS

↓

NATURE OF THE DISCIPLINE PROBLEM

↓

UNDERSTANDING WHY CHILDREN MISBEHAVE
Understanding Societal Change and Its Influence on Children's Behaviors
Recognizing Student Needs
Understanding Developmental Changes and Accompanying
Behaviors
Recognizing the Importance of Instructional Competence

PRINCIPLES OF CLASSROOM MANAGEMENT

8. Teachers' awareness of the causes of misbehavior enables them to use positive control techniques rather than negative approaches stemming from erroneously viewing misbehavior as a personal affront.

9. Basic human needs such as food, safety, belonging, and security are prerequisites for appropriate classroom behavior.

10. Students' need for a sense of significance, competence, and power exerts influences on their behavior.

11. Societal changes beyond the schools' control exert much influence on student behavior.

12. Cognitive and moral developmental changes result in normal student behavior that often is disruptive in learning environments.

13. Instructional competence can ameliorate the effects of negative outside influences as well as prevent the misbehavior that occurs as a direct result of poor instruction.

INTRODUCTION

"Kids aren't the way they used to be. When I went to school kids knew their place. Teachers wanted to teach and students wanted to learn. The students respected their teachers, and believe me, they sure didn't fool around in school like they do today." Such beliefs are commonly held by adults as they remember the "way it used to be." Are such perceptions a matter of fact? Not entirely!

There have always been some behavior problems in our schools because of students' normal developmental changes. In addition there have always been some schools and homes that have been unable to provide adequately for children's needs. However, recent rapid changes in society have not only caused additional behavior problems but also conpounded the already existing ones. There have been significant shifts in the family structure, the distribution of wealth and knowledge, the cultural and racial makeup of the population, and world economies, as well as advances in technology only fantasized about a few decades ago. These changes are evident in students' thoughts, attitudes, and behavior. Nonetheless, students still want to learn.

Teachers still want to teach. However, if they want to maximize their teaching time, they must minimize the effect of societal changes on student behavior in their classrooms. Teachers must (1) not expect students to think and act the way they did years ago; (2) not demand respect from students solely on the basis of a title or position; (3) understand the methods and behaviors young people employ to find their place in today's society; and (4) understand the ongoing societal changes and their influence on students' lives. To assist teachers in reaching this goal, this chapter describes some of the main factors that have caused students to change and provides an explanation of why students now misbehave.

SOCIETAL CHANGES

That schools are microcosms of the larger society (Kindsvatter, 1978) has been recognized for over 50 years (Dewey, 1916). Therefore, discipline problems in the schools reflect the problems that face our society. The social climate of the nation, city, or town and the surrounding community that each school serves has profound effects on students' perceptions of the value of an education and their behavior in school (Menacker, Weldon, and Hurwitz, 1989).

It is widely recognized that our society is plagued by the ills of drug and alchohol use, crime, unemployment, child abuse, adolescent suicide, and teenage pregnancy. It is no coincidence that as these social problems increase, so do discipline problems in the schools. This relationship highlights the fact that many factors that contribute to discipline problems are beyond the schools' control (Bayh, 1978).

Although the relationship between school discipline and the problems facing society is somewhat obvious, less obvious, subtle changes are having long-range, significant influences on children's behavior in the schools.

Many discipline problems in the school reflect problems that face our society. (James Carroll)

Regardless of society's ills, disruptive behavior may still be expected in the schools because it is an institution that brings together many of the conditions that facilitate misbehavior. Large numbers of young people, many of whom would rather be elsewhere and who are still learning socially acceptable behaviors, are concentrated in one place for long periods of time. These students come from a wide range of backgrounds, with different ethnic, racial, and parental attitudes and expectations concerning education. Schools expose all students to norm-violating behaviors and make failure visible (Elliott and Voss, 1974; Feldhusen, 1978).

Changes in society have a profound effect on student attitudes and behaviors. Children no longer grow up in a society that provides them with constant, consistent sets of guidelines and expectations, and they grow up in a society that is vastly more complex than it was even 30 years ago. The stimulus for such change and complexity has been the intense, rapid technological advancements in mass communication, involving the exchange of a multitude of varying viewpoints, ideas, and philosophies. With young people's exposure to this array of new information, the direct influence of parents, community, and school has begun to wane. Children now have different role models. Schools are faced with children who are exposed to more and more varied types of information than any children before. As a result they think and act differently.

Knowledge Explosion and the Erosion of Respect
for Authority

In 1957 the Russians launched Sputnik, the first satellite. This event caused a national fear that the Russians were outdistancing us in scientific knowledge and technological advancements. This event and the resultant national concern was, in all probability, one of the major initiating factors of the most recent explosion of knowledge.

Since the 1950s this explosion has been unabated and has increased at an ever-escalating rate. It has resulted in technological advances creating consumer products only dreamed of previously. Personal computers, microwave ovens, VCRs, color TVs, TV satellite dishes, and compact disk players, to name a few, are commonplace today. It is estimated that by the time children born in 1980 graduate from high school, the world's knowledge will have increased four times. When these children reach the age of 50, knowledge will have increased 32 times, and 97 percent of all knowledge will have been learned since they were born (Toffler, 1970).

Such rapid expansion of knowledge causes generation gaps characterized by discontinuities rather than mere differences. By the end of elementary school many children possess knowledge that their parents only vaguely comprehend. This is poignantly clear in such areas as personal computing,

The unabated knowledge explosion has influenced the erosion of respect for traditional authority figures. (Ken Karp)

ecology, and astronomy. In addition, because of the almost instantaneous telecommunication of national and world events, children are keenly aware of the state of the present world. They see famine, terrorist attacks, political corruption, drug busts, and chemical spills on a daily basis.

Such knowledge causes children to view adults as ineffective in managing their own world, and they perceive past solutions of life's problems as irrelevant to the world in which they live. Therefore, respect, which was once given to adults because of their worldliness and expertise, begins to erode and adults exercise less influence on the young. When talking to adolescents, it is common to hear such statements as "My parents don't understand," "Why do we have to do it by hand when there are calculators that can do it for you?" and "Why do I have to be always honest when government officials are always lying?"

As the world becomes a more complex and frightening place and as children perceive their parents and teachers to be less relevant sources for solutions, the future grows more remote, uncertain, and unpredictable, producing such feelings as "live for today." This view of the future seems to be related to student behavior. Stinchcombe (1964) demonstrated a direct relationship between adolescents' image of the future and their present attitudes and behaviors. Those adolescents who saw themselves as gaining little or nothing in their future by attending school were most likely to exhibit rebellious, alienated behavior. Therefore instructional variables such as the teachers' ability to maximize student success and demonstrate the present and future usefulness of the material play a very important role in students' perceived value of education.

Television and Violence

Ninety-six percent of all American homes have at least one television set, and the average American child spends more time viewing television than she does in a classroom (Zuckerman and Zuckerman, 1985). Television has become a major source of information and influence on the lives of children.

The format of television in the United States consists of brief sequences of fast-paced action with frequent interruptions by unrelated commercial messages. Television provides a very different experience than any stimulus available earlier in human history. Television transmits to a viewer incredible amounts of information and gives the viewer a "window on the world." The inhabitants of the TV world often act and think in ways that contrast sharply with the attitudes and behaviors of parents, teachers, and peers.

Most studies have concentrated on the amount of violence portrayed on television and its effects on children. Content analysis of television shows in the early 1950s indicated that on the average there were 11 threats or acts of violence per hour. In the 1970s it was reported that the average American child witnessed 18,000 televised murders by the time she graduated from high school (Rothenberg, 1975). More recent analysis confirmed that TV violence has been increasing and that it has increased more rapidly on programs that appeal to young audiences (Pearl, 1984).

Violence is not solely a characteristic of fictional TV programming. News programs depict considerable amounts of real violence for the more than one-third of elementary-aged children and the more than one-half of adolescents who are regular news viewers. The "eyewitness" local news format features many more violent stories than the traditional formats of the past. Content analysis indicated that stories about murder, rape, and assault are disproportionately covered as local news, and stories of international violence and crime predominate in national newscasts (Atkin, 1983).

Many researchers have studied the effects of TV violence on children's development. In the 1950s psychologists suggested that it had a cathartic effect and reduced a viewer's aggressive behaviors. More recent laboratory and field studies do not support this finding (Pearl, Bouthilet, and Lazar, 1982).

The National Institute of Mental Health's report on the relationship between television and behavior concluded that (1) research findings support a causal relationship between television violence and aggressive behavior; (2) there is a consensus among researchers that television violence leads to aggressive behavior; (3) despite slight variations over the past decade, the amount of violence on television remains at consistently high levels; and (4) television cultivates television-influenced attitudes among viewers, heavy viewers being more fearful and less trusting of others than are light viewers (Bouthilet and Lazar, 1982).

A later study indicated that heavy TV viewing was significantly associated with elementary school children's belief in a "mean and scary world" and that poor school behavior (restlessness, disruptiveness, inattentiveness, aggressiveness) was significantly correlated with the home TV environment (number of sets, hours of viewing, and type of programs) (Singer, Singer, and Rapaczynski, 1984). In trying to explain the effects of TV on school behavior, Rice, Huston, and Wright (1982) hypothesized that the stimuli of sound effects, exciting music, and fast-action images may generate an arousal reaction, with an accompanying inability to tolerate the sometimes long conversations, explanations, and long delays characteristic of the real world of school.

There have been various processes proposed to explain the relationship between TV viewing and children's behavior (Pearl, 1984). The observational modeling theory is the most widely accepted. This theory proposes that aggression is learned from the models portrayed on TV and is practiced through imitation (Bondura, 1973). This learning and imitation is substantially influenced by real-life simulations portrayed on TV.

The effect of prolonged viewing of TV violence on children's behavior has been well documented. Less studied is its psychological effect, especially of the real-life violence shown on news broadcasts. A hypothesis is that violence on TV produces stress in children, and too much exposure to too much violence over too long a time may create emotional upset and insecurity, leading to resultant disturbed behavior (Rice, 1981).

Television and Alternative Role Models

In addition to violence, TV influences children's behaviors by presenting a wide range of alternative models and life-styles. For instance, Music Television, a very popular network with young people, broadcasts 24 hours a day the audio and video imagery of the latest rock concerts. What once were mostly inaudible lyrics are now visual depictions of songs, along with the lights and sounds of a rock concert. Popular groups sing about drug and alcohol use, sexual promiscuity, and distrust of school and teachers. Past "top ten" songs such as "Another Brick in the Wall," with the lyric "we don't need no education," "Hot for Teacher," and "Smoking in the Boys Room" are perfect examples of songs that communicate negative messages and may cause school and classroom disruptions.

Television brings big-city life into the rural areas; displays alternative life-styles that are contrary to the traditional "mother, father, and two children" households; and presents different messages than do parents and

Television exposes children to both frequent violence and alternative role models that can influence their behavior. (Charles Gatewood)

teachers. Television communicates to children pluralistic standards, changing customs, and shifting beliefs and values.

Because of its overwhelming influence, TV serves as a very important stimulus to motivate changes in childrens' behavior as they attempt to determine who they are, what they can do, and how far they can go in testing the limits of their parents' and teachers' authority. Such behavioral experimentation is both a prerequisite and a necessary component of the cognitive and moral developmental growth of young people. Uncertainty, erratic behavior, and inconsistencies have always been characteristic of preadolescents and adolescents. However, today's world is not as simple as it once was, and parents and teachers have more alternative models with which to compete. It is imperative that teachers be aware of these outside influences on student behaviors so that they are able to work constructively with and be supportive of today's youth.

FAILURE OF THE HOME TO MEET CHILDREN'S BASIC NEEDS

Educators have long recognized the significant influence of a child's home life on behavior as well as on academic progress. Particularly crucial is the home's ability to meet students' basic needs.

Case 8: Hanging on the Corner

Teresa, a fifth-grade student, is in the school's playground at 7:45 every morning even though school doesn't start until 9:00. Often she is eating a bag of potato chips and drinking a can of soda. On cold snowy mornings she huddles in the doorway wearing a spring jacket and sneakers, waiting for the door to be unlocked so that she can stand in the hallway until the rest of the students arrive. She brags to the other students that she hangs out on the corner with the teenagers in the neighborhood until 12:00 or 1:00 A.M. In fact this is substantiated by the home and school coordinator who eventually is called on to investigate her home environment.

Teresa is the youngest of four children. Her father left his family before she started school. Her mother works for a janitorial service and leaves for work by 7:00 A.M. When she returns home in the evening she either goes out with her boyfriend or goes to sleep early, basically entrusting Teresa's care to her 16-year-old brother, who has recently quit school.

Academically Teresa is two years below grade in both reading and mathematics. She never completes homework assignments, is never prepared for class with the necessary books and materials, and usually chooses not to participate in learning activities. Her classroom behavior is excessively off-task, characterized by noisy movements both in and out of her seat, calling out, and disruption of other students by talking to them or physically touching them. Occasionally she becomes abusive, using a loud, challenging voice and vulgarities to students and to the teacher.

When considering Teresa's home environment, is it surprising that she has academic and behavior problems in school? Abraham Maslow's theory of basic human needs predicts that in such a case this behavior is to be expected.

Maslow (1968) postulated that basic human needs align themselves into a hierarchy of the following levels:

1. Physiological needs: hunger, thirst, breathing
2. Safety and security needs: protection from injury, pain, extremes of heat and cold
3. Belonging and affection needs: giving and receiving love, warmth, and affection
4. Esteem and self-respect needs: feeling adequate, competent, worthy; being appreciated and respected by others
5. Self-actualization needs: self-fulfillment by using one's talents and potential

If the lower-level needs are not met, an individual may experience difficulty, frustration, and a lack of motivation in attempting to meet the higher-order needs.

Maslow's hierarchy also represents a series of developmental levels. Although the meeting of these needs is important to and occurs throughout an individual's life, younger children spend considerably more time and effort meeting the lower-level needs. From preadolescence on, assuming the lower-level needs are met, emphasis shifts to the higher-order needs of esteem and self-actualization. (Further discussion of self-esteem is found in a later section.)

Academic achievement and appropriate behavior are most likely to occur in school when a student's home environment has met her physiological safety and belonging needs. This enables her to begin to work on meeting the needs of esteem and self-actualization both at home and at school.

Let's now examine Teresa's home environment in light of Maslow's hierarchy of basic needs. Her home environment is deficient in meeting her physiological, safety, and belonging needs. This is evident in her breakfast of potato chips and soda, her clothing on cold days (a light jacket and sneakers), and no father at home and a mother rarely present. Because of her inadequate home environment, she attempts to meet her need for belonging and esteem by bragging about hanging out with the teenagers or by using loud, vulgar statements in class and disturbing other students. It is surprising that Teresa still attends school on a regular basis. However if her home environment remains the same, if she continues to achieve below grade academically and if she continues to exhibit behavior problems, she most likely will quit school at an early age, still unable to control her own behavior.

The importance of the home environment on school behavior was clearly indicated by a longitudinal study of third-, sixth-, and ninth-grade students (Feldhusen, Thuroton, and Benning, 1973). Persistently disruptive students differed substantially from persistently prosocial students in a number of home and family variables:

1. The supervision and discipline of the parents were inadequate, being too lax, too strict, or erratic.
2. The parents were indifferent or hostile to the child. They disapproved of many things about the child and handed out angry physical punishment.
3. The family operated only partially as a unit, if at all, and the marital relationship lacked closeness and equality of partnership.
4. The parents found it difficult to discuss concerns regarding the child and believed that they had little influence on the child. They believed that other children exerted bad influences on their child.

Both the case of Teresa and Feldhusen's longitudinal investigation describe homes that could be considered abusive or at least neglectful environments. However many nonabusive or nonneglectful home environments also create situations that are quite stressful to children. This stress may be symptomatically displayed as a behavior problem.

Case 9: Marital Conflict

Seth was a typical eleventh-grade student from a middle-class home attending a suburban high school. For the most part he was motivated and attentive. Occasionally he had to be reminded to stop talking or to take his seat when class started. His grades were B's with a few C's. He planned to attend a state college and major in liberal arts. Teachers enjoyed having Seth in their classes.

Now, at the end of eleventh grade, Seth has changed. He doesn't turn in homework, is often off-task, and his motivation is reduced. His future plans are to get a job after high school rather than attend college.

Conferences with his teachers and counselors reveal that his parents have begun to discuss divorce. Since Seth is the oldest of three children, he often is involved in discussions with his parents concerning how the family will manage in the future. Both his mother and father now ask him for assistance in meeting family responsibilities rather than asking each other.

Seth's home environment is significantly different from Teresa's; however both have a detrimental effect on their behavior in school. Seth's situation is similar to that which an increasing number of children have to face. The relationship of changing home environments and school performance was stressed in an address given in 1984 by the then U.S. Secretary of Education Bell to educational leaders. He stated, "The problems of American education today are at least partly attributed to changes that have taken place over the past decade in the lifestyle, stability, and commitment of parents."

It was proposed that "Over the past quarter century changes in children's out-of-school experience have been much more substantial than changes in what they experience in school" (Levine, 1984, p. 3). It was further stated that children's out-of-school experiences are stronger predictors of school behavior than their in-school experiences.

What are these significant changes that have occurred in the home environment of American children? Between 1960 and 1980, the divorce rate increased over 150 percent (U.S. Bureau of the Census, 1981), with the probability that one in two new marriages will end in divorce (U.S. Bureau of the Census, 1984). Unmarried-couple households tripled since 1970 (Levine, 1984). Such family structures have resulted in a 66 percent increase since 1970 in the number of children living in single-parent homes, and it is estimated that at least 50 percent of all the children born in the 1970s will live in a single-parent home at some time (Levine, 1984). Remarriage is not always a solution since it often creates additional problems for children (Visher and Visher, 1978). Any form of marital conflict increases the likelihood that children will develop behavior problems (Rutter, 1978).

Not only does divorce change the family structure, but also many times it results in a decrease in the family's standard of living, with an increasing number of children and their single mothers moving into poverty status (Levine, 1984). During the late 1970s and early 1980s the number of preschool children in families living below the poverty level was greater than the comparable growth of children entering elementary school (U.S. Bu-

The number of school-age children living in poverty is increasing, which can result in many of a child's basic needs going unmet. (Charles Gatewood)

reau of the Census, 1984). Thus the proportion of children entering school who come from poverty backgrounds is increasing.

It is well documented that because of poverty, many of a child's basic needs are not met. Such children are also at a greater risk of developing academic and/or behavioral problems (Gelfand, Jenson, & Drew, 1982; Parke, 1978).

SCHOOL'S FAILURE TO MEET CHILDREN'S BASIC NEEDS

Physiological Needs

Students are in school to learn. They are continually asked to demonstrate their new understanding and skills. In essence schools are attempting to aid students in the process that Maslow calls self-actualization. When students successfully demonstrate new learnings, they usually are positively reinforced, which leads to the development of self-esteem and self-respect. Positive self-esteem further motivates students to learn, which results in the further development of self-actualization. The self-esteem, learning, self-actualization cycle continues only if the schools create environments in which the lower-level needs—physiological, safety and security, belonging and affection—are met.

Case 10: Forgetting to Sit Down

Sarah, a second-grade student, is a bright, happy, friendly child. She is very active, always being the first child to be ready for recess and the last to stop playing before returning to the classroom. When going to or from school, she is often seen skipping, jumping, or doing cartwheels.

Sarah's desk is second from the front. When given seat work, she either stands at her desk or half stands with one knee on the chair. The teacher always reminds her to sit, but no sooner has she sat down then she is back up on her feet.

After a good number of reminders, Sarah is kept in from recess. When this occurs, it is noted that she begins to walk around the room when class is in progress. This leads to further reprimands by the teacher, until her parents are notified.

The parents inform the teacher that at home Sarah is always jumping rope, playing catch, dancing, and even standing rather than sitting for piano lessons and practice. Also she stands at the table at mealtimes. It is decided that Sarah's seat will be moved to the back of the room so that her standing doesn't interfere with the other students. After this is explained to Sarah, she agrees to the move. The reprimands stop. Sarah continues to do excellent work, and by the end of second grade she is able to sit in her seat while working.

Case 10 illustrates how a young child attempts to meet the physiological need of movement and activity. This need was met by recess and standing at her desk. However, when the teacher demanded that Sarah sit and eventually removed recess, the need was no longer being met. This resulted in Sarah's further disruptive behavior of excessive movement around the room.

The importance of meeting students' physiological needs as a prerequisite to learning is quite evident in the construction of new schools and the renovation of older school buildings. Considerable attention is given to providing each classroom with adequate space and proper lighting, temperature, and ventilation. Almost every teacher, from personal experience, can attest to the importance of maintaining proper environmental conditions in a classroom if learning is to take place. Ask any teacher how much learning occurs on the first cold day of fall before the heating system is functional, or on the first hot day of early spring before the heating system has been turned off.

Somewhat less evident, but no less important than the environmental conditions, are concerns about hunger, overcrowding, noise, and frequent interruptions. Teachers are often heard voicing concern over the lack of attention of students in classes held just before lunch. When schools are overcrowded and/or lunch facilities are inadequate, lunch can span a three-hour period. Some students eat at the earliest lunch, sometimes before 11:00 A.M., whereas others eat at the latest lunch, sometimes after 1:00 P.M. This can produce a group of students who are hungry periodically every day, resulting in a lack of attention toward learning tasks.

Case 11: There Must Be a Better Way

One of the requirements of a certain university's secondary student teacher practicum is that student teachers follow a student's schedule of classes for an entire day. Their reactions are recorded. Some remarks that reflect common reactions of the student teachers are as follows:

No sooner were we in our seats in the first-period class than the V.P. was on the intercom system. She spent at least five minutes with announcements mostly directed for the teachers' attention. The speaker was loud and very annoying. After the announcements most of the students were talking among themselves. By the time we got down to work 15 minutes had passed. Halfway through the period a student messenger interrupted the class when he brought the morning office notices to the teacher. And believe it or not five minutes before the end of class the V.P. was back on the intercom with additional announcements. It was quite evident to me that these interruptions were a direct cause of inattentiveness and reduction in effective instruction. Much time was wasted both during the announcements and in obtaining student on-task behavior after the interruptions. There must be a better way.

Probably the most eye-opening experience I had was remembering how crowded and noisy schools can be. This was most evident to me when we changed classes. We had three minutes between classes. The halls were very crowded, with frequent pushing, shoving, and just bumping into each other. The noise level was so loud that it really bothered me. On arriving at the next class all I really wanted to do was to sit quietly for a few minutes before starting to work. The changes from hallways to classrooms are dramatic. I can see why it is difficult for some students to settle down and get on-task at the beginning of class. As bad as the hallways were it didn't prepare me for lunch. The lunch room was even noisier. By the time I waited in line I only had 15 minutes to eat and then back to the hallways to class. By the end of the day I was drained.

Case 12: Too Much Noise

Karen is a third-grade student who is well behaved and does well academically. One day her class is taken to the all-purpose room to observe a film. All of the third-grade classes are dismissed from their classrooms simultaneously. The children in the hallway are very noisy because of excitement. Karen is seen walking in the hallway holding her ears with a very sad face. When entering the room she goes directly to the back corner of the room and sits against the wall. The teacher asks her what is the matter. She says the noise hurts her ears; she feels like crying and she doesn't want to be there if it is going to be so noisy.

After the teachers quiet the students down, Karen rejoins her class. Referral to an ear specialist discloses that Karen has no problems with her hearing that would have caused such a reaction.

Interruptions, noise, and overcrowding, such as described in Cases 11 and 12, produce in students, regardless of age, emotional uneasiness that may result in nervousness, anxiety, a need to withdraw, or overactivity. All of these symptoms interfere with on-task behavior and reduce the effectiveness of the teaching/learning environment. Schools must pay particular attention to minimizing these serious distractions if they want to reduce student misbehavior that is caused by unmet physiological needs.

Safety and Security Needs

Case 13: Afraid of Going to School

Keith, an eighth-grade student, achieves at an average level in his social studies class. This class meets during the last period of the day. Approximately midway through the year his behavior in this class begins to change. He goes from a student who is attentive and participates freely to one who rarely participates and often has to be called back to attention by the teacher. He often is seen nervously looking out the window and is the first out of his seat and room at the end of class.

After a few days of such behavior the teacher requests that Keith stay a few minutes after class to discuss his changed behavior. At this time Keith informs his teacher that he has to be the first to leave school because if Greg sees him he will beat him up. He is fearful of Greg because Greg had threatened him for telling the gym teacher that he was throwing Keith's clothing around the locker room after gym class.

Generally schools create environments in which students feel safe from physical harm. Therefore it is assumed that students are safe from physical harm while attending school. While for the most part this is true, there are occasions when students, like Keith, do fear for their physical safety. Students in some schools sometimes are assaulted, coerced, bribed, or robbed. Also there are students in all schools who occasionally experience anxiety about walking to and from school, going to the restroom, changing in locker rooms, or changing classes. The more students feel insecure about their physical safety, the less likely they will be able to exhibit the on-task behaviors necessary for learning.

Belonging and Affection Needs

Whereas these needs are most often met by family at home or by the students' peers in and out of school, there must also be elements of caring, trust, and respect in the interpersonal relationships between teacher and students. In other words, there should be a caring, supportive classroom climate.

Withall (1969) stressed that the most important variable in determining the climate of a classroom is the teacher's verbal and nonverbal behaviors. Appropriate student behavior can be enhanced when teachers communicate the following to the learners:

Trust: "I believe you are able to learn and want to learn."
Respect: "Insofar as I try to help you learn, you are, by the same token, helping me to learn."
Caring: "I perceive you as a unique and worthwhile person who I want to help to learn and grow." (Whithall, 1979)

Case 14: Turning Off Students

Ms. Washington, senior high school science teacher, is quite concerned over what is perceived to be a significant decrease in student participation throughout the year. She views the problem as follows: "I ask a lot of questions. Early in the year many students volunteer but within a few weeks I find that volunteering has almost ceased and the only way I can get students to participate is to call on them."

Arrangements are made to observe her to determine the causes of this problem. Teacher questions, student responses, and teacher feedback are recorded. An example of one such interaction is this:

TEACHER QUESTION: "We know that man is in the family of Hominidae. What is man's taxonomic order?"
STUDENT RESPONSE: "Mammals."
TEACHER FEEDBACK: "No it's not mammals. We had this material last week; you should know it. The answer is Primates."

This observation reveals that about 70 percent of Ms. Washington's feedback is totally or partially negative. Upon speaking to the students, they are quick to point out that they don't feel like being put down because their answer isn't exactly what she wants. One student states, "I only answer when I know I'm correct. If I don't understand something I often just let it go rather than be drilled."

For students to learn effectively, they must fully participate in the learning process. Students must be encouraged to ask and answer questions, attempt new approaches, make mistakes, and ask for assistance. Learners only engage in these behaviors in settings in which they feel safe from being ridiculed or made to feel inadequate. As the year progressed Ms. Washington failed to demonstrate her trust, respect, and caring for her students. Thus, they were discouraged from fully participating in the learning process.

Teacher comments such as "Why do you ask so many questions?", "You should know this; we studied it last week", or "Everyone should understand this; there should be no questions" serve no useful purpose. Instead they communicate unproductive expectations toward learning and serve to hinder learner participation, confidence, and motivation, which in turn lead to off-task behavior.

The importance of schools being places where students are "cared for" is also stressed by Glasser (1978). He sees failure as the root of misbehavior, stressing that when students don't learn at the expected rate, they get less "care" and recognition. This produces a situation in which students see themselves as trapped and there is no acceptance and no recognition except for what can be gained through misbehavior.

In sharp contrast to the feelings of Ms. Washington's students are the feelings of the following fifth-grade students.

Case 15: I'm Going to Be Sorry When Fifth Grade Is Over

One afternoon last May we overheard a group of fifth-grade students say, "I'm going to be sorry when fifth grade is over." I stopped and asked them if they would be willing to tell me why they felt this way. The following were their comments.

"She lets us give our opinions."
"If we say something stupid, she doesn't say anything."
"She lets us decide how we are going to do things."
"She gives us suggestions and helps us when we get stuck."
"You can say how you feel."
"She gives us choices."
"She tells us what she thinks, but doesn't want us to think like her. Some teachers tell us their opinions, but you know that they really want you to think the same way."
"We learn a lot."

Self-Esteem

All individuals have a need for self-esteem. Learners must feel good about themselves before they can dedicate their energies toward learning.

Students who achieve academically at unsatisfactory levels are continually reminded of their shortcomings and incompetence throughout the school day. Unless these students succeed in cocurricular areas, such as athletics or music, school attendance results in a continual erosion of their self-esteem. For such students, misbehavior gives them some of this lost self-esteem. We have heard chronically misbehaving students rationalize their behaviors with such comments as "At least I get some attention," "The students know that they can count on me to liven the class up," and "The teacher knows not to fool with me." Such rationalizations have a hidden meaning; what the student is really saying is "I'm important because I have the power to disrupt this class."

Self-esteem has three major components (Jones, 1980):

Significance: a learner's belief that she is liked by and important to others who are important to her.

Competence: a learner's success at some task that has value to her.

Power: a learner's ability to control important parts of her environment.

Since self-esteem is such a basic need, individuals continually strive to meet it. Therefore if teachers fail to provide opportunities for students to experience a sense of significance, competence, and power, they increase the likelihood that children will express their significance, competence, and power in undesirable ways.

CHILDREN'S PURSUIT OF SOCIAL RECOGNITION

Closely akin to our discussion of children's basic needs is Adlerian psychology's explanation of children's pursuit of social recognition and acceptance.

The renowned psychiatrist Alfred Adler and his student and colleague Rudolph Driekurs believed that behavior is best understood from a few key premises.

1. People are social beings who have a need to belong, be recognized, and accepted.
2. Behavior is goal-directed and has the purpose of gaining the recognition and acceptance that people want.
3. People can choose how they behave; they can behave or misbehave. Their behavior is not outside their control.

Putting these key ideas together, Adler and Driekurs believed that people choose to try a wide variety of behaviors to see if it gains them the recognition and acceptance they want. When socially accepted means do not produce the needed recognition and acceptance, people then choose to misbehave under the mistaken belief that these socially unacceptable behaviors will produce the recognition they seek. In summary, misbehavior reflects the mistaken belief that such behaviors are the only way to receive recognition.

Applying these premises to children's conduct, Dreikurs, Grundwald, and Pepper (1982) identified four mistaken goals of their disruptive behaviors. These goals are attention getting, power seeking, revenge seeking, and inadequacy. The goals are usually sought after in a sequential order if not rewarded. According to this theory, these goals are strongest in elementary-aged children but are also present in adolescents.

Case 16: Seeking Faulty Goals

Bob is a sixth-grade student of average academic ability. During the first day of class when students are asked to choose seats, Bob chooses the one next to the window in the back of the room. Between classes he rarely interacts with classmates. Instead he either bolts out of the class first or slowly swaggers out last.

During instructional times he either nonchalantly leans back in his seat or jumps up and calls out answers. During seat work he often has to be reminded to begin, and once he finishes, he taps his pencil, wanders around the back of the room, or noisily moves his chair and desk.

Bob's behavior often improves for short periods of time after excessive teacher attention that ranges from positive reinforcement to reprimands. These periods of improvement are followed by a return to similar disruptive behaviors. Bob's attention-seeking behavior continues throughout the first half of the school year. The teacher's response usually is to yell at him, send him to the principal, or make comments in front of the class that reflect the teacher's extreme frustration.

The teacher's behavior eventually is characterized by threats, such as "You will stay after school longer every day until you begin to behave," or "Every day that you don't turn in your homework, you will have 20 more problems to do." Bob sees immediately the impossibility of some of the threats and boldly says, "If I have to stay after school longer each day, in two weeks I'll have to sleep here." There are tremendous amounts of laughter from his classmates at such comments. However, eventually he says, "I'm not coming for your detention" and "You can't make me do homework if I don't want to." The teacher no longer feels annoyed but now feels threatened and challenged.

Whenever problems arise in the classroom, the teacher and students are quick to blame Bob. Occasionally he is accused of things that he does not do, and he is quick to shout, "I didn't do it; I'm always the one who gets blamed for everything around here." His classmates now also show extreme annoyance with his behaviors. Once this happens, he resorts to acts directed against individuals. He kicks students' chairs and intentionally knocks over others' books as he walks down the aisles.

One day another boy accuses Bob of taking his book. Without warning Bob flips the student's desk. The student falls backward, lands on his arm, and breaks it. As a result, Bob is suspended.

When Bob returns from his suspension, he is notified that he will be sent to the office for any violation of a classroom rule. He is completely ignored by his classmates.

For the rest of the year Bob comes in, goes to the back of the room, does no work, and bothers no one. At first the teacher tries to get Bob involved, but all efforts are refused. The teacher thinks to herself that she has tried everything she knows. "If he wants to just sit there, let him. At least he isn't bothering anyone any more."

Bob was a child who felt that he was not getting the recognition he desired. He saw no chance of gaining this recognition through socially accepted or constructive contributions. He first channeled his energies into gaining attention. Like all attention-seeking students, he had the faulty notion that he was important only when others took notice of him and acknowledged his presence.

Attention-seeking students make up a large part of the misbehaving population in the schools. These students may ask question after question, use excessive charm, continually need help or assistance, continually ask for the teacher's approval, call out, or show off. The teacher usually becomes annoyed at such children. When the teacher reprimands or gives these children attention, they temporarily stop their attention-seeking behavior. When attention-getting behavior no longer gives the students the recognition they want, many of them seek this recognition through the next goal, power, which is exactly what Bob did when he began to confront the teacher openly.

Students who seek power through misbehavior believe, "I can do what I want to and nobody can make me do anything I don't want to do." They feel important because they perceive that they are in control. By challenging teachers, they often gain social acceptance from their peers. Students seeking power argue, lie, ignore, become stubborn, have temper tantrums, and generally become disobedient to show that they are in command of the situation. Teachers feel threatened or challenged by these children and often feel compelled to force them into compliance. Once the teacher enters into a power struggle with power-seeking students, the students usually win. Whether or not the students succeed in getting what they want, they have succeeded in getting the teacher to fight, thereby giving them undue attention and time. If the teacher "wins" the power struggle, the winning reinforces the students' idea that power is what really counts.

With a power-seeking student, reprimands from the teacher result in intensified challenges or temporary withdrawal before new power-seeking behaviors reappear. As power struggles develop between a teacher and a student, both teacher controlling and student power-seeking behaviors usually become more severe and the student-teacher relationship deteriorates further. With continued power struggles, which the student sees herself as losing, the student often moves to the next goal—seeking revenge.

When students have no control over their environment, they experience an increased sense of inferiority and futility. These young people feel that they have been treated unfairly and are deeply hurt by what they consider to be others' disregard for their feelings. They seek revenge by hurting others, often not just those that they think have hurt them. For instance Bob sought his revenge on random individuals who happened to be sitting along his aisle. Such children destroy property, hit, engage in extremely rough play, and use obscenities.

When working with such students, teachers feel defeated and hurt and have a difficult time being concerned with what is best for the student. Instead teachers feel a strong desire "to get even." Teacher reprimands usually result in an explosive display of anger and abusiveness from the student.

Unfortunately revenge-seeking behaviors elicit dislike and more hurt from others. The students continually feel a deep sense of despair and worthlessness. Their interactions with other people often result in negative feelings about themselves, which eventually move them to the last goal—the desire to be left alone in order to avoid further attacks on their self-esteem. They cannot be motivated and refuse to participate in class activities. Their message is clear: "Don't expect anything from me because I have nothing worthwhile to give." They are often heard saying, "Why don't you just leave me alone; I'm not bothering anyone," "Why try, I'll just get it wrong," or "I can't do it."

Teachers often feel that they have tried everything in the world with these students and finally give up. Further attempts usually result in very little, if any, change in the students' refusal to show interest, to participate, or to interact with others. Bob's teacher actually felt somewhat relieved that he no longer was a disturbing influence in class. However if the teacher had been able to stop his progression toward the faulty goal of inadequacy, Bob would have had a much more meaningful and valuable sixth-grade learning experience.

Most of the goals of misbehavior are pursued one at a time, but some students switch back and forth between goals and some goal-seeking behaviors are situational. The hierarchical approach to classroom management presented in this book offers many strategies for working with children seeking the four mistaken goals. In addition specific management techniques for each goal are discussed in detail in Charles (1989), Dreikurs, Grundwald, and Pepper (1982), Dubelle and Hoffman (1984), and Sweeney (1981).

STAGES OF COGNITIVE AND MORAL DEVELOPMENT

Not too long ago it was believed that children thought exactly the same way as adults. However, work in the area of cognitive development by the child psychologist Jean Piaget helped lay this misconception to rest. It is now largely accepted that children move through distinct stages of cognitive and moral development. At each stage children think and interpret their environment differently than children at other stages. This causes variance in behavior as children move from one stage to another. An understanding of these stages enables a teacher to better understand student behavior patterns.

Cognitive Development

Throughout his lifetime, Piaget studied the manner in which children interacted with their environment and how their intellect developed. He considered knowledge to be the transformation of an individual's experience with the environment and not the accumulation of facts and pieces of information. His research resulted in the formulation of a four-stage age-related cognitive development theory (Piaget, 1970), which has significantly influenced the manner in which children are educated. These stages are the sensorimotor, the preoperational, the concrete operational, and the formal operational stages.

The sensorimotor stage of development occurs from birth to approximately two years of age. It is characterized by the refinement of motor skills and the use of the five senses to explore the environment. This stage obviously has little importance for teachers working with school-age children.

The preoperational stage occurs from approximately two to seven years and is the stage most children have reached when they begin their school experience. Children at this stage are egocentric, with an inability to conceive that others may see things differently than they do. Although their ability to give some thought to decisions is developing, the great majority of the time they act only on perceptive impulses. Their short attention span interacts with their static thinking, resulting in an inability to think of a sequence of steps or operations. Their sense of time and space is limited to short duration and close proximity.

The concrete operational stage occurs from approximately seven to twelve years. Children now are able to order and classify objects and consider several variables simultaneously as long as they have experiences with "concrete" content. Step-by-step instructions are needed by these children if they are expected to work through lengthy procedures. What can be frustrating to teachers who do not understand the characteristics of this stage is that these children do not attempt to check their conclusions, have difficulty thinking about thinking (how they arrived at certain conclusions), and seem unaware and unconcerned with inconsistencies in their own reasoning.

At the earliest, about twelve years of age, children begin to move into the formal operational stage. They begin to develop independent critical thinking skills, plan lengthy procedures, and consider a number of possible answers to problems. They no longer are tied to concrete examples but instead are able to use symbols and verbal examples. These children or adolescents also begin to think about their own and others' thinking, leading them to consider motives; the past, present, and future; the abstract; the remote; and the ideal. The methodological implications for teaching students at each stage are somewhat obvious and have been researched and written about extensively (Adler, 1966; Gorman, 1972; Karplus, 1977).

Moral Development

Piaget's cognitive development theory is directly related to a child's progress through the stages of moral development. Piaget demonstrated that a child is close to or at the formal operational stage of cognitive development before she possesses the intellectual ability to evaluate, consider, and act on abstract moral dilemmas. Piaget further demonstrated that what an elementary child thinks is bad or wrong is vastly different from what an adolescent thinks is wrong (Piaget, 1965).

Piaget's work formed the basis for Laurence Kohlberg's theory of moral development. Kohlberg saw moral development as progressing through six levels of moral reasoning: punishment-obedience, exchange of favors, good boy–nice girl, law and order, social contract, and universal ethical principles (Kohlberg, 1969, 1975).

Children between the ages of four and six have a "punishment-obedience" orientation to moral reasoning. Their decisions are based on the physical consequences of an act; will they be punished or rewarded? Outcomes of situations are paramount, and there is very little comprehension of a person's motive or intention. Their egocentrism limits their ability to see other points of view or alternatives.

Between the ages of six and nine, children move into the "exchange of favors" orientation. At this level judgments are made on the basis of reciprocal favors; you do this for me and I will do this for you. Fulfilling one's own needs comes first. Children are just beginning to understand the motives behind behaviors and outcomes.

Children move into the "good boy–nice girl" orientation between the ages of ten and fifteen. Conformity dictates behavior and reasoning ability. Peer review is strong, and judgments about how to behave are made on the basis of avoiding criticism and pleasing others. Peer conformity is so strong that it is quite common to follow peers unquestionably, but at the same time, continually to ask "why" when requests are made by adults.

The "law and order" orientation dominates young people's moral reasoning between the ages of fifteen and eighteen. Individuals at this stage of development are quite rigid. Judgments are made on the basis of obeying the law. Motives are understood but not whole-heartedly considered if the behavior has broken a law. At this stage teenagers are quick to recognize and point out inconsistencies in expected behavior. It is quite common to hear teenagers say to adults, "Why do I have to do this? You don't." Finally they also are beginning to recognize the consequences of their actions.

According to Kohlberg, few people reach the next two levels of moral reasoning. For those who do, the "social contract" orientation is reached between the ages of eighteen and twenty. Moral judgments are made on the basis of upholding individual rights and democratic principles. People at this level recognize that individuals differ in their values and do not accept "because I said so" or "that's the way it is" as rationales for rules.

The highest level of moral reasoning is the "universal ethical" orientation. Judgments are based on respect for the dignity of human beings and on what is good for humanity, not on selfish interests or standards upheld by authority.

As in cognitive development, the ages within any moral development stage are approximations. Individuals continually move back and forth between stages, depending on the moral situation at hand, especially at transitional points between stages.

Behavior: The Interaction of Cognitive and Moral Development

It is important for teachers to be very familiar with the moral and cognitive growth of school-age children to understand how they perceive what is right and wrong, what cognitive skills they are able to use, and what motivates their social and academic behavior. It is also important to recognize common developmental behaviors that are a result of the interaction of the cognitive and moral stages through which the children pass. This interaction does not and cannot explain all disruptive classroom behaviors. However, it does provide a basis on which we can begin to understand many of the disruptive behaviors exhibited in classrooms.

At the beginning of elementary school, students are in the "preoperational" stage cognitively and the "punishment-obedience" stage morally. Their behavior is a result of the interplay of such factors as their egocentricity, limited sense of time and space, little comprehension of other's motives, and short attention span. Typical behaviors of this stage are to become frustrated easily, have difficulty sharing, argue frequently, believe that they are right and their classmates wrong, and tattle a lot.

By middle to upper elementary school and beginning junior high or middle school, children are in the "concrete operational" stage cognitively and the "exchange of favors" to the "good boy–nice girl" stages morally. Typical behaviors early in this period are frequent forming and re-forming of cliques, acting on opinions based on a single or very few concrete characteristics, and telling secrets. These students employ many annoying attention-seeking behaviors to please the teacher. Later the effects of peer conformity appear. Children are often off-task because they are constantly in conversation with their friends. Those who do not fit into the conforming peer group often are excluded and ridiculed.

Students still have little patience with long discussions and lengthy explanations. They are unaware or unconcerned about their inconsistencies and are closed-minded. They often employ such phrases as "I know!" or "Do we have to discuss this?" or "I don't care!" with a tone that communicates a nonchalant lack of interest.

By the time students are leaving junior high school and entering high school, most of them will be in the "formal operational" stage cognitively and moving from the "good boy–nice girl" to the "law and order" stage, a few reaching the "social contract" level by the end of high school.

Adolescents can deal with abstractness and conceive of many possibilities and ideals as well as the reality of their environment. Although peer pressure is still strong, they begin to see the need and rationale for rules and policies and eventually the need to protect rights and principles. They are now attempting to discover who they are, what they believe in, and what they are competent in.

Because of the young persons' search for a self-identity and their ability to think abstractedly, they may often challenge and question the

Misbehavior can result when the instruction is not matched with the student's cognitive development stage. (Ken Karp)

Age-specific behavior is often the result of interaction between cognitive and moral development.

traditional values taught in school and home. These students need to have a valid reason for "why" everything is the way it is. They will not accept the rationale "because I said so" as a legitimate reason to conform to a rule. Some students hold to a particular behavior, explanation, or judgment, even in the face of punishment, if they feel that their individual rights have been challenged or violated. Unfortunately many of these behaviors are carried out in an argumentative format. Table 3-1 lists the cognitive and moral stages, their characteristics, and associated behaviors.

A longitudinal study provides support for the idea that normal developmental changes can lead to disruptive behavior. Jessor and Jessor (1977) found that the correlates of misbehavior in school are (1) growth in independence; (2) decline in traditional ideology; (3) increase in relativistic morality; (4) increase in peer orientation; and (5) increase in modeling problem behaviors. This finding led the researchers to conclude that the normal course of developmental change is in the direction of greater possibility of problems. However, Clarizio and McCoy (1983) stated that normal problem behaviors that occur as a developmental phenomenon seem to have a very high probability of being resolved with increasing age. Support for such a statement is offered by a study of 400 famous twentieth-century men and women, which concluded that four out of five had experienced difficulties and problems related to school and schooling (Goertzel and Goertzel, 1962).

INSTRUCTIONAL COMPETENCE

At first glance it may seem that the teacher has none or little control over the five causes of misbehavior that thus far have been discussed. However although a teacher cannot significantly alter the course of most of these

TABLE 3-1 Cognitive and Moral Development with Common Associated Behaviors

COGNITIVE STAGE	COGNITIVE ABILITIES	MORAL STAGE	MORAL REASONING	COMMON BEHAVIOR
Sensorimotor (0–2)	use of senses to "know" environment			
Preoperational (2–7)	—difficulty with conceiving others' points of view (egocentric) —sense of time & space limited to short duration/close proximity —difficulty thinking through steps or decisions; acts impulsively	Punishment-obedience (4–6)	—actions based on physical outcome —little comprehension of motives —egocentric	—inattentiveness —easily frustrated —difficulty sharing —arguments during play
Concrete operational (7–12)	—limited ability to think about thinking —often will not check conclusions —unaware and unconcerned with their own inconsistencies	Exchange of favors (6–9)	—actions based on reciprocal favors —fulfilling one's own needs comes first —beginning to understand motives	—cliques —attention-getting behavior —exclusion of certain classmates —inattentiveness during periods of discussion —"know it all" attitude

Formal operational (12–)	Good boy–nice girl (10–15)	
—ability to think about thinking has developed	—actions based on peer conformity	—point out inconsistencies between behaviors and rules
—can use independent critical thinking skills	**Law and order (15–18)**	—challenge rules and policies
—can consider motives; the past, present, & future; the abstract; and the ideal	—rigid judgments based on following the law	—demand rationale behind rules
	—recognize motives and consequences	—will not unquestionably accept authority
		—argumentative
	Social contract (18–20)	
	—actions based on upholding individual rights and democratic principles	
	—actions based on respect for human dignity	
	Universal ethical (few people reach this level)	

A teacher has total control over the use of effective teaching strategies. (Susan Woog Wagner)

societal, familial, and developmental events, she does have total control over ensuring that she has excellent instructional competence. In this way the teacher can minimize the effects of these ongoing events and prevent additional misbehavior caused by poor instructional methodology. At the same time, of course, she will be maximizing the learning potential in her classroom.

Case 17: Not Being Able to Teach

Ms. Cook loves mathematics and enjoys working with young people, which she does often in camp and youth organizations. After graduating with a B.S. degree in mathematics, she decides to continue her education, eventually earning a master's degree in mathematics and teaching certification at the secondary level. She obtains a teaching position at a progressive suburban junior high school.

Ms. Cook conscientiously plans for all of her algebra and geometry classes and knows the material thoroughly. However, within a few months Ms. Cook's classes are characterized by significant discipline problems, such as most of the students being out of their seats, talking, throwing paper, calling out jokes, coming in unprepared, and in a few instances openly confronting Ms. Cook's procedures and competence.

Even though she is given assistance, supervision, and support from the administration, Ms. Cook decides not to return for her second year of teaching. In an attempt to understand the students' behavior, they are interviewed at the end of the school year. The following are the most common responses concerning Ms. Cook's methods:

1. Gave unclear explanations
2. Discussed topics having nothing or little to do with the subject at hand
3. Kept repeating understood material
4. Wrote things on the board but never explained them and her board work was sloppy
5. Would say, "We already did this" when asked for help
6. Did not involve the class and only called on the same people
7. Had difficulty giving clear answers to our questions
8. Didn't explain how we could use the material
9. Always used her note cards
10. Could not determine why the class was having difficulty understanding the material
11. Either gave us the answers to the homework or didn't go over it, so no one had to do it

---

Why would a teacher who is quite knowledgeable and enthusiastic about the subject matter and enjoys working with young people have such management problems? Why would otherwise well-behaved students misbehave to such an extent in one particular class? The students' responses indicate a reasonable answer: the teacher's lack of skill in basic instructional methodology.

Because of instructional skill deficiencies, the students perceived the teacher as lacking "expert power." Expert power is the social authority and respect a teacher receives because she possesses special knowledge and expertness (French and Raven, 1960). (This and other authority bases are discussed in depth in Chapter Four.) Even though the teacher did possess expertness in the field of mathematics, it was not perceived by the students because of her inability to communicate the content clearly, evaluate and remediate student misunderstandings, and explain the relevancy of the content to students' lives. The likelihood that students will respect a teacher increases when they view teachers as having expertness.

A teacher's ability to explain and clarify is foremost in developing authority (Tanner, 1978). Tanner stated that "Teacher effectiveness, as perceived by pupils, invests the teacher with classroom authority" (p. 67). To students, teacher effectiveness translates to "explaining the material so that we can understand it." When this occurs, students regard the teacher as competent and the teacher is invested with authority. Unlike Ms. Cook's students, who indicated that instructional clarity was a problem, students who respect and like their teachers often respond that "the teacher explains things well."

It has been shown that when students like their teachers, they are more likely to behave appropriately and are more motivated to learn (Kounin, 1970). Upon further investigation Kounin found that liked teachers are described by students as those who can explain the content well, whereas those who are disliked leave students in some state of confusion.

SUMMARY

Although there are innumerable causes of misbehavior in schools, this chapter focused on six of the major ones.

Societal changes, most notably the effects of the knowledge explosion and the media revolution, have created an environment that is vastly different from that in which children of previous generations grew up. In addition home life for children is significantly different. For instance more children now than ever before live in single-parent homes. Also, more children are living at or below the poverty level. Because of these and other factors, some children's basic needs are not being met by the home. Such out-of-school experiences have been much more significant predictors of school behavior than children's in-school experiences.

Within the schools themselves, some children's basic needs are not being met, which may cause discipline problems. In addition, throughout the school years children's developmental cognitive and moral growth, as well as their continual need for social recognition, is reflected in their behavior.

A teacher has little or no control over many of these developments. What she does have control over is her own instructional competence. Excellent instruction can ameliorate the effects of these outside influences as well as prevent the misbehavior that occurs as a direct result of poor instruction. Effective teaching techniques are covered in detail in Chapter Five.

REFERENCES

ADLER, I. (1966, December). Mental growth and the art of teaching. *The Mathematics Teacher, 59*, 706–715.

ATKIN, C. (1983). Effects of realistic TV violence vs. fictional violence on aggression. *Journalism Quarterly, 60*, 4, 615–621.

BANDURA, A. (1973). *Aggression: A Social Learning Analysis.* Englewood Cliffs, NJ: Prentice-Hall.

BAYH, B. (1978). Seeking solutions to school violence and vandalism. *Phi Delta Kappan, 59*, 5, 299–302.

BOUTHILET, P. D., and LAZAR, J. (Eds.). (1982). *Television and Behavior: Ten Years of Scientific Progress and Implications for the Eighties.* Washington, DC: U.S. Department of Health and Human Services, National Institute of Mental Health.

CHARLES, C. M. (1989). *Building Classroom Discipline from Models to Practice,* 2nd ed. New York: Longman.

CLARIZIO, H. F., and McCOY, G. F. (1983). *Behavior Disorders in Children,* 3rd ed. New York: Harper & Row.

DEWEY, J. (1916). *Democracy and Education.* New York: Macmillan.

DREIKURS, R., GRUNDWALD, B., and PEPPER, F. (1982). *Maintaining Sanity in the Classroom: Classroom Management Techniques,* 2nd ed. New York: Harper & Row.

DUBELLE, S. T., and HOFFMAN, C. M. (1984). *Misbehaving—Solving the Disciplinary Puzzle for Educators.* Lancaster, PA: Technomic.

ELLIOT, D. S., and VOSS, H. L. (1974). *Delinquency and Dropout.* Lexington, MA: Lexington Books.

FELDHUSEN, J. F. (1978). Behavior problems in secondary schools. *Journal of Research and Development in Education, 11*, 4, 17–28.

FELDHUSEN, J. F., THUROTON, J. R., and BENNING, J. J. (1973). A longitudinal study of delinquency and other aspects of children's behavior. *International Journal of Criminology and Penology, 1*, 341–351.

FRENCH, J. R. P., and RAVEN, B. (1960). In D. Cartwright and A. Zander (Eds.), *Group Dynamics: Research and Theory.* Evamotor, IL: Row-Peterson

GELFAND, D. M., JENSON, W. R., and DREW, C. J. (1982). *Understanding Child Behavior Disorders.* New York: Holt, Rinehart & Winston.

GLASSER, W. (1978). Disorders in our schools: Causes and remedies. *Phi Delta Kappan, 59*, 5, 331–333.

GOERTZEL, V., and GOERTZEL, M. (1962). *Cradles of Eminence.* Boston: Little, Brown.

GORMAN, R. M. (1972). *Discovering Piaget: A Guide for Teachers.* Columbus, OH: Charles E. Merrill.

JESSOR, J., and JESSOR, S. L. (1977). *Problem Behavior and Psychosocial Development.* New York: Academic Press.

JONES, V. F. (1980). *Adolescents with Behavior Problems.* Boston: Allyn & Bacon.

KARPLUS, R. (1977). *Science Teaching and the Development of Reasoning.* Berkeley: University of California Press.

KINDSVATTER, R. (1978). A new view of the dynamics of discipline. *Phi Delta Kappan, 59*, 5, 322–325.

KOHLBERG, L. (1969). *Stages in the Development of Moral Thought and Action.* New York: Holt, Rinehart & Winston.

KOHLBERG, L. (1975). The cognitive-developmental approach to moral education. *Phi Delta Kappan, 56*, 10, 610–677.

KOUNIN, J. S. (1970). *Discipline and Group Management in Classrooms.* New York: Holt, Rinehart & Winston.

LEVINE, V. (1984, August). Time use and student achievement: A critical assessment of the National Commission Report. *Forum* (College of Education, The Pennsylvania State University), *11*, 12.

MASLOW, A. (1968). *Toward a Psychology of Being.* New York: D. Von Nostrand.

MENACKER, J., WELDON, W., and HURWITZ, E. (1989). School order and safety as community issues. *Phi Delta Kappan, 71*, 1, 39.

PARKE, R. D. (1978). Children's home environments: Social and cognitive effects. In I. Altman and J. F. Wohlwill (Eds.), *Children and the Environment.* New York: Plenum Press.

PEARL, D. (1984). Violence and aggression. *Society, 21,* 6, 15–16.

PEARL, D., BOUTHILET, L., and LAZAR, J. (Eds.). (1982). *Television and Behavior: Ten Years of Scientific Progress and Implications for the Eighties,* Vol. 2. Washington, DC: U.S. Government Printing Office.

PIAGET, J. (1965). *The Moral Judgment of the Child.* Glencoe, IL: Free Press.

PIAGET, J. (1970). Piaget's theory. In P. H. Mussen (Ed.), *Carmichael's Manual of Child Psychology,* Vol. 1. New York: Wiley.

RICE, M. L., HUSTON, A. C., and WRIGHT, J. C. (1982). The forms and codes of television: Effects on children's attention, comprehension and social behavior. In D. Pearl, L. Bouthilet, and J. Lazar (Eds.), *Television and Behavior: Ten Years of Scientific Progress and Implications for the Eighties,* Vol. 2. Washington, DC: U.S. Government Printing Office.

RICE, P. F. (1981). *The Adolescent Development, Relationships, and Culture,* 3rd ed. Boston: Allyn & Bacon.

ROTHENBERG, M. B. (1975). Effects of television violence on children and youth. *Journal of the American Medical Association, 234,* 1043–1046.

RUTTER, M. (1978). Family, area, and school influences in the genesis of conduct disorders. In L. Herson, M. Berger, and D. Shaffer (Eds.), *Aggression and Anti-Social Behaviour in Childhood and Adolescence.* Oxford: Pergamon Press.

SINGER, D. G., SINGER, J. L., and Zuckerman, D. M. (1981). *Teaching Television.* New York: Dial Press, 1981.

SINGER, J. L., SINGER, D. G., and RAPACZYNSKI, W. S. (1984). Family patterns and television viewing as predictors of children's beliefs and aggression. *Journal of Communications, 34,* 2, 73–89.

STINCHCOMBE, A. L. (1964). *Rebellion in a High School.* Chicago: Quadrangle Books.

SWEENEY, J. J. (1981). *Adlerian Counseling Proven Concepts and Strategies,* 2nd ed. Muncie, IN: Accelerated Development.

TANNER, L. N. (1978). *Classroom Discipline for Effective Teaching and Learning.* New York: Holt, Rinehart & Winston.

TOFFLER, A. (1970). *Future Shock.* New York: Random House.

U.S. Bureau of the Census. (1981, June). *Population Profile of the United States: 1980,* Series p. 20, No. 363. Washington, DC: U.S. Government Printing Office.

U.S. Bureau of the Census. (1984). *Estimates of Poverty Including the Value of Noncash Benefits: 1979 to 1982.* Washington, DC: U.S. Government Printing Office.

VISHER, E. B., and VISHER, J. S. (1978). Common problems of stepparents and their spouses. *American Journal of Orthopsychiatry,* 48, 252–262.

WITHALL, J. (1969, March). Evaluation of classroom climate. *Childhood Education,* pp. 403–408.

WITHALL, J. (1979). Problem behavior: Function of social-emotional climate? *Journal of Education, 161,* 2, 89–101.

ZUCKERMAN, D. M., and ZUCKERMAN, B. S. (1985). Television's impact on children. *Pediatrics, 75,* 2, 223–240.

EXERCISES

1. In your own school experiences, what are some instructional techniques your teacher used that had the potential to change disruptive student behaviors?

2. What if anything can schools and classroom teachers do to help students meet the following basic human needs: (a) physiological, (b) safety and security, and (c) belonging and affection?

3. What can classroom teachers do to help students satisfy the three components of self-esteem: (a) significance, (b) competence, and (c) power?

4. Even though they are beyond the school's control, changes in society can influence student behavior in school. What changes in society during the last ten years do you feel have had negative influences on classroom behavior?

5. In your opinion, can television programs and films cause students to misbehave in the classroom? If so, list some specific examples to support your opinion. If not, explain why.

6. Explain why some educational researchers believe that cognitive development is a prerequisite for moral development.

7. Considering students' cognitive development, how might a teacher teach the following concepts in the third, seventh, and eleventh grades?
   a. Volume of a rectangular solid $= L \times W \times H$
   b. Civil rights and equality
   c. Subject-predicate agreement
   d. Gravity

8. How might inappropriate teaching of these concepts for the cognitive level of the students contribute to classroom discipline problems?

9. Considering students' moral development, what can we expect as typical reactions to the following events at each of the following grade levels.

	First	Fourth	Seventh	Twelfth
a. A student from a poor family steals the lunch ticket of a student from a fairly wealthy family.				
b. A teacher keeps the entire class on a detention because of the disruptive behavior of a few.				
c. A student destroys school property and allows another student to be falsely accused and punished for the vandalism.				
d. A student has points subtracted from her test score for talking after her test paper was already turned in.				

10. What are some normal behaviors (considering their developmental level) for elementary students, junior high school students, and senior high students that can be disruptive in a classroom?

11. What might a teacher do to allow the normal behaviors (listed in the answer to question 10) to be expressed, while at the same time to prevent them from disrupting learning?

CHAPTER 4

Philosophical Approaches to Classroom Management

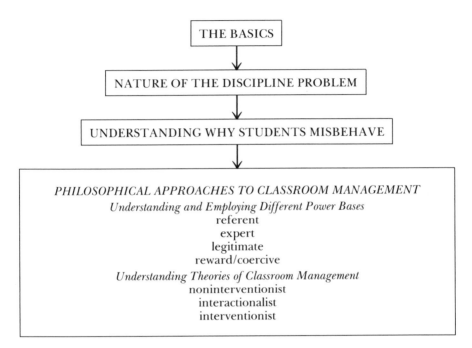

THE BASICS

↓

NATURE OF THE DISCIPLINE PROBLEM

↓

UNDERSTANDING WHY STUDENTS MISBEHAVE

↓

PHILOSOPHICAL APPROACHES TO CLASSROOM MANAGEMENT
Understanding and Employing Different Power Bases
referent
expert
legitimate
reward/coercive
Understanding Theories of Classroom Management
noninterventionist
interactionalist
interventionist

PRINCIPLES OF CLASSROOM MANAGEMENT

14. Theoretical approaches to classroom management are useful to teachers because they offer a basis whereby student and teacher behavior can be analyzed, understood, and controlled.
15. As social agents, teachers have access to a variety of power bases, which can be used to influence student behavior.
16. The techniques a teacher employs to control student behavior should be consistent with the teacher's beliefs about how students learn and develop.

INTRODUCTION

Case 18: The Tricks of the Trade Approach

Ms. Judy Knepp is a first-year teacher in Armstrong Middle School. She is having a great deal of difficulty with her sixth-grade developmental reading class. Many of the students seem disinterested in school, lazy, immature, and very rebellious. As a result of continuous widespread chattering, Ms. Knepp spends the vast majority of each class period yelling and reprimanding individual students. She has considered using detention to control students, but there are so many disruptive students that she just doesn't know whom to give detention to first. Although most of her other classes are going well, this one class has become such a battlefield that she finds herself hating to go to school in the morning.

After struggling with this class on her own for a couple of long weeks, Ms. Knepp decides that she better ask somebody for help. She is reluctant to go to any of the administrators since she thinks that revealing a problem to any of them probably will result in a very low official evaluation for her first semester's work. Finally, she decides that the best person to go to is Ms. Hoffman, a veteran teacher of 14 years with a reputation for striking fear into the hearts of her sixth-grade students. After she tells Ms. Hoffman all about her horrendous fifth-period class, Ms. Knepp waits anxiously for the words of wisdom that will help her to get this class under control. Finally the long-needed advice arrives: "I'd just keep the whole class in for detention. Keep them until about 4:30 just one day, and I guarantee you won't have any more trouble with them. These kids think they're tough, but when they see that you're just as mean and tough as they are, they'll melt pretty quickly." Ms. Knepp is dismayed. Her first and only thoughts are "that's just not fair. What about those four or five kids who don't misbehave? Why should they have to stay in too?" She does not voice her objections to Ms. Hoffman. She feels that Ms. Hoffman will see her as rude and ungrateful if she turns down advice for which she herself had asked. She does ask, "What about parents who object to such punishment?" However, Ms. Hoffman assures her that she has never had any trouble from parents and that the principal, Dr. Kropa, will support the disciplinary action even if any parents do try to butt in. Ms. Knepp feels trapped. She knows that Ms. Hoffman expects her to follow through and will be upset if she doesn't. She also fears that Ms. Hoffman will spread the word about her ingratitude to the other veteran teachers if she doesn't take the advice, and she longs to be accepted by the other teachers.

Despite her misgivings, Ms. Knepp decides that she will follow the advice and do it quickly before she loses her nerve. The next day in class, she announces that one more disruption—no matter who is the guilty culprit—will bring detention for the entire class. For five minutes silence reigns, and the class actually accomplishes some work. Ms. Knepp begins to breathe a long sigh of relief when suddenly she hears a loud "you pig" from the back right-hand corner of the room. She is positive that all the students have heard the epithet and knows that she cannot ignore it. She also knows that an unenforced threat will mean disaster. "That does it. Everyone in this class has detention tomorrow after school." Immediately the air fills with a chorus of "That ain't fair," "I didn't do nothing," "You wish," and "Don't hold your breath." Naturally, most of these complaints come from the biggest troublemakers. However, several students who never cause trouble also complain bitterly of this unfair treatment. Deep down, Ms. Knepp agrees with them, but she feels compelled to dismiss their legitimate complaints with a faint-hearted, "Well, life just isn't always fair, and you might as well learn that now." She stonewalls it through the rest of the class, and is deeply relieved when the class is over.

When Ms. Knepp arrives at school the next morning, there is a note from Dr. Kropa in her box stating that Mr. and Mrs. Pennsi are coming in during the free period to talk about the detention of their son, Fred. Fred is one of the few students who rarely causes trouble. Ms. Knepp feels unable to defend her action. It contradicts her beliefs about fairness and how students should be treated. The conference is a disaster. Ms. Knepp begins by trying to convince the Pennsies that she is right, but she ends up admitting that she too feels that she has been unfair to Fred. After the conference, she discusses the punishment with Dr. Kropa, who suggests that it is best to call it off. Ms. Knepp drags herself, half in tears, to her class. She is going to back down and rescind the punishment. She knows that the kids will see this as a sign of weakness, and she genuinely is afraid of the consequences.

The problem facing Ms. Knepp is not an uncommon one for teachers. Teaching can be a very threatening and frustrating experience, and all of us entertain at some time doubts about our ability to maintain effective classroom discipline. These self-doubts are especially common early in a teaching career. The consequence of these normal self-doubts for many teachers, however, is a frantic search for gimmicks, techniques, or tricks, which they hope will allow them to survive in the real classroom world. This is indeed unfortunate. When classroom management problems are approached with a frenetically sought-after bag of tricks instead of with a carefully developed systematic plan for decision making, teachers are likely to find themselves, as Ms. Knepp did, behaving in ways they regret later, after careful reflection. Teachers who are most successful at creating a positive classroom atmosphere that enhances student learning are those who employ a carefully developed plan for classroom management. The plan is congruent with their basic beliefs about the nature of the teaching and learning process. Such teachers avoid the dilemma that Ms. Knepp encountered.

There are multiple models or systems of classroom management that encompass hundreds of techniques for promoting positive student behavior. Most of these are effective in some situations but not others, for some students but not others, and for some teachers but not others. "What most of the experts fail to mention is that the efficacy of a technique is contextually dependent. Who the teacher teaches and who the teacher is dictate what technique will have the greatest potential for addressing the complex management problems evidenced in classrooms (Lasley, 1989). Additionally, all of these techniques are based implicitly or explicitly on some belief system concerning how human beings behave and why, and they contain powerful messages about the nature of students, teachers, and learning. The task of the classroom teacher is to find prototypes of classroom management that are consistent with his beliefs and to employ them under appropriate circumstances.

How can teachers ensure that their behavior in dealing with classroom management and classroom discipline problems will be effective and will match their beliefs about students, teachers, and learning? There are two things teachers can do. First, they can develop a systematic plan for promoting positive student behavior and dealing with inappropriate behavior. Second, they can understand their own basic beliefs about classroom management. Chapters Five through Nine are designed to help teachers develop a systematic plan, and they provide multiple options for dealing with any single classroom management problem. Numerous options are provided to allow each individual teacher to develop a personal plan for encouraging appropriate student behavior and dealing with unacceptable behavior congruent with his own basic beliefs about management. This also allows the teacher to prioritize his options in a hierarchical format so that they may be used deliberately.

This chapter is designed to help teachers and future teachers begin to lay the philosophical foundation for their own classroom management plan by providing an overview of a variety of philosophical approaches to classroom management. So they may be considered in a more systematic and orderly fashion, they are grouped under two major headings: teacher power bases and theories of classroom management. The section dealing with power bases discusses the various types of power or influence that are available to teachers to promote appropriate student behavior. The second section explains three theories of classroom management and their underlying beliefs and includes models and techniques falling within each of the theoretical approaches.

It is important to be aware of the inherent connection between the three theories of classroom management and the four power bases. Each of the three theories of classroom management relies primarily on the dominant use of one or two power bases. Teachers can examine the foundation for their own classroom management plans by comparing their beliefs with those inherent in each of the various teacher power bases and theories of classroom management.

TEACHER POWER BASES

French and Raven (1960) identified five different types of power that teachers as social agents might use to control student behavior. The effective teacher is aware of what type of power he wants to use to control student behavior and is also aware of the type of power that is implicit in each of the various techniques available. It cannot be emphasized enough that when teachers' beliefs and behavior are consistent, they are much more likely to be successful. Congruence between beliefs and behavior makes teachers more effective for two reasons: (1) The teacher is more likely to follow through and be consistent in dealing with student behavior because he believes that it is the right thing to do (unlike Ms. Knepp), and (2) students are more likely to perceive the teacher as a genuine person who practices what he preaches. As you read the explanation of the four types of power, ask yourself which type or types fit your beliefs and which types you could use comfortably. Although every teacher probably uses each of the four types of power at some time, each teacher has a dominant power base that he uses most often.

The four teacher power bases are presented in a hierarchical format, beginning with those more likely to engender student control over their own behavior and proceeding to power bases that foster increasing teacher control. If a teacher believes, as we do, that one of the important long-range goals of schooling is to foster student self-direction, using those power bases at the top of the hierarchy as often as possible results in consistency between this major tenet and teacher behavior. If a teacher does not share this belief, this hierarchical arrangement of power bases is not so important for him. Whatever one's beliefs about the long-range goals of education, it is still necessary to understand all of the various teacher power bases since no single one is effective for all students, all classrooms, or all teachers. Thus, effective classroom management requires use of a variety of teacher power.

Referent Power

Case 19: The Involved Teacher

Mr. Emig was envied by administrators and teachers alike at Spring Grove Junior High. Even though he taught eighth-grade

English to all types of students, he never sent students to the office, rarely gave detentions, and never needed parent conferences to discuss student behavior. In fact, it seemed as if he never had any discipline problems with students. Mr. Karr, the principal, decided that other teachers might be able to learn some techniques from Mr. Emig and so asked some of his students why his classes were so well behaved. Students said that they liked Mr. Emig because he was always involved in activities with them. He sponsored the school newspaper, went on ski club trips, went to athletic events, coached track, chaperoned dances, and advised the student council. Because of his heavy involvement with them, students got a chance to see him as a person, not just as a teacher, and they felt that he was a really good person who cared a lot about kids. As a result, nobody hassled him in class.

The type of power Mr. Emig uses to influence student behavior has been termed *referent power* by French and Raven. When the teacher has referent power, students behave as the teacher wishes because they like the teacher as a person. Students view the teacher as a good person who is concerned about them, cares about their learning, and demands a certain type of behavior because it is in the students' best interest.

Teachers who enjoy this type of relationship with students are able to appeal directly to students to act a certain way, and most often students do so. Examples of such direct appeals are "I'm really not feeling well today. Please keep the noise level at a minimum" and "It really makes me angry when you hand assignments in late. Please have your assignments ready on time." The teacher who enjoys a referent power base with his students might handle Ms. Knepp's problem with a statement such as "You disappoint me and make me very angry when you misbehave and disrupt class time. I spend a great deal of time planning activities which you will enjoy and which will help you to learn, but I must spend so much time on discipline that we don't get to them. I would really appreciate it if you would stop the misbehavior."

Referent power must not be confused with the situation in which the teacher attempts to be the students' friend. A teacher who wants to be friends with students generally is dependent on students to fill his personal needs. This dependency creates an environment in which students are able to manipulate the teacher, so that teacher and students gradually become equals. Eventually the teacher completely loses the ability to influence students to behave appropriately and thus has no power base whatsoever. In contrast, the teacher who uses referent power is still an authority figure and does make demands on students. Students carry out the teacher's wishes because they like the teacher as a teacher, not as a friend.

It is neither possible nor wise to use referent power all the time. Most teachers use referent power with some classes but not others, with some students but not others, in some situations but not others. Sometimes teachers simply do not like students or particular classes, and vice versa. Using referent power with students who genuinely dislike the teacher may result in disaster. One need only consider the possible and probable response from students who see their primary goal as making the teacher's life miserable to direct appeals such as the examples given previously.

There are two requirements for the effective use of referent power: (1) The teacher must perceive that the students like him, and (2) the teacher must communicate that he cares about and likes the students. Caring and liking alone are not enough. They must be communicated to students through behaviors such as using positive nonverbal gestures; giving positive oral and written comments; offering some extra time and attention to students; expressing sincere interest in students' ideas, activities, and most especially, learning; and being supportive of students as people regardless of their ability in the teacher's particular subject. When students make it clear that they like the teacher through their general reactions to him before, during, and after class, and when the teacher has communicated his caring and concern to students, the use of referent power can make classroom management easy.

Expert Power

Case 20: Her Reputation Precedes Her

Ms. Sanchez is the chemistry teacher at Lakefront High School. Each year, Ms. Sanchez teaches an advanced placement (AP) chemistry course to college-bound seniors. For the last five years, none of her AP students has received less than a three on the AP exam. As a result each student has received college credit for AP chemistry. Students in Ms. Sanchez's class recognize that she is very knowledgeable about chemistry and knows how to teach. If an observer walks into Ms. Sanchez's class, even during April and May, he will find all of the seniors heavily involved in class activities, with very little off-task behavior.

Ms. Sanchez is an excellent example of a teacher who uses expert power to control student behavior. When the teacher enjoys expert power, students behave as the teacher wishes because they view him as a good, knowledgeable teacher who can really help them learn. This is the power of professional competence. For expert power to be present, two important conditions must be fulfilled: (1) The students perceive the teacher as having special knowledge as well as the teaching skills to help students acquire that knowledge, and (2) the students value learning what the teacher is teaching them. Students may value what they are learning for any number of reasons: The subject matter is inherently interesting, they can use it in the real world, they want good grades, or to reach some personal goal such as college or a job. However, students must value it for some reason or expert power is not an effective power base.

Teachers who employ expert power successfully have students who make comments similar to these: "I behave because he is a really good teacher," "She makes biology interesting," and "He makes you really want to learn." A teacher with an expert power base might say to Ms. Knepp's disruptive class: "I'm sure you realize how important reading is. If you can't read, you will have a rough time being successful in our society. You know that I can help you learn to read and to read well, but I can't do that if you won't behave as I've asked you to behave."

As was the case with referent power, an individual teacher may be able to use expert power with some classes and some students but not with others. A math teacher may be able to use expert power with the advanced calculus group but not with the remedial general math group, and the knowledgeable auto mechanics teacher may be able to use expert power with the vocational-technical students but not with students who take auto mechanics just to fill up their schedules. The teacher who wishes to use expert power successfully communicates his competence through mastery of content material, the use of motivating teaching techniques, clear explanations, and thorough class preparation, in other words, using his professional knowledge to help students learn. Chapter Five summarizes the professional knowledge teachers may use to establish expert power in the classroom.

One final caveat concerning this type of power: Whereas most primary school teachers are perceived as experts by their students, expert power does not seem to be effective in motivating primary school students to behave appropriately. Thus, unlike the other four power bases, which can be employed at all levels of basic education, the appropriate use of expert power seems to be confined to students above the primary grades.

Legitimate Power

Case 21: School Is Your Job

Mr. Davis looked at the fourth-graders in front of him, many of whom were talking or staring into space instead of doing the seat work assignment. He said, "You are really disappointing me. You're sitting there wasting precious time. School is not a place for wasting time. School is your job, just like your parents have jobs, and my job is to see to it that you work hard and learn during school. Your parents pay taxes so that you'll have the chance to come to school and learn. You and I both have the responsibility to do what we're supposed to do. Now, cut out the talking and the daydreaming, and do your math."

The third type of power identified by French and Raven and utilized by Mr. Davis in the example is legitimate power. The teacher who seeks to influence students through legitimate power expects students to behave appropriately because the teacher has the legal and formal authority as well as the legal and formal responsibility for maintaining appropriate behavior in the classroom. Students behave because the teacher is the teacher, and inherent in that role is certain authority and power. Students who behave because of legitimate power make statements such as "I behave because the teacher asked us to. You're supposed to do what the teacher says." A teacher who employs legitimate power might use a statement in Ms. Knepp's class such as "I do not like the way you people are treating me. I am your teacher. I will not put up with disrespectful behavior. I am responsible for making sure that you learn, and I'm going to do that. If that means using the principal and other school authorities to help me do my job, I'll do just that."

Because of the societal changes discussed in Chapter Three, most teachers rightly believe that today's students are much less likely to behave because of legitimate teacher power than the students of 30 or 40 years ago. However, it is still possible to use legitimate power with some classes and some students. Groups of students who generally accept teacher-set rules and assignments without question or challenge are appropriate groups with whom to use legitimate power.

Teachers must demonstrate through their behavior that they accept the responsibilities as well as the power inherent in the role of teacher. If they wish to operate from a legitimate power base, teachers must be viewed by students as fitting the stereotypical image of teacher (e.g., in dress, speech, and mannerisms). It is also important that teachers and school administrators be perceived as working together if teachers expect students to see them as legitimate authorities. School administrators help teachers gain legitimate power by making clear to students through words and actions that they expect students to treat teachers as legitimate authority figures. Teachers help themselves gain legitimate power by following and enforcing school rules and by supporting school policies and administrators.

Reward/Coercive Power

Case 22: Going to Recess

"O.K., second-graders, it's time to put your spelling books away and get ready for recess. Now, we all remember that we get ready by putting all books and supplies neatly and quietly in our desks and then folding our hands on top of the desk and looking at me quietly. Let's see which row can get ready first. I see that Tammy's row is ready. O.K., Tammy's row, you can walk quietly out to the playground. "Oh, no, wait a minute. Where are you going, Joe? You're not allowed to go out to recess this week because of your misbehavior on the bus. You can go over to Mr. Li's room and do your math assignment. I'll check it when I get back."

This teacher is using reward and coercive power to influence student behavior. Although they may be considered two separate types of teacher authority, reward and coercive power are discussed together because they are really two sides of the same coin. They are both based on behavioral notions of learning, foster teacher control over student behavior, and are governed by the same principles of application.

Teachers who operate from this power base reward students for appropriate behavior and punish students who misbehave. There are a variety of rewards, such as oral or written praise, gold stars, free time, "good news" notes to parents, and release from required assignments, as well as a variety of punishments, including verbal reprimands, loss of recess or free time, detention, in-school suspension, out-of-school suspension, and corporal punishment. An example of a statement by a student who behaves appropriately because of reward/coercive power is "I behave because if I don't, I have to write out a stupid saying 50 times and get it signed by my parents." A teacher using reward/coercive power to solve Ms. Knepp's problem might say, "I've decided that for every five minutes without a disruption this class will earn one point. At the end of each week, the class may buy one night free from homework during the following week for every ten points it has accumulated. Remember, if there are any disturbances at all, you will not receive a point for the five-minute period." This point system is an example of a behavior modification technique. More information on the use of behavior modification in the classroom may be obtained from Axelrod (1977).

There are several requirements for the effective use of reward/

coercive power: (1) the teacher must be consistent in assigning and with-holding rewards and punishments; (2) the teacher must ensure that students see the connection between their behavior and the reward or punishment; (3) the rewards or punishments actually must be perceived as rewards or punishments by the student (many students view a three-day out-of-school suspension as a vacation, not a punishment).

As is true for the other three power bases, reward/coercive power cannot be used all the time. As students become older, they often resent obvious attempts to manipulate their behavior through rewards and punishments. It is also more difficult with older students to find rewards and punishments under the classroom teacher's control that are powerful enough to motivate students to behave appropriately. Still, it is possible to use reward/coercive power successfully with some students and some classes at all levels of schooling. For example, one reward and/or punishment that teachers do control is student time during school. Finally, there are some inherent dangers in the use of reward/coercive power. Research indicates that when students are rewarded for engaging in an activity, they are likely to perceive that activity as less inherently interesting in the future and are less likely to engage in that activity without external rewards (Lepper and Green, 1978). Also overuse of punishment is likely to engender in students very negative attitudes toward school and learning.

As stated earlier, most teachers use a combination of these power bases. They use different types of power with different types of classes and different types of students. They may even use a variety of types of power bases with the same students. This may, indeed, be the most practical and effective approach, although combining certain power bases, for example, coercive and referent, may be very difficult to do.

Punishments and rewards are often used by teachers; however, they may not be the most effective means to manage student behavior.

It is important for the teacher to recognize what type of power he uses to influence students in a given situation and to recognize why that type of power is appropriate or not appropriate for the given students and situation. It is also important to recognize the power base that the teacher uses most frequently at present as well as the power base he feels most comfortable with and would like to use most often. For some teachers, the two may be quite different. Examining your beliefs about teacher power bases is one important step toward ensuring that your beliefs about classroom management and your actions in influencing student behavior are compatible. Table 4-1 offers a brief comparison of the four power bases on several significant dimensions.

TABLE 4-1

	REFERENT	EXPERT	LEGITIMATE	REWARD/ COERCIVE
Motivation to behave	Student likes teacher as person	Teacher has special knowledge	Teacher has legal authority	Teacher can reward and punish
Need for teacher control of student behavior	Very low	Very low	Moderate	High
Requirements for use	Students must like the teacher as a person	Teacher expertise must be perceived and valued	Students must respect legal authority	Rewards and punishments must be effective
Key teacher behaviors	Communicates caring for students	Demonstrates mastery of content and teaching skills	Acts as a teacher is expected to act	Has and uses knowledge of student likes and dislikes
Age limitations	Useful for all levels	Less useful at primary level	Useful at all levels	Useful at all levels but less useful at senior high level
Caveats	Teacher is not the student's friend	Heavily dependent on student values	Societal changes have lessened the usefulness of this power base	Emphasizes extrinsic over instrinsic motivation

THEORIES OF CLASSROOM MANAGEMENT

The purpose of this section is to describe three theories of classroom management. Inherent in each of these theories are answers either explicit or implicit to seven basic questions about classroom management. Before reading further it is best to answer the seven questions from your point of view so that you can compare your answers to the answers given by the various theories and identify the theory that fits your own thinking most closely. The seven basic questions follow:

1. Who has the primary responsibility for controlling student behavior in the classroom?
2. Who should develop the rules and standards for appropriate classroom behavior?
3. Which is more important, overt behavior or inner thoughts and feelings?
4. How important are individual student differences in dealing with management problems?
5. How quickly should the teacher intervene when management problems occur?
6. What types of interventions should be used when management problems do occur?
7. What teacher power bases should be used most frequently to control student behavior?

The conceptualization of classroom management as three theoretical points on a continuum, going from primarily student control to joint student-teacher control to primarily teacher control, as well as the names for the three theories, were taken from Wolfgang and Glickman (1980). This text, however, takes the Wolfgang and Glickman conceptualization one step further by relating the theories to our seven basic questions about classroom management. Keep in mind that question 7 revolves around the notion of teacher power bases, which was discussed in the previous section.

Case 23: Handling Disruptive David

Ms. Koskowski, Ms. Sweely, and Mr. Green all teach on the fourth-grade team at Longmeadow School. Although they work well together and like each other, they all have very different approaches to classroom discipline. To illustrate their differing approaches, let's examine their behavior as each one deals with the same situation.

In the classroom there are three students at the reading center in the far right-hand corner and two students working quietly on insects at the science interest center near the blackboard located in the front of the room. Five students are correcting math problems with a teacher's aide, and ten students are working with the teacher in a reading group. David, one of the students with the teacher's aide, begins to mutter out loud, "I hate this math. It's too hard to do. I never get them right. Why do we have to learn about fractions anyway?" As his monologue continues, David's voice begins to get louder and clearly becomes a disruption for the other students.

Ms. Koskowski

Ms. Koskowski looks pointedly in David's direction and motions with her index finger in front of her lips. David doesn't get the hint and continues to vent his frustrations. Finally, she walks over to David, pulls him aside, and whispers, "I can see you are very frustrated, David, and it's O.K. to be frustrated, but it's not O.K. to yell about it so no one else can learn. When you yell like that, it stops everyone else from learning, and I get angry because I don't like to see other students being disturbed. I'd like you to go over to the reading center for a few minutes and read your library book. After you calm down and you're ready to try the math again, come back to your seat and give it a try. I think you can handle it if you just get control of yourself and settle down."

Ms. Sweely

As soon as she sees that David is beginning to interrupt the other students, Ms. Sweely gives the reading group a question to think about silently and walks toward David's desk. She puts her hand gently on his shoulder, but the muttering continues. She says, "David, you are disrupting others; please stop talking and get back to math." David stops for about five seconds but then begins complaining out loud again. "David, since you can't work with the group without disrupting other people, you will have to go back to the castle (a desk and rocking chair partitioned off from the rest of the class) and finish your math there by yourself. Tomorrow, if you believe that you can handle it, you may rejoin your math group."

Mr. Green

As soon as David's muttering becomes audible, Mr. Green says, "David, that behavior is against our class rules. Stop talking and concentrate on your math." David stops talking momentarily but begins again. Mr. Green walks calmly to David's desk and removes a small, round, blue chip. As he does, he says, "Well, David, you've lost them all now. That means no more recess for the rest of the week and no good news note to your Mom and Dad."

Noninterventionist

Ms. Koskowski embodies the noninterventionist theory of classroom management in her handling of David's disruption. Notice that she allows David a considerable amount of time to control his own behavior. She interrupts the reading group for an extended individual interaction with David in which she focuses on his underlying feelings, expresses belief that he can control his own behavior, and uses an "I message" (see Chapter Eight) to communicate her feelings.

The noninterventionist conception of classroom management is based on a philosophical and psychological belief system that is commonly referred to as humanistic or student-centered. Its underlying belief is that students must have the primary responsibility for controlling their own behavior. Noninterventionists believe that students are inherently capable of controlling their own behavior, and if given the opportunity to do so, they will. The teacher's primary role is to structure the classroom environment to facilitate the students' control over their own behavior. Guidelines for acceptable student behavior are usually developed by the students with guidance from the teacher. In helping the students to arrive at reasonable classroom rules, the teacher acts as a facilitator and helps the students to recognize that appropriate behavior is determined by the particular learning activity and by the needs of the students and teacher in that particular situation.

Noninterventionists see behavior as a symptom of inner thoughts and feelings. Controlling outward behavior is seen as a necessary but insufficient method for solving discipline problems. The teacher must help the student deal with the thoughts and feelings that motivated the disruptive behavior if resolution of the problem is going to occur. Each individual student must be treated in accordance with his own individual needs and preferences. Therefore individual differences among students are a very important factor in teacher decision making about how to react to classroom problems.

When discipline problems do occur, the teacher is slow to become involved. He tries to give the disruptive student nonverbal indicators that his behavior is inappropriate and gives the student time to control his own behavior without intervention.

When teacher intervention does occur because the student can't control his own behavior, the primary method of resolving discipline problems is extended private conferences between the teacher and the student. During these conferences, the teacher uses communication skills such as reflective listening and questioning to help the student arrive at a realistic solution to his problem. Solutions are not forced on the student by the teacher. Other techniques often used by teachers include nonverbal or low-profile correction methods to deal with disruptive behavior in the group situation, restructuring the classroom to ensure that student needs are met, and allowing students to have choices concerning the classroom activities in which they engage.

The teacher power bases that are most compatible with the noninterventionist theory are referent and expert power. Each of these power bases emphasizes students' control over their own behavior. The noninterventionist theory adds a new dimension to the notion of expert power. The teacher's expertise in this case consists of his ability to help students sort through their thoughts and feelings to enable them to see the real cause of their problems and regain control over their own behavior.

Some of the better-known systems of classroom management that are derived primarily from this noninterventionist viewpoint are Gordon's teacher effectiveness training (1974), Ginott's positive communication model (1972), and the transactional analysis model of Berne (1964) and Harris (1969). In Ms. Knepp's chaotic classroom, a noninterventionist teacher would first try to find out why students seemed unable to have their needs met by the class. He would discuss the situation with the class in order to work out any problems that were causing students to misbehave. Then he would hold private, problem-solving conferences with individual students who continued to be disruptive.

Teachers who wish to employ noninterventionist systems and techniques truly must believe that students can and will control their own behavior if they are given the opportunity to do so. The teacher sees student control as a long-range goal that takes time rather than a transformation that occurs overnight. Since most classroom teachers do not employ noninterventionist systems, students have not been given many opportunities in school to control their own behavior. As a result, many students have some initial difficulty in doing so. Students expect the teacher to jump in and take charge, and when the teacher fails to stop misbehavior immediately, they may assume that the teacher condones the misbehavior. Therefore, it is imperative that the teacher explain his expectations and beliefs about controlling behavior to the students very early in the school year. Lasley (1989) suggests that noninterventionist strategies are most appropriate for students who are self-directed and mature. He posits that most elementary and secondary students do not fit into this category.

Finally, it is important to recognize that the noninterventionist philosophy is not an "anything goes" attitude. There are definite standards of behavior that students have helped to develop and have committed themselves to, and these standards of behavior are upheld. Though methods of intervention are usually private, student-centered, and designed to encourage student control over behavior, intervention does occur and continues until student behavior meets acceptable standards. Many teachers, who wish to apply the noninterventionist theory but find it very difficult to do so initially, move to the interactionalist position and then gradually introduce noninterventionist techniques when students are more prepared for them.

Interactionalist

In Case 23, Ms. Sweely exemplifies the interactionalist theory of classroom management. Her interactionalist ideas are illustrated primarily by her desire to protect the reading group activity while dealing with David simultaneously, by her initial use of touch control (see Chapter Seven) to signal David that he should control his behavior, by her emphasis on the effect of David's behavior on others, and by her separation of David from the group to help him recognize the logical consequence of being disruptive in a group situation.

Interactionalist models of classroom management, as the name implies, are based on the underlying belief that control of student behavior is the joint responsibility of student and teacher. Interactionalists accept many of the basic beliefs of humanistic or student-centered psychology but recognize that the group nature of the classroom requires that the teacher place the needs of the group as a whole above the needs of individual students. They believe that students must be given some opportunity to control their own behavior because a long-range, and often implicit, goal of education is to help students learn to control their own behavior. The teacher, however, must also take responsibility for controlling student behavior because the classroom is a group learning situation. The interactionalist teacher promotes individual student control over behavior when possible but sometimes must subordinate this goal to the right of all students to learn.

Classroom rules and guidelines are generally developed jointly by the teacher and students. Some teachers begin with a minimal number of rules, those that are most necessary, and allow students to develop additional ones. Others retain veto power over rules that are suggested by students. Both of these techniques, insisting on certain rules and retaining veto power, are intended to help the teacher maintain the ability to use classroom rules to protect the rights of all the students as a whole. As do noninterventionists, interactionalist teachers also try to help students recognize that appropriate behavior is determined by the rational demands of the learning activity and by student and teacher needs during a particular learning activity. Teachers often conduct classroom meetings (see Glasser, 1969) to discuss general student compliance with classroom rules, to modify the rules if necessary, and to give students an opportunity to help solve management problems

Classroom meetings can help students realize that they have responsibilities to both themselves and the class. (University of Virginia Summer Enrichment Program)

that are affecting several students. The use of classroom meetings is intended to help students see their responsibilities both to themselves and to the other members of the class.

Interactionalists believe that both outward behavior and inner thoughts and feelings are important in the classroom. Outward behavior must be controlled to protect the rights of the group, and thoughts and feelings must be explored to get at the root of problems. In accordance with these beliefs, teachers often use coping skills (described in Chapter Seven) to control student behavior in the group situation and then follow up with an individual conference with the student to discuss the student's motivation for misbehaving. In contrast to noninterventionists, they are likely to intervene much more quickly when disruptions occur and view their primary goal as stopping the disruption as quickly as possible.

Many interactionalist theorists advocate using techniques for controlling behavior that directly point out to the student the natural link between the behavior and its consequences. The outcomes of misbehavior should be linked as closely as possible to the misbehavior itself, for example, requiring a student who comes five minutes late to remain five minutes after school to make up the work or removing a student from a small group learning situation until he is able to work in the group without disrupting other group members. Interactionalist teachers believe that relating student behavior to its direct or logical consequences is an effective method for helping students learn to control their behavior by anticipating its consequences.

The teacher power bases most compatible with the interactionalist theory are expert and legitimate power. Each of these power bases emphasizes that the primary purpose of schools is to help students learn important information that will be valuable to them. Therefore, the teacher must protect the rights of the class as a whole and must stop individual behavior problems that interfere with group rights.

Two well-known models of classroom management that are derived from the interactionalist point of view are Dreikurs' and Bassel's model (1971) and Glasser's reality therapy (1969). An interactionalist teacher in Ms. Knepp's situation might decide to hold a classroom meeting in which students are told that their behavior is unacceptable and that they must work out a satisfactory solution. Students might also be told that any individuals who are unable to work without disrupting others have to work in isolation until they learn how to work in a group setting without being disruptive.

Interventionist

The interventionist theory of classroom management is portrayed by Mr. Green's handling of David's misbehavior. His interventionist ideas can be seen when he very quickly moves to stop the misbehavior, emphasizes classroom rules, employs blue chips as rewards, and uses punishment in the form of loss of recess privileges and in the loss of good news notes.

Interventionist systems of classroom management are based on the basic tenets of behavioral psychology and the underlying belief that controlling student behavior is the primary responsibility of the teacher. Interventionists believe that students want the teacher to be in charge in the classroom and expect the teacher to ensure that students behave appropriately. They think that the key to positive classroom discipline is the creation by the teacher of an environment that motivates students to behave in appropriate ways. The environment is seen as the primary motivator of behavior. The teacher sets the rules and guidelines for classroom behavior and makes sure that his expectations are clear to students. The teacher then uses reward and coercive power in systematic ways to ensure student compliance with the prestated classroom rules. Reward and coercive power bases are most compatible with interventionist theories because they emphasize teacher control over student behavior.

Controlling external behavior is viewed by interventionists as more important than dealing with students' thoughts and emotions. Whereas noninterventionists believe that behavior changes only after a change in attitude has occurred, interventionists believe that once external behavior changes, changes in attitudes follow. Consistency in enforcing rules and applying rewards and punishments is important. Individual differences among students are not seen as particularly significant in dealing with misbehavior. Lasley (1989) suggests that interventionist strategies are most appropriate for developmentally immature students.

When classroom disruptions occur, interventionists usually move quickly to stop them. Halting the disruption and redirecting the misbe-having student to more positive behavior are seen as the primary goals of dealing with misbehavior. Techniques commonly employed by interven-tionist teachers include behavior modification, behavioral contracting, to-ken economy systems, consistent reinforcement of appropriate behavior, and group systems of rewards and punishments. Some well-known models of classroom management derived from the interventionist point of view include Canter's assertive discipline model (1978), Axelrod's behavior mod-ification model (1977), and Dobson's punishment model (1970).

An interventionist teacher might handle Ms. Knepp's class by setting up a group behavior modification program in which the group earned points for appropriate behavior and could exchange these points for mean-ingful rewards. At the same time, the interventionist teacher would swiftly punish individuals who misbehaved, using a predetermined course of pun-ishments.

The teacher who wants to employ an interventionist model of classroom management should be aware of some important considerations. A thorough understanding of the principles of behavioral psychology is necessary to implement behavior modification appropriately. Most inter-ventionists are concerned about student thoughts and emotions; however, their primary objective in dealing with classroom management is the control of outward student behavior. Also, individual student differences do play a minor role since they must be considered when determining which rein-forcers and punishment will be effective for the individual student. What is reinforcing for one student may be a punishment for another and vice versa. Finally, effective use of behavior modification tends to be more difficult with secondary students since the reactions of other students to behavior is usually more powerful than the reactions of the teacher; students have reached a higher stage of moral reasoning (see Chapter Three), and in-school rewards are not as powerful as out-of-school rewards.

Table 4-2 provides an overview of the three theories of classroom management in reference to their answers to the seven basic questions about classroom management.

SUMMARY

The first section of the chapter provides an explanation of the four teacher power bases: referent, expert, legitimate, and reward/coercive. Each of the power bases is presented in terms of the underlying assumptions about student motivation to behave, the assumed need for teacher control over student behavior, the requirements for employing the power base effec-tively, key teacher behaviors in using the power base, and limitations and caveats concerning its use.

TABLE 4-2

	NONINTERVENTIONIST	INTERACTIONALIST	INTERVENTIONIST
Primary responsibility for control	student	student and teacher	teacher
Development of rules	student with teacher guidance	teacher with some student input	teacher
Primary focus	major focus on inner feelings and thoughts	initial focus on behavior; secondary focus on feelings and thoughts	major focus on behavior
Importance of individual differences	major emphasis	moderate emphasis	minor emphasis
Time until intervention	allow time for student to control own behavior	allow some time for student to control own behavior but protect group	teacher moves quickly to redirect behavior
Types of intervention used	nonverbal moves, private conferences, communication, skills, I messages	coping skills, consequences, group meetings, anecdotal records	rewards, punishments, token economy, contracting
Most compatible power bases	referent, expert	expert, legitimate	reward/coercive
Proponents	Gordon, Ginott, Berne, Harris	Dreikurs, Glasser	Canter, Dobson, Axelrod

The second section discusses seven basic questions that are useful for articulating beliefs about classroom management: (1) Who has the primary responsibility for controlling student behavior in the classroom? (2) Who should develop the rules and standards for appropriate classroom behavior? (3) Which is more important, overt behavior or inner thoughts and feelings? (4) How important are individual student differences in dealing with management problems? (5) How quickly should the teacher intervene when management problems occur? (6) What types of interventions should be used when management problems do occur? (7) What teacher power bases should be used most frequently to control student behavior?

Articulating one's beliefs is the initial step toward developing a systematic plan for controlling student behavior. These seven basic questions are used to analyze three theories of classroom management: noninterventionist, interactionalist, and interventionist.

The information and questions provided in this chapter may be used by teachers to develop a plan for preventing classroom management problems and for dealing with disruptive student behavior that is congruent with their basic beliefs about teaching and learning.

REFERENCES

AXELROD, S. (1977). *Behavior Modification for the Classroom Teacher*. New York: McGraw-Hill.

Berne, E. (1964). *Games People Play: The Psychology of Human Relations*. New York: Grove Press.

CANTER, L. (1978). *Assertive Discipline*. New York: Wadsworth.

DOBSON, J. (1970). *Dare to Discipline*. Wheaton, IL: Tyndale House.

DREIKURS, R., AND BASSEL, P. (1971). *Discipline Without Tears*. New York: Hawthorne.

FRENCH, J. R. P., AND RAVEN, B. (1960). In D. Cartwright and A. Zander (Eds.), *Group Dynamics: Research and Theory*. Evanston, IL: Row-Peterson.

GINOTT, H. (1972). *Between Teacher and Child*. New York: Peter H. Wyden.

GLASSER, W. (1969). *Schools without Failure*. New York: Harper & Row.

GORDON, T. (1974). *Teacher Effectiveness Training*. New York: Peter H. Wyden.

HARRIS, T. (1969). *I'm O.K.; You're O.K.: A Practical Guide to Transactional Analysis*. New York: Harper & Row.

LASLEY, T. J. (1989). A teacher development model for classroom management. *Phi Delta Kappan, 71,* I, 36–38.

LEPPER, M., AND GREEN, D. (1978). *The Hidden Costs of Reward: New Perspectives on Human Motivation*. Hillsdale, NJ: Erlbaum.

WOLFGANG, C., AND GLICKMAN, C. (1980). *Solving Discipline Problems: Strategies for Classroom Teachers*. Boston: Allyn & Bacon.

EXERCISES

1. If one of the long-term goals of classroom management and discipline is for students to gain control over their own behavior, what are some advantages and disadvantages of using each of the four teacher power bases to help students to achieve that goal?

2. Given your knowledge of cognitive and moral development, what factors facilitate or limit the use of each of the four teacher power bases at (a) the primary elementary grades, (b) the intermediate elementary grades, (c) the junior high level, and (d) the senior high level?

3. Do you think there is any relationship between job satisfaction and the power base the teacher uses most frequently to influence student behavior?

4. What specific teacher behaviors would indicate to you that a teacher was trying to use (a) referent power and (b) expert power?

5. Using referent authority successfully requires the teacher to communicate caring to students. (a) How can a teacher communicate caring without initiating personal friendships? (b) As you see it, is there a danger in initiating personal friendships with students?

6. How would teachers operating at each of the four authority bases respond differently to the following situations?

	REFERENT	EXPERT	LEGITIMATE	REWARD/ COERCIVE
a. A student throws a paper airplane across the room.				
b. A student publicly shows disrespect for the teacher.				
c. A student makes funny noises while another student is giving an oral report.				

7. Circle the choice that best describes your answer to each of the following questions:
   a. Who has the primary responsibility for controlling student behavior?
      the teacher   the student   both teacher and student
   b. Who should develop rules for classroom behavior?
      the teacher   the students   both teacher and students
   c. In handling discipline problems, should the teacher focus more on overt behavior or more on inner feelings and thoughts?
      primarily on behavior   primarily on feelings and thoughts
   d. How important are individual differences among students in dealing with discipline?
      very important   somewhat important   not important
   e. When discipline problems occur, is it more important to help the disruptive student solve the problem or to protect the right of the group to learn?
      protecting the group   helping the individual
   Use the chart on theories of classroom management and your preceding answers to classify yourself as a noninterventionist, an interactionalist, or an interventionist.

8. If one of the long-range goals of classroom management is to help students gain control over their own behavior, what are the advantages and disadvantages of each of the three theories of classroom management in helping students meet that goal?

9. Given your knowledge of cognitive and moral development, what factors facilitate or limit the use of each of the three theories of classroom management at (a) the primary elementary level, (b) the intermediate elementary level, (c) the junior high level, and (d) the senior high level?

10. How would teachers using each of the theories of classroom management respond differently to the following situations?

	NONINTER-VENTIONIST	INTER-ACTIONALIST	INTER-VENTIONIST
a. A student uses power equipment in a dangerous way.			
b. A student chews gum loudly and blows bubbles.			
c. A student draws mustaches and beards on all the pictures in a textbook.			

11. Is there any danger in using techniques to control student behavior that are not consistent with your basic beliefs about student learning and behavior?

CHAPTER 5

The Professional Teacher

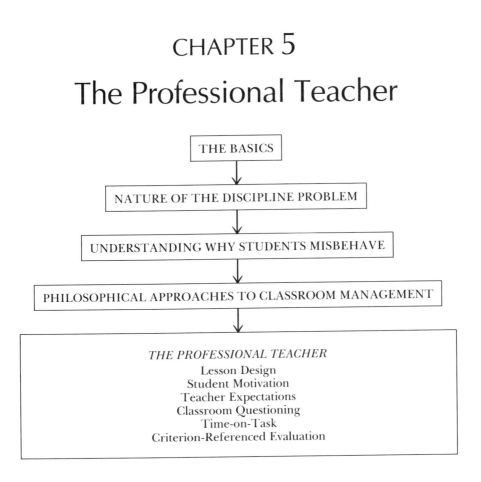

THE BASICS

↓

NATURE OF THE DISCIPLINE PROBLEM

↓

UNDERSTANDING WHY STUDENTS MISBEHAVE

↓

PHILOSOPHICAL APPROACHES TO CLASSROOM MANAGEMENT

↓

THE PROFESSIONAL TEACHER
Lesson Design
Student Motivation
Teacher Expectations
Classroom Questioning
Time-on-Task
Criterion-Referenced Evaluation

PRINCIPLES OF CLASSROOM MANAGEMENT

17. Student learning and on-task student behavior are maximized when teaching strategies are based on what educators know about how people learn and effective teaching.
18. Understanding and using the research on effective teaching enhances the teacher's instructional competence and helps to prevent classroom management problems.

INTRODUCTION

Classroom management frequently is conceptualized solely as a matter of student control rather than a dimension of curriculum, instruction, and overall school climate (Duke, 1982). In reality, classroom management is closely intertwined with effective instruction. "Research findings converge on the conclusion that teachers who approach classroom management as a process of establishing and maintaining effective learning environments tend to be more successful than teachers who place more emphasis on their roles as authority figures or disciplinarians" (Brophy, 1988a, p. 1). In the hierarchical decision-making model of classroom management, the teacher must ensure that she has done all that can be done to prevent problems from occurring before moving on to coping techniques. This means that the teacher must ensure that her classroom instructional behavior matches the behaviors defined by best professional practice as most likely to maximize student learning and enhance appropriate student behavior. If this is not the case, moving on to later rungs on the hierarchy and employing techniques to remediate misbehavior is likely to prove fruitless since misbehavior will inevitably reoccur.

One of the problems that has plagued classroom teachers historically, however, is identifying the yardstick that should be used to measure whether their teaching behavior matches best professional practice. Fortunately, at this point in the history of our profession, there is a reliable knowledge base, which when used appropriately, can be a useful tool to help teachers ensure that their behavior is most likely to enhance student learning and appropriate behavior.

The purpose of this chapter is to present a synopsis of that knowledge base as it relates to several dimensions of the teaching-learning process, including (1) lesson design, (2) student motivation, (3) teacher expectations, (4) teacher questioning, (5) time-on-task, and (6) criterion-referenced self-evaluation. Before discussing specific research findings on teacher effects on students, it is important for the reader to develop a general understanding of (1) specific assumptions and limitations associated with these research findings and (2) the process utilized in identifying them.

Most of the research findings synthesized in this chapter were derived from studies of teacher behaviors that were effective in promoting student achievement, specifically student achievement as defined by lower-level cognitive objectives, which are efficiently measured by paper-and-pencil tests (Brophy, 1988b). Specifically, it appears that general principles for teaching behavior derived from these research studies apply to "instruction in any body of knowledge or set of skills that has been sufficiently well organized and analyzed so that: 1) it can be presented systematically, and then 2) practiced or applied during activities that call for student performance that 3) can be evaluated for quality and 4) can be given corrective feedback (where incorrect or imperfect). This would include not only basic knowledge and skills in any subject matter but also certain aspects of higher level activities such as reading comprehension and study skills, mathematics problem-solving, and scientific experimentation" (p. 8).

Although these principles will apply to the vast majority of instructional situations in which all elementary and secondary teachers will be engaged, they are not universally applicable. For example, "they will not apply to teacher behavior during lessons designed primarily to create a process rather than a product (e.g., debate, discussion, role play, simulation, etcetera) or during activities that call for students to discover or invent their own responses rather than to follow a prescribed process to reach a predetermined outcome (for example, interpretation of poetry or literature, creative writing, and artistic expression)" (p. 9).

Now let us turn our attention to a brief description of the process by which most of these generalizations were derived. The research findings in this chapter resulted from various long-term research projects, which usually followed a three-step process.

In step 1 of the research process, teams of researchers observed classroom teachers who were considered to be either very effective or very ineffective. Effectiveness was most often defined as enhanced student achievement on paper-and-pencil tests. The result of these classroom observations was a list of teaching behaviors that were used frequently by the effective teachers but not by the ineffective teachers. The researchers hypothesized that at least some of these "effective" teaching behaviors were responsible for the success of the effective teachers.

In step 2 of the research process, correlational studies were conducted that attempted to find positive relationships between the use of these "effective" teaching behaviors and student behavior or student learning as measured by paper-and-pencil achievement test scores. These correlational studies indicated that some of the effective teaching behaviors were positively related to student behavior and achievement, whereas others were not. Thus, the result of step 2 was a narrowing of the list of effective teaching behaviors to those that were used typically by the effective teachers *and* had a positive relationship with student behavior or student achievement test scores.

In step 3 of the process, experimental studies were conducted. The researchers trained an experimental group of teachers to use the narrowed-down list of effective teaching behaviors consistently in their teaching. The achievement scores and classroom behavior of students taught by these experimental teachers were then compared with the achievement test scores and behavior of students taught by a control group of teachers, who had not been trained to use the effective teaching behaviors. The results of these experimental comparison studies showed that students of the experimental teachers had significantly higher achievement test scores or significantly better classroom behavior.

Thus, this chapter gives you, the teacher, a list of generalizations derived from research on teacher effects. These generalizations hold true for most teachers, most classrooms, and most students. How well they apply to your students or your individual teaching situation, however, must be determined by you as you use them and then evaluate their effectiveness in promoting better learning and more positive behavior for your students; that is, teachers must use their professional judgment and their knowledge of their own students to apply these generalizations most effectively. "Even relevant and valid guidelines need to be used and understood as general principles rather than rigid rules" (Brophy, 1988b, p. 15). This is not to say that it is all right to ignore these generalizations. They represent the profession's accumulated knowledge concerning best practice. All teachers have a professional obligation to use them when appropriate. We simply are saying that any generalizations must be applied to individual cases wisely and with an eye toward evaluating their effectiveness. Just as a doctor must regulate the "normal" dosage of medicine to fit individual patients, so too teachers must modify these research findings to fit their individual students.

LESSON DESIGN

Over the last decade, Madeline Hunter (1982), Barak Rosenshine (Rosenshine and Stevens, 1986), and other researchers have spent a great deal of time and energy trying to identify the most effective type of lesson structure to enhance student learning. Although the various researchers tend to use their own specialized vocabulary, giving the essential elements of a lesson different names, they agree that lessons that include the following components are most effective in helping students learn: a lesson introduction, clear explanations of the content, checking for student understanding, a period of coached practice, a lesson summary or closure, a period of solitary practice, and periodic reviews. These principles apply to lessons designed to produce the types of outcomes identified in the introduction to the chapter.

INTRODUCTION

1. A good introduction makes students aware of what they are supposed to learn, activates their prior knowledge of the topic, focuses their attention on the main elements of the lesson to come, and motivates them to be interested in the lesson.

CLARITY

2. Clear explanations of the content of the lesson proceed in step-by-step fashion, illustrate the content by using concrete examples familiar to the students, and are interspersed with questions to check for student understanding. "Lessons in which learners perceive links among the main ideas are more likely to contribute to content learning than are lessons in which links among the main ideas are less easily perceived by learners" (Anderson, 1989, p. 102). The teacher can aid learners in the processing of linking ideas by making sure that

presentations are well organized. Techniques for ensuring that presentations are well organized include (a) use of structured overviews, use of advance organizers, and stating objectives near the beginning of the presentation; (b) outlining the content, signaling transactions between ideas, calling attention to main ideas, and summarizing subsections of the lesson during the presentation; and (c) summarizing main ideas near the end of the presentation. Well-organized presentations aid student comprehension by telling students what prior knowledge is relevant and should be activated and by pointing out what pieces of information are important in using activated prior knowledge (Anderson, 1989).

COACHED PRACTICE

3. Effective lessons include a period of coached or guided practice during which students practice using the skill or knowledge, either through seat work exercises, oral questions and answers, or some type of group work. This initial practice is closely monitored by the teacher so that students receive frequent feedback and correction, for example, after every two or three problems. It is very important that the teacher check to make sure that the students are experiencing high amounts of success (over 75 percent) with the coached practice exercises before moving on to solitary practice. Otherwise, students may spend a large portion of the solitary practice period practicing and learning the wrong information or skill.

Wang and Palinscar (1989) have pointed out an additional important aspect of the guided practice portion of lessons designed to help students acquire cognitive strategies (such as study skills, problem-solving skills, and critical thinking skills). They cite scaffolding as a critical teacher behavior in enhancing student comprehension. "Scaffolding occurs when the teacher supports students' attempts to use a cognitive strategy; adjusts that support according to learner characteristics, the nature of the material, and the nature of the task; and treats the support as temporary, removing it as students show increased competence in using the cognitive strategy" (p. 79). In other words, the teacher plans instruction to move from modeling and instruction to feedback and coaching, and increasingly transfers control to students.

CLOSURE

4. A lesson summary or closure asks students to become actively involved in summarizing the key ideas that have been learned in the lesson and gives them some ideas about where future lessons will take them.

SOLITARY PRACTICE

5. Effective lessons also include a period of solitary or independent practice during which students practice the skill on their own and experience significant amounts of success (over 75 percent). This practice often takes the form

of independent seat work or homework. The effectiveness of homework as a tool for promoting learning is directly related to whether it is checked and feedback is provided to students.

REVIEW

6. Finally, periodic reviews conducted on a weekly and monthly basis help students consolidate their learning and provide additional reinforcement.

These components are especially necessary and effective in lessons designed to impart basic information or specific skills and procedures. They should not be viewed as putting the teacher in a straightjacket, which constrains the teacher's creativity and individuality. They provide the basic framework for effective lessons, which teachers can embellish with their own creative ideas and tailor to fit their unique teaching situations.

It is important to remember that a lesson does not equal a class period. A lesson is defined as the amount of instructional time required for students to achieve a specific learning objective. Since a lesson may extend over several class periods, it is not essential to have all of these components in each class period. On the other hand, if one class period contains two lessons, one would expect the components to be repeated twice.

Using these six research-based components in designing lessons helps to cut down on student confusion about what they are supposed to learn and ensures that learning proceeds in an orderly sequence of steps. When students are trying to learn level three before they have mastered level one, and when they are not given sufficient practice to master skills, they become confused, disinterested, and much more likely to cause discipline problems in the classroom.

STUDENT MOTIVATION

Student motivation refers to an inner drive that focuses student behavior on a particular goal or task and causes the student to be persistent in trying to achieve the goal or complete the task successfully. When students are motivated to learn, they usually pay attention to the lesson, become actively involved in the learning, and direct their energies to the learning task. When students are not motivated to learn, they lose interest in lessons quickly, look for sources of entertainment, and may direct their energies at amusing themselves and disrupting the learning process of others. Fostering motivation to learn in students is undoubtedly one of the most powerful tools the teacher has in preventing classroom discipline problems. There are many variables that the professional teacher can manipulate to increase student motivation to learn. According to a recent review of research on student motivation (Brophy, 1987), some of the most powerful variables are the following:

1. Student interest. Teachers can increase student motivation by relating subject content to student interest in life outside of school. For example, an English teacher relates poetry to lyrics of popular music, and a chemistry teacher allows students to analyze the chemical composition of products that they use. Admittedly, there is no subject in which every topic can be related to the real world. However, student interest may also be increased by using classroom activities that students enjoy, such as games, simulations, videos, and group work, and by allowing students to plan or select activities in which they will be engaged. Although these strategies can't be used effectively every day, they can be employed by all teachers at some time.

2. Student needs. Motivation to learn is increased when students perceive that learning activities provide an opportunity to meet some of their basic human needs as identified by Maslow (see Chapter Three). For example, simply providing elementary students with the opportunity to talk while the whole group listens can be an easy way to help meet students' needs for self-esteem. At the secondary level, allowing students to work together with peers on learning activities helps to meet students' needs for a sense of belonging and acceptance by others. Additionally, providing a pleasant, task-oriented climate in which expectations are clear helps to meet students' needs for psychological safety and security.

3. Novelty and variety. When the teacher has designed learning activities that include novel events, situations, and materials, students are much more likely to become involved in lessons. The popcorn lesson that follows is an excellent example of the use of novelty to gain student attention. Once student attention has been captured, the teacher is much more likely to be able to keep it focused on the lesson if she plans a variety of short learning activities.

Human attention spans can be remarkably long when persons are involved in an activity that they find utterly fascinating. Most students, however, do not find typical school activities fascinating. Therefore, student attention spans tend to be rather short. The professional teacher recognizes this fact and plans activities that last no longer than 15 to 20 minutes. For instance, the teacher who gives a lecture in two 15-minute halves with a 5-minute oral exercise interspersed is much more likely to maintain student interest than a teacher who gives a 30-minute lecture followed by the 5-minute oral exercise. Soap operas on television are an excellent example of changing the focus of activity every 5 to 10 minutes, and we all realize how captivating they are.

Case 24: The Popcorn Popper

As the students walk into their tenth-grade creative writing class, they hear an unusual noise. On the teacher's desk is an electric popcorn popper, which is filled with unpopped kernels and turned on. Soon, the room is filled with the aroma of fresh popcorn. When the popping is finished, the teacher passes a bowl of popcorn around for everyone to eat. After the students finish eating, the teacher asks them to recreate orally, the sights, sounds, smells, taste, and feel of the popcorn. The teacher uses their accounts as an introduction to a writing exercise on the five senses.

---

4. Success. When students are successful at tasks that they perceive as at least somewhat challenging, their motivation for future learning is greatly enhanced. Is it any wonder that students who are continually unsuccessful become disruptive influences in the classroom? It is unreasonable to expect that students who fail constantly will have any motivation whatever to participate in future learning activities since they have no hope of succeeding. Thus, it is especially important for teachers to create success for students who are not normally successful. Teachers help to ensure that all students experience success by making goals and objectives clear, by teaching content clearly in small steps, and by checking to see that students understand each step. In addition, success is encouraged by helping students acquire the study skills necessary to succeed when they must work on their own—outlining, note taking, and using textbooks correctly. It cannot be stressed enough that the most powerful technique for helping students succeed is to ensure that the material is at the appropriate level of difficulty. Material should be appropriate for the students, given the students' prior learning in that subject.

5. Student attributions for success and failure. Human beings have a natural tendency to search for causes of success and failure. Research on classroom learning has identified five factors to which students normally attribute success and failure in the classroom (Ames and Ames, 1984). These factors are effort, ability, luck, others, and the difficulty of the task. The only one of these five factors that can be controlled by the student herself is effort. The other factors are out of her control. "Students who believe that their personal efforts influence their learning and achievement are more likely to learn than those who believe that learning depends on teachers or other factors such as luck or the difficulty of the tasks" (Wang and Palinscar, 1989, p. 77). When a student fails, it is important for the student to believe that she has the power to change that failure into success in the future.

The teacher must help the student to attribute the past failure to lack of effort or the use of ineffective strategies, but not to ability. This assumes that the material is at the appropriate level of difficulty and that the student is capable of learning it, given a reasonable effort. When students are successful, it is important to have them attribute the success to both ability and effort because this influences students to believe that they have the ability necessary to repeat the success in the future, given the appropriate effort. When students fail, teachers should influence them to attribute it to lack of effort (or use of ineffective strategies) and try to get them to plan for the future to decrease the likelihood of failing again. When students succeed, teachers should influence them to attribute it to ability and effort.

6. Tension.   Tension refers to a feeling of concern or anxiety on the part of the student because she knows that she will be required to demonstrate her learning. A moderate amount of tension increases student learning. When there is no tension in the learning situation, students may be so relaxed that no learning occurs. On the other hand if there is an overwhelming amount of tension, students may expend more energy in dealing with the tension than they do in learning. Creating a moderate amount of tension results in motivation without tension overload.

In deciding whether to create tension in students, teachers must keep in mind the nature of the learning task itself. When the learning task is inherently interesting and challenging for students, there is little need for the teacher to add any tension. When the learning task is routine and generally uninteresting for students, a moderate amount of tension created by the teacher generally enhances motivation and learning. Teacher behaviors that hold students accountable for individual learning and raise the level of tension include moving around the room, calling on volunteers and nonvolunteers to answer questions in a random pattern, giving quizzes on class material, checking homework and seat work, and reminding students that they will be tested on the material and are responsible for learning it.

7. Feeling tone.   Feeling tone refers to the emotional atmosphere or climate in the classroom. According to Madeline Hunter, classroom feeling tone can be extremely positive, moderately positive, neutral, moderately negative, and extremely negative. An extremely positive feeling tone can be sickeningly sweet and actually direct student attention away from the learning task. A neutral tone is very bland and nonstimulating, and an extremely negative feeling tone is very threatening and may produce a tension overload. The most effective feeling tone is a moderately positive atmosphere in which the climate is pleasant and friendly but clearly focused on the learning task at hand. Although a moderately positive feeling tone is most motivating, it is sometimes necessary to create, temporarily, a moderately negative feeling tone. For example, if students are not doing their work and not living up to their responsibilities, it is necessary to shake them out of their complacency with some well-chosen, negative comments. The wise teacher understands that undesirable consequences may result from a classroom feeling tone that is continuously negative and, therefore, works at creating a moderately positive classroom climate. The teacher helps to create such a feeling tone by making the room comfortable and pleasantly decorated, treating students in a courteous and friendly manner, expressing sincere interest in students, getting to know students as individuals, and communicating positively with students both verbally and nonverbally. See how one teacher expresses his sincere interest in students in the case below.

Case 25: Talking Between Classes

Mr. Dailey, the eighth-grade English teacher, does not spend the time in between classes standing out in the hallway or visiting with friends. Instead he uses the three minutes to chat with individual students. During these chats, he talks with students about their out-of-school activities, their hobbies, their feelings about school and his class in particular, their plans and aspirations, and everyday school events. He feels that these three-minute chats really promote a more positive feeling tone in his classroom and allow him to relate to his students as individuals.

---

8. Feedback.   Motivation to learn is also increased by giving specific feedback to students concerning their performance. Knowledge concerning both degree of effort and degree of success motivates students by providing information that can be used to improve performance in the future and by providing a yardstick or criterion by which progress in learning can be measured. Feedback is most effective when it is specific and is delivered soon after or at the time of performance. Teachers most often provide feedback in the form of oral and written comments about student work and grades on tests and assignments. One additional way to use feedback as a motivator is to have students keep track of their own progress over time and to provide periodic opportunities for them to reflect on their progress.

9. Encouragement.   Children are often reminded of their limitations by adults. Teachers and parents get into the habit of pointing out how children have fallen short and failed to meet expectations rather than emphasizing that definite accomplishments have taken place and that progress has been made. For example, a child who gets a 68 on a test has learned twice as much as she has failed to learn; however, most adults would tend to emphasize what has not been learned.

Encouragement, on the other hand, emphasizes the positive aspects of behavior; recognizes and rewards real effort; communicates positive expectations for future behavior; and communicates that the teacher trusts, respects, and believes in the child. Finally, encouraging communication as defined by Sweeny (1981) puts the emphasis on present and future behavior rather than on past transgressions and on what is being learned and done correctly rather than on what has not been learned.

Whereas criticism, pointing out shortcomings, and focusing on past transgressions erode children's self-esteem, encouraging communication enhances self-esteem. Dreikur's *Children the Challenge* (1964) presents an excellent discussion of encouragement.

In the following case, the negative impact of poorly constructed feedback on students will be clear. Ms. Johnson would have had a much more positive impact on Heidi's motivation if she had pointed out the positive aspects of Heidi's work as well as the error in spelling.

Case 26: Nonconstructive Feedback

Ms. Johnson was handing back the seventh-graders' reports on their library books. Heidi waited anxiously to get her report back. She had read a book on archaeology and had really gotten into it. She spent quite a bit of time explaining in her report how neat it must be to be able to relive the past by examining the artifacts people left behind. When she received her book report, Heidi was dejected. The word *artifact*—Heidi had spelled it *artafact*—was circled twice on her paper with *sp* written above it. At the bottom of the paper, Ms. Johnson had written, "spelling errors are careless and are not acceptable." The only other mark Ms. Johnson had made on the paper was a grade of C.

How can classroom teachers use these research findings to improve student motivation in their own classrooms? Ask yourself the following questions in planning classroom activities for your students:

1. How can I make use of natural student interests in this learning activity?
2. How can I help students to meet their basic human needs in this activity?
3. How can I use novel events and/or materials in this activity?
4. How can I provide for variety in these learning activities?
5. How can I ensure that my students will be successful?
6. How can I create an appropriate level of tension for this learning task?
7. How can I create a moderately pleasant feeling tone for this activity?
8. How can I provide feedback to students and help them to recognize their progress in learning?
9. How can I encourage my students?

Additionally, when discipline problems do occur, it is important for the teacher to recognize what might be done to increase motivation to learn and decrease motivation to misbehave. The list of nine questions represents an important resource in redirecting student motivation toward appropriate behavior.

TEACHER EXPECTATIONS

Research on teacher expectations and their influence on student learning is closely connected to research on student motivation. In a famous study entitled *Pygmalion in the Classroom* (1968), Rosenthal and Jacobs began a line of inquiry that has yielded powerful discoveries concerning teacher behavior in the classroom. They told teachers in an inner-city elementary school that they had developed an intelligence test designed to identify "intellectual bloomers," that is, students who were just on the verge of taking a tremendous leap in their ability to learn. They also told these teachers that certain students in their classes had taken the test and had been so identified. This, however, was a total fabrication, as there was no such test. When Rosenthal and Jacobs checked student achievement test scores at the end of the year, amazingly, the intellectual bloomers had actually bloomed. Compared to a matched group of their peers, the researcher-identified bloomers had made much greater gains in achievement. As a result, the researchers assumed that the teachers must have treated the bloomers differently in some way in the classroom, but they had no observational data to support this assumption. This study has remained controversial even to the present time (Wineburg, 1987), but it provided the initial momentum for a very potent set of research findings (Good, 1987).

Beginning in the 1970s, researchers such as Thomas Good and Jere Brophy conducted observational studies to examine teacher behavior toward students whom they perceived as high achievers and students whom they perceived as low achievers. Multiple researchers and their research studies found that teachers often unintentionally communicate low expectations toward students whom they perceive as low achievers. These lower expectations are communicated by behaviors such as

1. Calling on low achievers less often to answer questions.
2. Giving low achievers less think time to answer questions when they are called on.
3. Providing fewer clues and hints to low achievers when they have initial difficulty in answering questions.
4. Praising correct answers from low achievers less often.
5. Criticizing wrong answers from low achievers more often.
6. Praising marginal answers from low achievers but demanding more precise answers from high achievers.
7. Staying further away physically and psychologically from low achievers in the classroom.

8. Rarely expressing personal interest in low achievers.
9. Smiling less frequently at low achievers.
10. Making eye contact less frequently with low achievers.
11. Complimenting low achievers less often.

Some of these teacher behaviors may be motivated by good intentions on the part of the teacher, such as giving low achievers less think time because she does not want to embarrass them if they don't know an answer. However, the cumulative effect of these behaviors is the communication of a powerful message: "I don't expect you to be able to do much." This message triggers a vicious cycle. Students begin to expect less of themselves, produce less, and confirm the teacher's original perception of them as not very capable. In many cases, the teacher may have a legitimate reason to expect less from some students, but communicating low expectations produces only negative effects.

Researchers have demonstrated that when teachers equalize response opportunities, teacher feedback, and personal involvement, student learning can improve. The message is clear. Communicating high expectations to all learners may influence low achievers to learn more, whereas communicating low expectations no matter how justified has a debilitating effect.

Although the empirical research in this area has been limited to the effects of teacher expectations on achievement, we believe that the generalizations hold true for student behavior as well. Communicating high expectations for student behavior is likely to bring about increased positive behavior, and communicating low expectations for student behavior may very well bring about increased negative behavior. A teacher who says, "I am sure that all of you will complete all of your homework assignments carefully because you realize that doing homework is an important way of practicing what you are learning" is more likely to have students complete homework assignments than a teacher who says, "I know you probably don't like to do homework, but if you fail to complete homework assignments, it will definitely lower your grades." Brophy (1988a) discussed his agreement with this premise in the following way: "Consistent projection of positive expectations, attributions and social labels to the students is important in fostering positive self-concepts and related motives that orient them toward prosocial behavior. In short, students who are consistently treated as if they are well-intentioned individuals who respect themselves and others and desire to act responsibly, morally, and prosocially are more likely to live up to those expectations and acquire those qualities than students who are treated as if they had the opposite qualities" (p. 11). The powerful research in this area makes it imperative for all teachers to step back and reflect on the expectations they communicate to students through their verbal and nonverbal classroom behavior.

CLASSROOM QUESTIONING

Of all the instructional tools and techniques classroom teachers possess, questioning is perhaps the most versatile. Questions may be used to assess readiness for new learning, to create interest and motivation in learning, to make concepts more precise, to check to ensure that students understand the materials, to redirect off-task students to more positive behavior, and to create the moderate amount of tension that enhances learning. Use of good questioning techniques is a very potent means of keeping students actively involved in lessons and thereby minimizing disruptive student behavior. Wilen (1986) has compiled a good summary of research on teacher questioning. Research findings on classroom questioning indicate that the following behaviors are very helpful in promoting student learning:

1. Ask questions at a variety of cognitive levels. Asking questions in a hierarchy that proceeds from knowledge and comprehension to application, analysis, synthesis, and evaluation promotes both critical thinking and better retention of basic information (Good and Brophy, 1987).
2. First ask the question; then call on someone to answer.
3. Call on both volunteers and nonvolunteers to answer questions in a random rather than predictable order (Note: In working with first- and second graders, research (Brophy and Good, 1986) indicates that the use of a predictable rather than a random order in selecting students to answer questions is more effective.)
4. After asking a question, allow students three to five seconds of think time before calling on someone to answer. This use of time is especially necessary when asking higher-level questions, which require students to make inferences, connections, and judgments.
5. Get many students to respond to a question before giving feedback. This may be done by asking for occasional choral responses from the entire group, by asking students to indicate their agreement or disagreement with answers by using signals, or by redirecting the question to obtain several individual answers.
6. After a student answers a question, wait three to five seconds before you respond. This planned silence, or Wait Time 2, is a powerful instructional tool. It tends to increase the number of students who respond, to increase the length of student answers, to increase the amount of student-student interaction, and to increase the diversity of student responses.
7. Vary the type of positive reinforcement that you give and make it clear why student answers are worthy of positive reinforcement.
8. Ask follow-up or probing questions to extend student thinking after both correct and incorrect responses. Some sample types of follow-up questions are (a) asking for clarification, (b) asking students to re-create the thought process they used to arrive at an answer, (c) asking for specific examples to support a statement, (d) asking for elaboration or expansion of an answer, and (e) asking students to relate their answers to previous answers or questions.

Teachers who employ these techniques as part of their normal use of questioning in the classroom and adapt these research findings to fit their

A teacher can use many different questioning techniques to increase student participation. (Lynn McLaren)

own classroom context are more likely to improve student learning and to increase student involvement in the learning activities, thereby minimizing disruptive student behavior.

MAXIMIZING LEARNING TIME

One of the variables that affects how much students learn is the amount of time they spend learning. In general, there is a statistically positive relationship between time devoted to learning and scores on achievement tests. (Lieberman and Denham, 1980). This is not, however, a simple relationship, although it does seem deceptively simple on the surface. Other factors such as the quality of instruction and the kinds of learning tasks must be considered in assessing the potential impact of increased time spent on learning. Spending more instructional time with a poor teacher or on poorly devised learning tasks will not increase student learning.

Assuming that the teacher is competent and the learning tasks are appropriate, students who spend more time learning will most likely learn more and will create fewer management problems since they are occupied by the learning activities. Two areas teachers can control to increase the amount of time students spend learning are the time allocated to instruction and the rate of student engagement in the learning tasks.

Allocated Time

Allocated time refers to the amount of time that the teacher makes available for students to learn a subject. Studies have found that the amount of time allocated to various subjects in elementary schools differs widely even among teachers in the same district at the same grade level (Karweit, 1984). For example, some teachers at the fourth-grade level allocate as much as 12 hours per week to reading and language arts, whereas other fourth-grade teachers allocate as little as 4 hours per week. Some fourth-grade teachers allocate as much as 10 hours per week to math, and others allocate as little as 3. Other factors being equal, a student who spends three times as many hours in learning is going to learn a great deal more.

In secondary schools, the amount of time actually allocated to instruction also varies widely among teachers. The need to deal with routine attendance and housekeeping chores (for example, who still owes lab reports; who needs to make up Friday's test) as well as the need to deal with disruptions such as discipline problems and public address announcements can steal large chunks of time from learning activities. (See Chapter Two). The implications are clear. Elementary school teachers should carefully examine how much time they make available for students to learn the various subjects that they teach. Secondary school teachers should investigate how to handle routine duties more efficiently and how to minimize other types of disruptions.

Time-on-Task

In addition to increasing allocated time, teachers need to maximize student time-on-task. "Research on teaching has established that the key to successful management (and to successful instruction as well) is the teacher's ability to maximize the time students spend actively engaged in worthwhile academic assignments and to minimize the time they spend waiting for activities to get started, making transitions between activities, sitting with nothing to do, or engaging in misconduct" (Brophy, 1988a, p. 3). This statement refers to the percentage of the total time allocated for learning that the student actually spends engaged in learning activities. Research provides some guidelines to increase student time-on-task.

1. Use of substantive interaction—a teaching mode in which the teacher presents information, asks questions to assess comprehension, provides feedback to students, and monitors student work generally—leads to higher student engagement rates than independent or small group work that is not led by the teacher.
2. Teacher monitoring of the entire class during the beginning and ending portions of seat work activities as well as at regular intervals during the activity leads to higher engagement rates.
3. Making sure that students understand what the activity directs them to do, that

they have the skills necessary to complete the task successfully, that each student has access to all necessary materials, and that each student is protected from disruption by others leads to greater student time-on-task during seat work.

4. Giving students clear oral directions concerning how to do a seat work activity and what to do when they have finished the activity, as well as posting directions in writing, also leads to greater time-on-task during seat work.

5. Communicating teacher awareness of student behavior seems to lead to greater student involvement during seat work activities.

6. "Providing a variety of seatwork activities with concern for students' attention spans helps keep students on task and allows the teacher more uninterrupted small group instruction" (Evertson, 1989, p. 64).

In short, there are several steps teachers can take to increase the amount of time that students spend on learning activities. The effective teacher uses these suggestions to increase student learning and to minimize disruptive student behavior.

CRITERION-REFERENCED EVALUATION

One of the most troublesome aspects of teaching for many of us is the process of evaluating student work and assigning student grades. Teachers are often caught in a dilemma that requires them to make choices between competing goals, such as the need to be fair to all students and the need to provide extra help and incentive to encourage individual students. Evaluation is also a thorny issue for students. Students have a great deal of ego invested in assignments and naturally have a difficult time accepting even valid criticism and negative feedback. This issue often presents real problems in teacher-student relationships.

Additionally, Doyle (1983) has demonstrated that academic tasks are clearly related to evaluation and rewards in students' minds. As Anderson (1989) explains, the connection between academic tasks and evaluation has a significant impact on the cognitive strategies students employ in completing required academic tasks. "Students become concerned with the ambiguity (the degree to which a correct answer can be predicted in advance) and the risk (the stringency of criteria for performance) involved in academic tasks" (p. 110). Students attempt to reduce ambiguity and risk in a variety of ways, especially by attempting to make all tasks lower-level cognitive tasks; that is, they reduce or attempt to reduce all tasks to memory or procedural tasks. "This dilemma suggests that beginning [we'd suggest all] teachers need to give thought to students' perceptions of tasks and accountability and consider ways to reduce students' anxiety about evaluation while at the same time pressing for engagement" (p. 110). This section of the chapter describes the technique of criterion-referenced evaluation, which can be used to reduce student anxiety about task ambiguity and risk by making criteria clear and useful for students. Criterion-referenced self-evaluation will also help to make evaluation a fairer, more objective process, thereby avoiding the predicament that Mr. Farley faces.

Case 27: The Grade Explosion

As he received his term paper back from Mr. Farley, Bob, a twelfth-grader at Lincoln High, said in a voice loud enough to carry across the room, "Bullshit." "What did you say," asked Mr. Farley with a glare. Bob repeated, "Bullshit; I said bullshit. This grade you gave me sucks. I put a lot of time into this project, but you don't like me so you gave me a D. I'll bet all the brown noses in here got good grades. I'm sick and tired of this crap from you. You never like anything I do. That's all right because I don't like you either." Mr. Farley was speechless. He thought that he had taken great care in evaluating the students' term papers and had been able to justify each grade that he had given. Not knowing what else to say and not wanting to lose his authority in the eyes of the other students, Mr. Farley finally said, "You will not talk to me like that young man. Get down to the office and do not attempt to set foot in this room until you have apologized to me in front of this class".

To use criterion-referenced evaluation, the teacher devises criteria by which an assignment will be graded at the same time that the assignment is developed. These criteria generally take the form of a rating scale or checklist (see Tables 5-1 and 5-2). Although the process of developing the rating scale may look difficult if you've never done one before, it really isn't.

To develop the rating scale, the teacher begins with the objectives that the assignment has been designed to evaluate. Each objective is translated into one or two criteria. After the criteria have been listed, the teacher develops a rating scale for each criterion. To design the rating scale: (1) List the descriptor for high performance on this criterion; (2) list the descriptor for low performance on this criterion; (3) list the descriptor for average performance on this criterion; (4) assign a point value for low, average, and high performance on this criterion, depending on its importance.

By developing criteria at the same time that the assignment itself is developed, the teacher is able to provide students with the grading criteria when the assignment is initially given out. This helps to improve the quality of student work and to minimize student-teacher conflicts over fairness in

TABLE 5-1   Sample Criterion-Referenced Rating Scale 1

Project: Seventh-grade art—Design a puppet from a drawing which illustrates a stereotyped character or illustrates a particular occupation.

Rating Scale

A. Did you hand in a ditto with two drawings of the puppet?

No --------------- Only 1 --------------- Yes 2
0   3   5

B. How neatly were the drawings presented?

Not neat ---------- Somewhat neat ---------- Very neat
0   2   5

C. Does the puppet illustrate a stereotype or occupation?

No ----------------------------- Yes
0   20

D. Does the costume help to show the stereotype or occupation?

No ----------------------------- Yes
0   10

E. Does the puppet have 5 facial parts?

No Features --------------- 1 or 2 --------------- 3 or 4 --------------- 5
0   3   7   10

F. Does the puppet have at least 4 different applied materials?

None ---------- Only 1 ---------- Only 2 ---------- Only 3 ---------- All 4
0   2   5   7   10

G. Are there any added accessories or other points that you think should be included as part of your grade?

H. The grade I would give myself for this project is _____ because

_____

_____

_____

grading, such as that which occurred between Bob and Mr. Farley. In addition, the potential of criterion-referenced evaluation can be made even more powerful by requiring students to evaluate their own assignments by using the criteria which the teacher gave them and to hand in this criterion-referenced self-evaluation along with the assignment. This technique results in a more objective basis for student-teacher discussions of grading and helps students to be more realistic about the quality of their work.

In an experiment involving the use of criterion-referenced evaluation with high school English students (Levin and Heath, 1981), three matched groups of students were given an assignment to write a term paper for their

TABLE 5-2   Sample Criterion-Referenced Rating Scale 2

Project: Tenth grade life science research project and class oral presentation on sources of pollution within the local community.

Rating Scale

Part I-Research

A. Did the student locate one real example of pollution?
    No ----------------------------- Yes
    0   10

B. Did the student identify the type, source, cause, and effect of pollution?
    No ---------- 1/4 ---------- 2/4 ---------- 3/4 ---------- 4/4
    0   7.5   15   22.5   30

C. Did the student identify the responsible party and cite the source of identification?
    Neither ---------- Identified only party/source ---------- Both party and source
    0   10   20

D. Did the student identify 1 agency who has control over this problem?
    No ----------------------------- Yes
    0   20

E. Did the student propose 2 methods of correction?
    No ---------- Only 1 ---------- 2
    0   15   30

Part 2-Presentation

A. Was the presentation ready on time?
    No ----------------------------- Yes
    0   20

B. Was the presentation well organized?
    No ---------- Somewhat ---------- Clearly organized
    0   5   10

C. Was the student knowledgeable about the subject?
    No ---------- Not sure on 1 or 2 points ---------- Yes
    0   5   10

D. Did the student use audiovisual material?
    No ----------------------------- Yes
    0   10

Total Points out of 150

English course. One group of students was required to evaluate their own papers by using a criterion-referenced rating scale handed out by the teacher and to hand in the self-evaluation along with the term paper itself. A second group of students was given the criterion-referenced rating scale but was not required to use it. A third group was not given the rating scale at all. All of the term papers underwent a blind review by a panel of independent judges. The results showed that those students who used the rating scale to evaluate their own work did significantly better than the other two groups, and results also indicated that those students who were simply given the rating scale but not forced to use it did significantly better than those students who were not given the rating scale at all. Criterion-referenced self-evaluation and criterion-referenced evaluation seem to be promising techniques for improving student learning and also for minimizing potential relationship problems posed by the evaluation process.

SUMMARY

This chapter has provided an overview of the research on teacher effects, which constitutes a large portion of our profession's accumulated wisdom on best practice. All teachers have a professional obligation to examine their teaching behavior to ensure that it reflects best practice. This is a critical step to ensure that the teacher has done all that can be done to prevent classroom management problems from occurring.

Among the questions teachers should ask in assessing the congruence between best teaching practice and their own teaching behavior are the following: Do the lessons I design include an introduction, clear presentation of content, checking for student understanding, guided practice, independent practice, closure or summary, and periodic reviews? Have I used each of the following factors in trying to increase my students' motivation to learn: student interests, student needs, novelty and variety, success, student attributions, tension, feeling tone, feedback, and encouragement? Have I communicated high expectations for learning and behavior to all students by equalizing response opportunities, providing prompt and constructive feedback on performance, and treating all students with personal regard? Have I used classroom questioning to involve students actively in the learning process by asking questions at a variety of cognitive levels, using questions to increase student participation, and using questions to probe for and extend student thinking? Have I maximized student learning by allocating as much time as possible for student learning and by increasing the percentage of student engagement in learning activities? Have I made evaluation of student learning a fairer, more objective, more participatory process by using criterion-referenced evaluation?

The teacher who honestly can answer yes to each of these questions has made giant strides toward ensuring that her classroom will be a learning place for students in which discipline problems are kept to a minimum.

REFERENCES

AMES, R., AND AMES, C. (Eds.). (1984). *Research on Motivation in Education, Vol. 1: Student Motivation.* New York: Academic Press.

ANDERSON, L. M. (1989). Classroom instruction. In M. C. Reynolds (Ed.), *Knowledge Base for the Beginning Teacher.* New York: Pergamon Press.

BROPHY, J. E. (1987). Synthesis of research on strategies for motivating students to learn. *Educational Leadership, 45,* 2, 40–48.

BROPHY, J. E., AND GOOD, T. L. (1986). Teacher behavior and student achievement. In M. L. Witrock (Ed.), *Handbook of Research on Teaching,* 3rd ed. New York: Macmillan.

BROPHY, J. (1988a). Educating teachers about managing classrooms and students. *Teaching and Teacher Education, 4,* 1, 1–18.

BROPHY, J. (1988b). Research on teacher effects and abuses. *The Elementary School Journal, 89,* 1, 3–21.

DOYLE, W. (1983). Academic work. *Review of Educational Research, 53,* 159–199.

DREIKURS, R. (1964). *Children the Challenge.* New York: Hawthorne.

DUKE, D. L. (1982). *Helping Teachers Manage Classrooms.* Alexandria, Va: Association for Supervision and Curriculum Development.

EVERTSON, C. M. (1989). Classroom organization and management. In M. C. Reynolds (Ed.), *Knowledge Base for the Beginning Teacher.* New York: Pergamon Press.

GOOD, T. L. (1987). Two decades of research on teacher expectations: Findings and future directions. *Journal of Teacher Education,* July-August, pp. 32–47.

GOOD, T., AND BROPHY, J. (1987). *Looking in Classrooms,* 4th ed. New York: Harper & Row.

HUNTER, M. (1982). *Mastery Teaching.* El Segundo, CA: TIP Publications.

KARWEIT, N. (1984). Time on task reconsidered: Synthesis of research on time and learning. *Educational Leadership, 41,* 8, 32–35.

LEVIN, J., AND HEATH, R. (1981). *Criteria referenced evaluation: Its effect on student achievement, on task behavior and teacher behavior.* Paper presented at the Annual Conference of the Pennsylvania Association for Supervision and Curriculum Development, Harrisburg.

LIEBERMAN, A., AND DENHAM, C. (1980). *Time to Learn.* Sacramento: California Commission for Teacher Preparation and Licensing.

ROSENSHINE, B., AND STEVENS, R. (1986). Teaching functions. In M. L. Wittrock (Ed.), *Handbook of Research on Teaching,* 3rd ed. New York: Macmillan.

ROSENTHAL, R., AND JACOBS. L. (1968). *Pygmalion in the Classroom: Teacher Expectation and Pupil's Intellectual Development.* New York: Holt, Rinehart & Winston.

SWEENY, T. J. (1981). *Adlerian Counseling: Proven Concepts and Strategies,* 2nd ed. New York: Accelerated Development.

WANG, M. C., AND PALINSCAR, A. S. (1989). Teaching students to assume an active role in their learning. In M. C. Reynolds (Ed.), *Knowledge Base for the Beginning Teacher.* New York: Pergamon Press.

WILEN, W. W. (1986). *Questioning Skills for Teachers,* 2nd ed. Washington, DC: National Education Association.

WINEBURG, S. S. (1987). The self-fulfillment of the self-fulfilling prophecy. *Educational Researcher, 16,* 9, 28–36.

EXERCISES

1. Select a concept from any discipline with which you are familiar.

    a. Write a series of questions on the concept that contains questions on each of the following levels: knowledge, comprehension, application, analysis, synthesis, and evaluation.

    b. Would there be any difference in the use of wait time in asking the six questions you wrote for A? Why?

    c. Why is a hierarchical ordering of questions important in relation to classroom management?

2. With regard to classroom management, why do we suggest that it is better to ask the question first, and then call on someone to answer it? Would there be any justification for doing it the other way around?

3. What specifically can teachers do to communicate high expectations for learning and behavior to students?

4. What would be the effect on student learning if the following is omitted from the teaching act:
    a. The introduction?
    b. Checking for understanding?
    c. Closure or summary?

5. What are some things teachers can do to ensure that their explanation of content is presented clearly?

6. Using your knowledge of students' cognitive and moral development, what are some important techniques for motivating students at each of the following grade levels: (a) primary elementary, (b) intermediate elementary, (c) junior high, and (d) senior high?

7. If you were observing teachers, what specific behaviors would you look for to indicate that the teacher was attempting to maximize student time-on-task during (a) a lecture, (b) a discussion, and (c) a seat work activity?

8. How might secondary teachers handle routine chores such as taking attendance and receiving slips for excuses and early dismissals to maximize the time allocated for learning? What might elementary teachers do to ensure that all subjects receive the appropriate amount of allocated time?

9. What is the relationship between evaluation of student learning and student behavior? How would the use of criterion-referenced evaluation affect student behavior?

10. Choose an assignment that is typically graded subjectively and design a criterion-referenced evaluation device to grade the assignment.

CHAPTER 6

Structuring the Environment

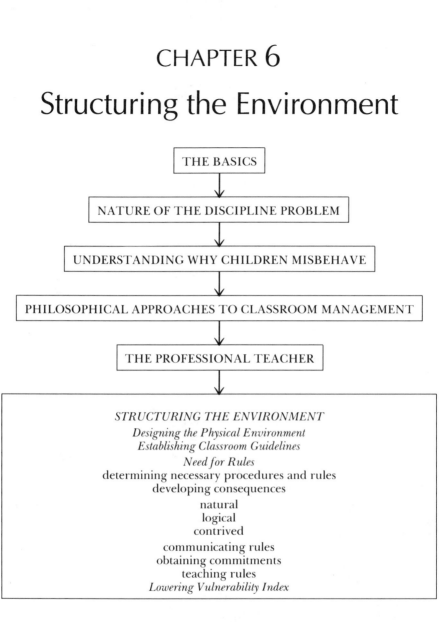

THE BASICS

↓

NATURE OF THE DISCIPLINE PROBLEM

↓

UNDERSTANDING WHY CHILDREN MISBEHAVE

↓

PHILOSOPHICAL APPROACHES TO CLASSROOM MANAGEMENT

↓

THE PROFESSIONAL TEACHER

↓

STRUCTURING THE ENVIRONMENT
Designing the Physical Environment
Establishing Classroom Guidelines
Need for Rules
determining necessary procedures and rules
developing consequences
natural
logical
contrived
communicating rules
obtaining commitments
teaching rules
Lowering Vulnerability Index

PRINCIPLES OF CLASSROOM MANAGEMENT

19. When environmental conditions are appropriate for learning, the likelihood of disruptive behavior is minimized.

20. Students are more likely to follow classroom guidelines when the teacher models appropriate behavior and explains the guidelines' relationship to learning, mutual student-teacher respect, and protection and safety of property and individuals.

21. Clearly communicating guidelines to students and obtaining their commitment to follow them enhances appropriate classroom behavior.

22. Enforcing teacher expectations by using natural and logical consequences helps students learn that they are responsible for the consequences of their behavior and for controlling their own behavior.

23. The probability of classroom discipline problems is reduced when teachers consider and modify, where necessary and possible, the interactions of student characteristics, teacher characteristics, environmental factors, and teaching/ learning activities.

INTRODUCTION

Misbehavior does not occur in a vacuum isolated from the surrounding classroom environment. Psychologists have long known that all behavior is controlled or influenced by events and conditions that precede (antecedents) as well as by events and conditions that follow (consequences) the behavior.

Antecedents may increase the likelihood that appropriate behavior will take place or set the stage for the occurrence of misbehavior. Therefore when teachers are preventing or modifying inappropriate behavior, they must examine antecedent events and conditions carefully before resorting to the delivery of consequences. The start of the school year and the introduction of novel learning activities are two critical times when very careful attention must be given to antecedent variables. Unfortunately teachers often give only cursory attention to antecedent variables at these times because their work load is high and planning time is limited. Understandably, many teachers decide to spend this restricted time on designing learning activities. However it must be stressed that learning activities are more successful when teachers have preplanned for appropriate seating arrangements and necessary supplies and materials and have developed rules and procedures (Brophy, 1988a).

Because of the impact of antecedent variables on student behavior, teachers must take the time to examine all of them, or at the very least, the two most crucial—the classroom's physical environment and classroom guidelines. This chapter discusses these important antecedents and also introduces the vulnerability index, a practical planning procedure to predict the potential development of discipline problems during any given classroom activity. If predicted to be too high, teachers can then reduce it by modifying relevant antecedents.

DESIGNING THE PHYSICAL CLASSROOM ENVIRONMENT

Environmental Conditions

Heating, lighting, ventilation, and noise affect behavior. Although there are some exceptions, today most schools have adequate lighting, heating, ventilation, and noise control. Many of these environmental variables are part of the school's physical plant and are basically out of the teacher's control.

Although teachers cannot install new lighting or remodel an inefficient heating system, they can ensure that the physical environment is the most appropriate for learning to take place, given what is available. For instance, teachers can control lighting intensity. Dim lighting during classwork, a flickering ceiling light, or inadequate darkening of the room for viewing movies or filmstrips causes unnecessary frustration, disinterest, and off-task behavior. Always checking on appropriate lighting before the start of a lesson avoids these problems. Since many schools are on predetermined heating schedules, there are some warm late winter or early spring days or cold early fall or late spring days when rooms may be uncomfortably hot or cold. Teachers have little influence over relevant physical plant matters, but when necessary they can open windows to allow fresh air into a too warm room, turn unnecessary lights off to cool the room, and remind students to bring sweaters on predicted cooler days.

Depending on the school's location, outside noise may be uncontrollable, but inside noise is often manageable. Teachers as a group should insist that noisy repairs to school buildings be completed either before or after school if possible. Likewise, insistence on predetermined times for public address announcements is necessary. Finally a strong school policy should dictate and enforce quiet hallway use by both teachers and students when classes are in session.

The importance of the optimization of environmental conditions that are conducive to learning cannot be stressed too much, as humans must be physically comfortable before their attention is voluntarily given to learning.

Use of Space

Teachers have no control over the size of their classrooms; however they usually can decide (except possibly in shops and labs) how to utilize best the given space within the classroom. Careful use of physical space makes a considerable difference in classroom behavior (Evans and Lovell, 1979).

SEATING ARRANGEMENTS

A teacher's first concern is the arrangement of seating. No matter what basic seating arrangement is used, it should be flexible enough to accommodate and facilitate the various learning activities that occur in a given classroom. If a teacher's primary instructional strategy involves a lot of group work, the teacher might put three or four desks together to facilitate these activities. On the other hand if a teacher emphasizes teacher-directed lecture and discussion, with individual seat work, an appropriate seating arrangement might be the traditional rows of desks separated by aisles. It is quite acceptable and often warranted for the teacher to change his primary seating arrangement to accommodate changing instructional activities.

In addition to flexibility, an effective seating arrangement allows the teacher to have close proximity to all students. Seating is planned so that the teacher may easily reach any student in the class without disturbing other students. Also seating is arranged so that all students are able to see instructional presentations. An effort should be made to avoid having students face distractions, such as windows or hallways. Finally, seating should not interfere with high-usage areas, where there are pencil sharpeners, sinks, closets, or wastepaper cans. Various seating arrangements for different learning activities are diagrammed and discussed, including their potential for discipline problems, in Howell and Howell (1979) and Rinne (1984).

Besides planning the location of seats and desks, which occupy most of the classroom space, the teacher decides where learning centers, bookcases, storage cabinets, and large work tables are placed. Appropriate placement helps the classroom reflect the excitement and variety of the learning that is occurring. Also classrooms should be neat and uncluttered. For many people a cluttered area is an uncomfortable environment in which to work and learn. Moreover, a cluttered, sloppy, unorganized classroom communicates to students that disorganization and sloppiness are acceptable, which may lead to behavior problems.

BULLETIN BOARDS AND DISPLAY AREAS

Case 28: Having Your Name Placed on the Board Isn't Always Bad

One by one the seventh-grade students enter Ms. White's room and cluster around the bulletin board. Today is the day after the test and the new lists go up. Cathy hollers, "Great; I made it!" Jimmy says, "I'm on both lists." One is for students who received A's or B's on the most recent test. The names are placed in alphabetical order and do not reflect a grade ranking. The other poster, "Commendable Improvements," lists those students who have made the best improvement from one test to another regardless of test grade. The interest students continually show towards this bulletin board surprises even Ms. White.

Case 29: Fourteen to Ten, Music Wins

The fifth-period bulletin board committee presents three ideas to the class. Mr. Jaffee reminds the students that they can vote for only one idea. Dana presents the first idea: "We would like to make a graph showing popular music sales of 1988." Tina presents the second idea: "I propose that we make bar graphs that compare the 1988 Olympic track and field outcomes to the world records." The third idea is presented by Jamie: "It would be interesting to have a display showing the many careers there are in mathematics."

After the class asks the presenting students questions about each idea, Mr. Jaffee calls for a vote. The popular music graphs receives 14 votes, the Olympics 10, and not surprisingly, mathematics careers only 4. The committee begins the research so that the bulletin board will be completed before parents' back-to-school night.

Each of Mr. Jaffee's five classes has a bulletin board committee, which is responsible for the design of one bulletin board during the year. The only criterion is that the topic has to be mathematically related or its design has to use some mathematical skill.

The bulletin boards in Mr. Jaffee's room serve two purposes: They publically recognize students' efforts, and they provide an opportunity for students to enrich their mathematics learning through their own efforts and using their own ideas. This is in striking contrast to some teachers' bulletin boards, which are packed away at the end of each school year only to reappear once again in September, or bulletin boards that contain yellowed notices dated a few months earlier.

The more bulletin boards are used to recognize students or provide students with opportunities for active participation, the more likely they will facilitate and enhance appropriate student behavior. Other excellent uses of bulletin boards and display areas are the posting of local or school newspaper articles mentioning students' names and the display of students' work. A part of a bulletin board or other wall space may be set aside for the posting of classroom guidelines.

ESTABLISHING CLASSROOM GUIDELINES

The development of classroom guidelines is one antecedent variable over which the teacher has major control. Classroom guidelines are necessary for the efficient and effective running of a classroom. A classroom is a complex interaction of students, teachers, and materials. Guidelines help to increase the likelihood that these interactions are orderly and the environment is conducive to learning. Properly designed guidelines should support teaching and learning and provide students with clear expectations and well-defined norms, which in turn give students the feeling of safety, security, and direction. This atmosphere often provides students with the motivation and rationale to compete with strong peer orientation, which often opposes the appropriate behaviors conducive for learning (Jones and Jones, 1981).

Classroom Procedures

There are two types of classroom guidelines, procedures and rules. Procedures are routines for behaviors that regularly occur at specified times or during particular activities. They are directed at accomplishing something rather than primarily aimed at managing disruptive behavior. Examples of procedures include standard ways of passing out and turning in materials, entering and leaving the room, and taking attendance. Procedures are clear-cut systematic steps or directions that reflect behaviors necessary for the smooth operation of the classroom.

Procedures are taught to students through examples and demonstrations, so they soon become an integral part of the running of the classroom. Properly designed and learned procedures maximize on-task student be-

Classroom procedures have to be taught to students. (Ken Karp)

havior by minimizing the need for students to ask for directions and the need for teachers continually to give instructions for everyday classroom events. Certain important procedures may be prominently displayed for students' reference. Steps to be followed during fire drills and appropriate heading information for tests and assignments are good examples of procedures to display.

Students often do not learn and use the procedures immediately after their introduction. At first, feedback and practice must be provided. However the time spent to learn the procedures is well invested and eventually leads to a successful management system (Brophy, 1988b). Often teachers in classrooms that are heavily procedurally oriented such as art, sciences, and elementary classrooms have students practice the procedures. In classrooms where procedures are directly related to safety or skill development (such as equipment handling in industrial arts or science laboratory techniques), instructional objectives involving the procedures are used in addition to the substantive subject matter objectives. Thus the procedures are an integral part of the classroom instruction.

The use of natural and logical consequences is quite appropriate for students who fail to follow procedural guidelines. Natural consequences are outcomes of behavior that occur without teacher intervention. Examples of natural consequences are the inability of a teacher to record a students' grade if an assignment is handed in without a name and incorrect results because of inappropriate laboratory procedures (if not a safety hazard).

The use of logical consequences is much more common and has wider applicability in school settings than natural ones. Logical consequences are generally defined as outcomes that are directly related to the behavior but need teacher intervention for them to occur. Examples of logical consequences are students having less time for recess because they did not line up correctly to leave the room and students having to pay for the damage to their textbooks because of careless use.

Natural and logical consequences are powerful management concepts because the consequences that the students experience are directly related to their behavior. In addition only the student is responsible for the consequences; therefore the teacher is removed from the role of punisher. The use of natural and logical consequences for managing behavior is covered in much more depth later in this chapter.

Classroom Rules

In contrast to procedures, rules focus on appropriate general behavior in order to avoid discipline problems. Because rules cover a wider spectrum of behavior than procedures, the development of rules is usually a more complex and consuming task.

THE NEED FOR RULES

Schools in general and classrooms in particular are dynamic places. As has been pointed out many times in this book, teaching and learning involve complex interactions in many different situations. Within almost any given classroom, learning activities vary widely and may range from individual seat work to large group projects that necessitate cooperative working arrangements among students.

One characteristic of human behavior is that it is highly sensitive to differing conditions across situations as well as to changing conditions within situations (Walker, 1979). Evidence indicates that children in general and disruptive children in particular are highly sensitive to changing situations and conditions (Johnson, Boadstad, and Lobitz, 1976; Kazdin and Bootzin, 1972). Couple the dynamic nature of schools and classrooms with the sensitivity of human behavior to changing conditions and the need for rules becomes apparent.

Rules provide the guidelines for those behaviors that are required if teaching and learning are to take place. Rules should be directed at organizing the learning environment to ensure the continuity and quality of teaching and learning and not at exerting control over students (Brophy, 1988a). Thus, appropriately designed rules increase on-task student behavior, resulting in improved learning.

DETERMINING NECESSARY RULES

One sure way to reduce the likelihood that rules will be effective is to present students with a long list of do's and don'ts. Teachers who attempt to cover every conceivable classroom behavior with a rule face an almost impossible task. They place themselves in the untenable position of having to observe and monitor the most minute and insignificant student behaviors, leaving little time for teaching. Students, especially·in upper elementary and secondary grades, view a long list of do's and don'ts as picky and impossible to follow. They look upon teachers who monitor and correct every behavior as nagging, unreasonable, and controlling.

Teachers must present students with a list of rules that is fair, realistic, and can be rationalized as necessary for the development of an appropriate classroom environment (Emmer et al., 1989). Therefore, before meeting a class for the first time, the teacher must seriously consider the question "What are the necessary student behaviors that I need in my classroom so that discipline problems will not occur?" To assist in answering this question, see our definition of a discipline problem in Chapter Two: *A discipline problem is any behavior that interferes with the teaching act, interferes with the rights of others to learn, is psychologically or physically unsafe, or destroys property.* Thus, any rule that is developed must be consistent with discouraging the problems and supporting appropriate behavior. In other words, any rule must be rationalized as being necessary to ensure that (1) the teacher's right to teach is protected, (2) the students' rights to learning are protected, (3) the students' psychological and physical safety are protected, and (4) property is protected. Rules that are so developed and rationalized make sense to students because they are not arbitrary. Such rules also lend themselves to the use of natural and logical consequences when students do not follow them.

DEVELOPING CONSEQUENCES

When students choose not to follow a classroom rule, they should experience a consequence (Canter, 1989). The development of appropriate consequences is as important, if not more important, than the development of the rules themselves. The type of consequences and how they are applied may make the difference between whether or not students follow rules and whether or not they respect the teacher.

Unfortunately teachers usually give considerably more thought to the design of rules than they do to consequences. When a rule is not followed, teachers often determine consequences on the spot. Such an approach may lead to inconsistent, irrational consequences, which are interpreted by students as being unfair, unreasonable, and unrelated to their behavior. This eventually undermines the teacher's effectiveness as a classroom manager, the ultimate outcome being more disruptive student behavior.

Without anyone's intervention, we will learn powerful lessons as we function as a part of society. For instance have you ever

> Had an accident because you ran a red light or a stop sign?
> Injured your foot while walking barefoot?
> Locked yourself out of your house because you forgot your key?
> Lost or broken something because of carelessness?
> Missed a bus or train because of lateness?

All of these events are powerful modifiers of future behavior and they all have certain characteristics. Each is an undesirable consequence, is experienced by all persons equally regardless of who they are, and comes about without the intervention of anyone else. Such consequences are called natural consequences because they are directly related to the behaviors and happen without anyone's outside influence. Dreikurs (1964) emphasized that by allowing children to experience the natural consequences of their behavior, they are provided with an honest and real learning situation.

Students are much more likely to experience natural consequences at home or in the general society than in school. However, allowing students to experience the natural consequences of their behavior, if at all possible, in classroom situations is a powerful control technique. It serves to remove the teacher from negative involvement with students and clearly communicates a cause-and-effect relationship between a student's chosen behavior and the experienced consequence.

Some examples of natural consequences in schools are

Obtaining a low test grade because of failure to study.

Losing assignments or books because of carelessness.

Ruining a shop project as a result of the inappropriate use of tools.

Losing a ball on a roof or over a school fence because of playing with it inappropriately.

The use of natural consequences in the classroom is somewhat limited because of inherent ethical, moral, and legal restraints that prohibit a teacher from allowing certain outcomes from happening. For instance, the natural consequences of failing to follow safety precautions in science laboratories or industrial arts classes could result in serious bodily injury or even death. Obviously such a consequence always must be avoided. Other natural consequences take a long time to develop and may put a student at an extreme disadvantage later in life, for example, being unable to gain entrance to college or meaningful employment because of behavior problems and poor grades.

When natural consequences are not appropriate or do not naturally follow a given behavior, the teacher needs to intervene and apply a second type of consequence called logical consequences.

Have you ever

Been subjected to a finance charge because you were late paying a bill?

Received a ticket for a traffic violation?

Had a check returned for insufficient funds because you didn't balance your checkbook?

Like natural consequences, logical consequences are directly and rationally related to the student's behavior and are powerful modifiers of future behavior. They differ from natural consequences in that the consequence is the result of the purposeful intervention of another person. In school that person is most likely the teacher, who optimally administers logical consequences in a calm, matter-of-fact manner. If, however, they are imposed in anger, they cease being logical consequences and tend to become punishment. Children are more likely to respond favorably or positively to logical consequences because they do not consider such consequences mean or unfair, whereas they often argue, fight back, or retaliate when punished (Dreikurs, 1964).

Logical consequences may be applied in two different ways. First the teacher prescribes the logical consequence without giving the student a choice. Examples are

"Joe, you spilled the paint; please clean it up."
"Sue, you continue to call out. When you raise your hand you will be called on."
"Andy, you wrote on your desk. You will have to clean it up during recess."

The second way is to give the student a choice of changing his behavior or experiencing the logical consequence. The effectiveness of this technique is that it puts the responsibility for appropriate behavior where it belongs, on the student. If the student chooses to continue with the disruptive behavior, the logical consequence is forthcoming. If the student chooses to cease the disruptive behavior, he remains an active classroom participant. Some examples are

"Sarah, you have a choice to walk down the hall without pushing or you will have to hold my hand."
"Heidi, you have the choice to stop disturbing Joey or you will have to change your seat."
"Mike, you have a choice to raise your hand or you will not be called on."

Notice that all the choices are phrased so the student being addressed is clearly identified, and the desired behavior as well as the logical consequence if the behavior does not change are succinctly stated.

Actually using the words "*you* have a choice" communicates to the student that the teacher is in a neutral position. It serves to remove the teacher from arguments and power struggles with the student, which are very detrimental to classroom management. This is extremely crucial, especially in highly explosive situations. Natural or logical consequences are not readily apparent to an extremely angry and upset student who lashes out by spewing vulgarities at his teacher during class. However suppose a teacher responds, "Your behavior is unacceptable. If this occurs again, your parents will be contacted immediately." The student is made aware of exactly what will happen if he chooses to continue his behavior, and perhaps more important, the teacher remains neutral in the eyes of both the student and the rest of the class.

A third form of consequences is contrived consequences, more commonly known as punishment. The strict definition of punishment is any adverse consequence of a targeted behavior that suppresses the behavior. However in day-to-day school practice, punishment is not defined in this way. In actuality punishment takes on two forms, removal of privileges and painful experiences, both of which may or may not suppress misbehavior.

Removal of privileges, if appropriately planned, may be not only punishment but a logical consequence. For example, taking away a students' recess time because he has to complete classwork that was missed while daydreaming is both punishment and a logical consequence. However, if the teacher cancels a student's participation in next week's trip to the zoo, this is punishment only and not a logical consequence because it is not directly related to helping the student complete his work.

Painful experiences may be physical (shaking, hitting, or pulling), verbal reprimands (yelling, sarcasm, or threats), or extra assignments (extra homework or writing something 100 times). Such consequences are often designed only to hurt and get even. The use of painful punishment in controlling human behavior has been and remains a highly controversial issue on the grounds of morality, ethics, law, and proven ineffectiveness.

Research has indicated consistently that painful punishment suppresses undesirable behavior for short periods of time without affecting lasting behavioral change. Because avoidance or escape behavior is often a side effect of painful experiences, frequent punishment teaches a child how to be "better at misbehaving" by avoiding detection and thus the punishment. Painful punishment is rarely an effective means of changing a person's behavior (Clarizio, 1980; Curwin and Mendler, 1980).

Punishment also deprives the student of the opportunity to learn prosocial, acceptable behavior because it seldom is logically related to the behavior and does not point to alternative acceptable behavior. In addition punishment reinforces a low level of moral development by modeling undesirable behaviors, which teach students that when one is in a position of authority, it is appropriate to act in punishing ways toward others (Clarizio, 1980: Curwin and Mendler, 1980; Jones and Jones, 1981).

When assisting children in controlling their disruptive behavior, it is important to have them examine both the motivation behind the behavior and the consequences of the behavior on themselves and others. Punishment obscures these issues by focusing the child's concern on the immediate punishment (Jones and Jones, 1981). It also limits the teacher's ability to

Punishment often leads to a student having feelings of rage, resentment, hostility, and an urge to get even.

help the child in this process because very frequently the child does not associate the punishment with his or her actions but with the punisher. This often leads to rage, resentment, hostility, and an urge to get even (Dreikurs, Grundwald, and Pepper, 1982).

Physical or corporal punishment is still used in many classrooms, although there has been an ever-increasing opposition to its use in schools. Epstein (1979) has stated, "There is no pedagogical justification for inflicting pain. . . . It does not merit any serious discussion of pros and cons" (pp. 229–230). Similarly Canter (1989) has stated, ". . . consequences should never be psychologically or physically harmful to the students . . . corporal punishment should never be administered" (p. 58). Clarizio (1980) has stated, ". . . there is very little in the way of evidence to suggest the benefit of physical punishment in the schools but there is a substantial body of research to suggest that this method can have undesirable long-term side effects" (p. 141). Some of the side effects of physical punishment are a resultant dislike and distrust of the teacher and school; an identification of a feeling of powerlessness, with negative effects on a child's motivation to learn; and the development of escape and avoidance behaviors that may take the form of lying, skipping class, or daydreaming (Clarizio, 1980; Epstein, 1979).

Two common myths surround the use of physical punishment (Clarizio, 1980). The first myth is that it is a tried and true method that aids students in developing a sense of personal responsibility, self-discipline, and moral character. In reality, studies have consistently indicated that physical punishment correlates with delinquency and low development of conscience.

The second myth is that it is the only form of discipline some children understand. In fact this has never been shown to be true. Perhaps it is a case of projection on the part of the teacher. In one study it was shown that teachers who relied heavily on physical punishment did not know other means of solving classroom management problems (Dayton Public Schools, 1973). Teachers must understand that if a technique has not worked in the past, more of the same will not produce desirable results. New approaches are needed.

The unproven effectiveness and the risk of harmful side effects has caused some of the largest school districts to prohibit corporal punishment (including Philadelphia; Washington, DC; and Chicago) even though many of these schools are plagued with discipline problems. The National Education Association and the American Federation of Teachers also have supported continually the abolition of physical punishment.

For teachers who occasionally use mild forms of punishment, guidelines for minimizing possible harmful side effects are discussed by Clarizio (1980) and Heitzman (1983).

Table 6-1 compares natural and logical consequences with punishment.

TABLE 6-1   Comparison of Consequences Versus Punishment

NATURAL/LOGICAL CONSEQUENCE	PUNISHMENT
Expresses the reality of a situation	Expresses the power of authority
Logically related to misbehavior	Contrived and arbitrary connection with misbehavior
Illustrates cause and effect	Does not illustrate cause and effect
Involves no moral judgment about person—"You are O.K.; your behavior isn't"	Often involves moral judgments
Concerned with the present	Concerned with the past
Administered without anger	Anger is often present
Helps develop self-discipline	Depends on extrinsic control
Choices often given	Alternatives are not given
Thoughtful, deliberate	Often impulsive
Does not develop escape and avoidance behaviors	Develops escape and avoidance behaviors
Does not produce resentment	Produces resentment
Teacher is removed from negative involvement with student	Teacher involvement is negative
Based on the concept of equality	Based on superior-inferior relationship
Communicates the expectation that the student is capable of controlling his own behavior	Communicates that the teacher must control the student's behavior

(Dreikurs, Grundwald, and Pepper 1982; Sweeney, 1981)

COMMUNICATING RULES

After classroom rules are developed and consequences thought through, the teacher must communicate the rules clearly to the students (Canter, 1989; Evertson and Emmer, 1982; Jones and Jones, 1981). Clear communication entails a discussion of what the rules are and a rationale for each and every one (Good and Brophy, 1973). The rationale for any rule necessarily involves the protection of a teacher's right to teach, the students' right to learn, and the students' right to psychological and physical safety and property. When students understand the purpose of rules, they are more likely to view them as reasonable and fair, thus increasing the likelihood of appropriate behavior.

The manner in which rules are phrased is important. Certain rules need to be stated, so that it is clear that they apply equally to both the teacher and the students. This is accomplished by using the phrase "We all need to" followed by the behavioral expectation and the rationale. For example, "We all need to respect each other's right to participate and voice his views. Therefore when someone is talking, pay attention and do not interrupt."

Such phrasing incorporates the principle that teachers must model the behaviors they expect (Brophy, 1988a).

Although it is essential that the teacher communicate behavioral expectations and the rationales behind them, this is not in many cases sufficient to ensure that the rules are obeyed. A final critical strategy is obtaining from each student a strong indication that he understands the rules as well as a commitment that he will attempt to abide by them (Jones and Jones, 1981).

OBTAINING COMMITMENTS

When two or more people reach an agreement, they often finalize it with a handshake or a signed contract, which demonstrates that the individuals intend to comply with the terms of the agreement. Even though agreements are often violated, a handshake, verbal promise, or written contract

---

Case 30: "I Don't Know If I Can Remember"

At the beginning of the school year, Mr. Merit has a discussion of class rules with his second-grade class. He explains each rule with examples. The reason for each rule is solicited from members of the class. Students are encouraged to ask questions about the rules, and Mr. Merit in turn asks the students questions to assess their understanding of the rules.

After the discussion Mr. Merit asks, "All those who understand the rules please raise your hand." Next he asks, "all those who will attempt to follow the rules please raise your hands." He notices that both Helen and Gary do not raise their hands and asks them why. Helen says, "I'm not sure if I'll always remember the rules and if I can't remember I can't promise to follow the rules." Mr. Merit replies, "Helen, I understand your concern, but I have written these rules on a poster, which I am going to place on the front bulletin board. Do you think that this will help you?" Helen answers, "Yes," and both Helen and Gary then raise their hands.

Mr. Merit then shows the class the poster of rules whose title is "I Will Try to Follow Our Classroom Rules." One by one each student comes up and signs his/her name at the bottom of the poster. Mr. Merit asks Helen to staple the poster to the front bulletin board and she does it immediately.

Case 31: "I'm Not Promising Anything"

On the first day of class, Ms. Loy explains the classroom rules to her tenth-grade mathematics classes. She discusses with the class why these rules are necessary for the teaching and learning of mathematics.

Ms. Loy then says to the class, "I am going to pass out two copies of the rules that we just discussed. You'll notice that at the bottom is the statement 'I am aware of these rules and understand them,' followed by a place for your signature. Please sign one copy and pass it up front so I can collect them. Place the other copy in your notebook."

Alex raises his hand and says, "I can't make any promises about my future behavior in this class. I'm not sure what the class is even going to be like." Ms. Loy replies, "Please read what you are signing." Alex reads "I am aware of these rules and understand them" and says out loud "Oh, I see; I'm not promising anything." Alex then signs the sheet and passes it to the front.

---

increases the probability that the agreements will be kept. With this idea in mind, teachers should attempt to have students express their understanding of the rules and their intent to abide by them.

Mr. Merit and Ms. Loy are both attempting to get their students to understand and agree to follow the classroom rules. However, notice that their methods are different because of the different level of maturity of their students. Ms. Loy only asks her students to confirm that they understand the rules, not that they will abide by them. This is an important distinction that should be made when working with older students because it reduces the potential of a student confrontation during a time in the school year when the development of teacher-student rapport is critical. In both cases, however, the rules are on display or available for quick reference, which is highly recommended (Evertson and Emmer, 1982; Jones and Jones, 1981).

Merely displaying rules in a classroom has little effect on maintaining appropriate student behavior (Madson, Becker, and Thomas, 1968). Teachers must refer to and use the displayed rules to assist individual students in learning the rules and developing self-control.

In the following case Mr. Martinez understands these principles and is able to carry them out.

Case 32: Calling Out Correct Answers

Mr. Martinez, a fourth-grade teacher, posts the classroom rules on the front bulletin board. One by one each student signs the poster, agreeing to follow the rules.

Mr. Martinez soon notices that Lowyn is having a difficult time remembering to raise her hand before answering questions. Instead Lowyn just calls out the answers. At first Mr. Martinez ignores the answer. The next time she calls out, he makes eye contact with her and nods his head in a disapproving fashion. Finally, he moves close to Lowyn and quietly says, "Lowyn, you have great answers, but you must raise your hand so that everyone has a equal chance to answer." Mr. Martinez half expects that this will not be the end of Lowyn's calling out so he is prepared for the next time she does not raise her hand.

The next lesson begins, and Mr. Martinez asks the class, "Who can summarize what we learned about magnets yesterday?" Enthusiastically Lowyn calls out, "Every magnet has a north and south pole." Mr. Martinez said, "Class, please, put down your hands. Lowyn, please look at the rules on the bulletin board and find the one that you are not obeying." Lowyn answers, "Number four. It says we need to raise our hands to answer a question." Mr. Martinez responds, "Yes it does, and why do we need such a rule?" "So that everyone in the class has a chance to answer questions," she replies. He next asks, "Lowyn did you agree to follow these rules when you signed the poster?" "Yes," Lowyn says. Mr. Martinez then requests that she try harder in the future and tells her that he will help her by pointing to the rules if she calls out again. The first time Lowyn raises her hand Mr. Martinez calls on her, and says, "Lowyn that was a great answer and thank you for raising your hand."

Mr. Martinez not only displays and teaches the rule to Lowyn but also, when she finally does raise her hand, reinforces the behavior. He understands that noting appropriate behavior and positively reinforcing it enhances the likelihood of appropriate behavior in the future (Clarizio, 1980; Evertson and Emmer, 1982; Madsen, Becker, and Thomas, 1968).

Teachers also may employ student self-analyses to remind students frequently of appropriate behavior and to help enhance their self-control, as Mr. Hite does.

Case 33: The Smiley Face Self-Analysis

Mr. Hite teaches first grade. After anlyzing the types of behaviors he feels are necessary for the proper running of his class, he shares the rules with the children and explains the Smiley Face Procedure. "We all know what smiley faces are, and we are going to use smiley faces to help you learn and obey the classroom rules." Holding up a sheet of paper (Figure 6-1), he continues, "As you can see this sheet has smiley faces next to each rule for every day of the week. At the end of class each day you will receive one of these sheets and you will circle the smiley face that is most like your behavior for the day." Each day Mr. Hite collects the sheets and reviews them. When a pattern of frowns are observed or when he disagrees with a student's rating, he is quick to work with the student in a positive, supportive manner to correct the behaviors.

After a few weeks Mr. Hite discontinues the self-analysis sheets on a regular basis. They are, however, readily employed whenever the class's behavior warrants it. Mr. Hite also uses the sheets for individual students who need assistance in self-control. He also develops sheets for new activities such as field trips and outdoor activities as they occur throughout the year.

Self-analysis of one's behavior can be used by any student, although the actual manner of employment of the technique varies. Whereas smiley faces are appropriate for younger elementary students, older students evaluate their behavior better by using rating continua. As with younger students self-analysis is requested of all students or individual students as the need arises. Figure 6-2 is an example of a continuum rating scale that was successfully used to manage a seventh-grade art class.

TEACHING AND EVALUATING

Teachers do not expect students to learn a mathematical skill on the first presentation. Effective instruction stresses the need for practice and feedback. This is often forgotten by teachers, who when it comes to rules, expect students to follow them immediately (Evertson and Emmer, 1982). Rules, like academic skills, must be taught (Brophy, 1988a; Canter, 1989; Evertson and Emmer, 1982; Jones and Jones, 1981). This entails practice and feedback. The amount of practice and feedback depends on the grade

CIRCLE THE APPLE THAT IS MOST LIKE YOUR BEHAVIOR TODAY

	MONDAY	TUESDAY	WEDNESDAY	THURSDAY	FRIDAY
Shared with Others					
Listened to the Teacher					
Listened While Others Talked					
Was Friendly to Others					
Worked Quietly					
Joined in Activities					
Stayed in My Seat					
Followed Directions					
Cleaned My Area					
Helped Put Away Materials					

FIGURE 6-1   Smiley Face Self-Analysis

NAME _____

CLASS _____

DATE _____

TEACHER-STUDENT EVALUATION

Class Behavior

1. Have you worked successfully with minimum supervision during the class period?

0% of time		50% of time		All the time
1	2	3	4	5

2. Have you been respectful and considerate to other students and their property?

0% of time		50% of time		All the time
1	2	3	4	5

3. Have you been cooperative with your teacher?

0% of time		50% of time		All the time
1	2	3	4	5

4. Have you used art materials properly?

0% of time		50% of time		All the time
1	2	3	4	5

5. Have you shown a high degree of maturity and responsibility for your age through proper class behavior?

0% of time		50% of time		All the time
1	2	3	4	5

6. Have you been considerate of your classmates and teacher by talking softly, remaining in your seat, and helping classmates if help is needed?

0% of time		50% of time		All the time
1	2	3	4	5

7. Have you cleaned your area and put your materials away?

0% of time		50% of time		All the time
1	2	3	· 4	5

FIGURE 6-2 Behavior Self-Analysis for Art Class

level and the novelty of the procedures and rules. Rules that students have not encountered before, such as those in a science lab, take longer to learn than rules that typically have been part of traditional classroom settings.

New activities often require students to learn new procedures and rules. Since learning is not instantaneous, only over time will students learn, understand, and abide by classroom rules. It is not uncommon for teachers to spend entire lessons on how students conduct a debate, cooperatively work on a group project, safely operate machinery, set up and care for science apparatus, or behave on field trips or outdoor activities. In such cases specific objectives directed toward the procedures and rules are formulated and incorporated into the lesson plans. Thus they become an integral part of the course content and their evaluation and consideration in grading decisions is warranted.

Some teachers evaluate students' understanding of rules by written exams or through student demonstrations (Curwin and Mendlen, 1980), particularly in the elementary grades. Also secondary science and industrial arts teachers insist that students pass safety exams and demonstrate appropriate use of equipment before being given permission to progress with the learning activities.

To summarize, teachers must communicate to students the importance of the rules for learning and teaching. This is best accomplished through a no-nonsense approach.

1. Analyzing the classroom environment to determine the necessary rules and procedures needed to protect teaching, learning, safety, and property
2. Clearly communicating the rules and their rationales to students
3. Obtaining students' commitments to abide by the rules
4. Teaching and evaluating students' understanding of the rules
5. Enforcing each rule with natural or logical consequences

ASSESSING THE POTENTIAL FOR DISRUPTIVE BEHAVIOR

Vulnerability Index

So far in this chapter the antecedent variables for structuring the physical environment and designing classroom procedures and rules have been discussed. Attention to these areas does much to reduce the probability of disruptive behavior throughout the school year. Concern given to these variables is also consistent with research that indicates that successful classroom managers are distinguished from ineffective managers based on what they do to prevent management problems from occurring (Emmer and Everston, 1982; Doyle, 1979; Kounin, 1970).

Although some modification is necessary throughout the year, much of the planning for structuring the physical environment as well as developing procedures and rules, as stated previously, is completed before the first day of class. However once students arrive, the teacher spends most of his time planning a variety of daily learning activities. Additional antecedent variables play an important part in diminishing the probability of discipline problems during these learning activities.

Brophy (1989a) and Doyle (1979) stressed that an integral aspect of the maintenance of order and the prevention of disruptive behavior is teacher planning prior to instruction. Such planning includes not only the design of learning objectives and activities commonly found in a teacher's lesson plan but also careful consideration of the specifics of student and teacher characteristics, teaching/learning activities, and environmental factors.

The vulnerability index is a tool for preinstructional decisionmaking that helps a teacher predict the likelihood of disruption during any given classroom activity. By identifying vulnerable components, the teacher is better able to modify the planned learning activities *before* the class actually is held to reduce the probability of classroom management problems (Nolan, 1986).

The vulnerability index involves four general variables: student characteristics, teacher characteristics, teaching/learning activities, and environmental factors.

1. *Student characteristics*
   a. *Students' ability to control their own behavior.* Some students are able to monitor and control their own behavior very well, whereas others are very impulsive and unable to control themselves. Those who have difficulty in exercising control often seek attention, are hyperactive, and come to school with unmet needs at home such as lack of proper nutrition or lack of rest. Teachers have very little control over this factor except through long-range strategies such as contracting, behavioral management, or referrals.
   b. *Students' interest and motivation in the subject.* Students who are very interested and motivated to do well in a particular subject are much less likely to cause discipline problems than are those with low interest and motivation. The inherent interest of the lesson material itself, students' record of past success or failure in the subject, and the closeness of the subject matter to student goals affect student interest and motivation. The teacher exerts some control over this factor by ensuring student success and by relating the material to short-term student interests and goals.
   c. *Students' ability in the subject matter.* When the subject material is moderately challenging but achievable, when the students have mastered the prerequisite learning, and when student learning styles are considered in planning, students are less likely to cause discipline problems. Teachers exercise influence over this factor by ensuring that students have the prerequisite knowledge and by teaching to a variety of learning styles.
   d. *Students' attention span.* When the length of the activities matches the attention span of students, disruptive behavior is less apt to occur. Therefore the teacher has a high degree of control by matching length of classroom activities to attention span.
2. *Teacher characteristics*
   a. *Level of preparation.* The more thorough the teacher's preparation for class, the less likely classroom discipline problems will occur. In judging the level of teacher preparation, the teacher considers his knowledge of the subject matter, the degree of organization of the activities, the continuity of activities, and anticipation of possible problems students may have with the material.

b. *Teacher energy level.* When the teacher exhibits a high energy level and generates enthusiasm for the learning activities, students are less likely to be disruptive. The teacher's energy level depends on the amount of rest the teacher has had, his general level of health, the time of day of the lesson, and the previous activities during the day. Teachers keep their energy at an adequate or high level by proper rest and by not planning too many high-energy lessons in a row.

c. *Teacher's relationship with students.* When the teacher has established a positive but professionally distant relationship with students and interacts positively with individual students, classroom discipline problems are likely to be few. On the other hand overly friendly relationships with students, hostile or sarcastic interactions with students, and failure to establish positive relationships with individual students have the opposite effect.

d. *Teacher's confidence.* When the teacher does not feel confident about his ability to deal with students and to handle discipline issues effectively, problems are more likely to arise. As the teacher begins to implement the strategies and techniques set forth in this book and his classroom management improves, his confidence will also rise.

3. *Teaching and learning activities*

a. *Teacher's ability to monitor individual student activity.* When the learning activities permit the teacher to observe easily what each individual student is doing during the lesson, it is much easier to prevent problems or to stop them quickly. Monitoring individual behavior is very difficult when students' attention is focused on multiple sources rather than on a single source, when students are engaged in individual or small group activities, or when the teacher is not able to see some students because of the room arrangement. The teacher manages this factor to some degree by the seating arrangement in the room and by his position in the room.

b. *Student's accountability for completing a definite task.* When each student is responsible for completion of a task in a given time period and when this accountability is monitored by the teacher, discipline problems are less likely to take place. Accountability is controlled to a large extent by specifying exactly what students are expected to do, by setting a time frame, by spelling out exact standards of performance, and by collecting and checking completed work promptly.

c. *Duration, sequence, and variety of activities.* When the duration of the learning activities match student attention spans, when the sequence of activities calls for gradual transitions from low-energy to high-energy activities and vice versa, and when learning activities are varied, the possibility of problems is reduced. Managing this component is accomplished by scheduling activities for shorter time periods, varying the types of activities during a lesson, planning complementary activities in sequence, and providing for smooth transitions between various activities.

4. *Environmental characteristics*

a. *Time of day.* Disruptive behavior in the classroom occurs more frequently at the end of the day, immediately before and after lunch, and before and after interruptions such as recess or assemblies.

b. *Time of year.* All other factors being equal, discipline problems are much more frequent later in the school year, on Fridays, and on days before school holidays or vacations.

c. *External events.* The first snowfall of the year, the first warm spell of the year, seasonal happenings, and any unusual events are likely to increase the lesson's vulnerability to classroom disruption.

External events have significant influence on student behavior. (Ken Karp)

    d. *School events.* School events such as assemblies, picture day, ring day, extended class or homeroom periods, birthday parties, pull-out programs, and frequent public address announcements also increase the opportunities for misbehavior.

    e. *Classroom environment.* Factors within the individual classroom such as large class size, lack of space, poor temperature control, and poor lighting may lead to an increase in misbehavior.

For the most part environmental factors cannot be significantly modified by the teacher. However, by concentrating on the other three variables—student characteristics, teacher characteristics, and activities—the environmental factors will have less impact on student behavior.

Determining the Vulnerability Index

An efficient systematic assessment of the vulnerability index for any given classroom activity is set forth in Table 6-2. By using the assessment instrument, the teacher conducts a "preinstructional thought experiment" (Doyle, 1979) by carefully thinking through the planned lesson, including proposed teacher behaviors, anticipated student reactions, and possible alternative courses of action.

By assessing a lesson's vulnerability in relationship to student charac-

TABLE 6-2 Vulnerability Index for a Given Lesson

Evaluate all of the factors in each area, determining vulnerability. Then make changes in those factors found to have high vulnerability in order to lessen the possibility of misbehavior.

Area 1: STUDENT CHARACTERISTICS

a. Students' Ability to Control Their Own Behavior

   (Are there many students who are attention seekers, hyperactive, or have needs that are unmet by their home environments?)

   vulnerability

low	medium	high

b. Students' Interest and Motivation in Subject

   (Is subject interesting to students? Does subject relate to student goals? Have students experienced past success with subject material?)

   vulnerability

low	medium	high

c. Students' Ability in Subject

   (Is material at the proper difficulty level? Do students have prerequisite knowledge? Have student learning styles been considered?)

   vulnerability

low	medium	high

d. Students' Attention Span

   (Does the length of the learning activities match students' attention spans?)

   vulnerability

low	medium	high

Area 2: TEACHER CHARACTERISTICS

a. Teacher's Preparation Level

   (Are you highly knowledgeable of the subject material? Has your planning considered the organization and continuity of the activities? Have you anticipated and planned for any problems students may have with the material?)

   vulnerability

low	medium	high

(continued)

TABLE 6-2 *(Continued)*

b. Teacher's Energy Level

(Are you well rested and in good health? Does the activity require a lot of teacher energy? Are you generally interested in the activity and can you generate enthusiasm?)

vulnerability

low	medium	high

c. Teacher's Relationships with Students

(Do you interact positively and professionally with students?)

vulnerability

low	medium	high

d. Teacher's Confidence

(Have you had experience successfully managing discipline problems?)

vulnerability

low	medium	high

Area 3: TEACHING/LEARNING ACTIVITIES

a. Teacher's Ability to Monitor Individual Student Activity

(Will students be working on one or more than one learning activity at a given time? Will students be engaged in individual or group work? Is the seating arrangement and your position in the classroom appropriate for the planned activities?)

vulnerability

low	medium	high

b. Students' Accountability for Definite Task Accomplishment

(Have you planned for student accountability by determining and communicating a time frame, expectations, and evaluation criteria?)

vulnerability

low	medium	high

c. Duration, Sequence, and Variety of Activities

(Have you planned for a variety of activities and for transition between activities?)

vulnerability

low	medium	high

(continued)

TABLE 6-2 (*Continued*)

Area 4: ENVIRONMENTAL CHARACTERISTICS

a. Time of Day

(Is the lesson late in the day or before or after lunch, recess, or a special school activity?)

	vulnerability	
low	medium	high

b. Time of Year

(Is the learning activity late in the school year, on a Friday, or before a school holiday?)

	vulnerability	
low	medium	high

c. External Events

(Is it snowing or a very warm spring day?)

	vulnerability	
low	medium	high

d. School Events

(Is a special school event occurring?)

	vulnerability	
low	medium	high

e. Classroom Environment

(Is your class size large or the room size small? Does your classroom have proper light, temperature control, and ventilation?)

	vulnerability	
low	medium	high

teristics, teacher characteristics, activities and environment, the teacher identifies individual and combinations of circumstances that may create discipline problems. Once identified, these factors are altered to reduce the lesson's vulnerability. Keep in mind that the teacher has the greatest control over teaching and learning activities, less over teacher characteristics, and the least over student characteristics and environmental factors. Therefore, when revising these factors teachers should spend the most time and effort on teaching and learning activities.

Research to date has indicated that by using the vulnerability index, teachers are able to predict management problems. They make changes in proposed activities to lower the lesson's vulnerability and plan more novel learning activities that capture student attention, thus reducing the potential for disruptive behavior (Nolan, 1986).

SUMMARY

This chapter first examined two of the most critical variables that influence behavior in the classroom, the physical environment and classroom guidelines. This discussion was then followed by an explanation of a practical planning procedure, the vulnerability index, which is used to predict the potential of disruptive behavior during any given learning activity.

Concerning environment, although teachers have no control of the size of their classrooms, they can control the seating arrangement and the use of bulletin boards to lesson the possibility of disruption. The seating arrangement should accommodate the learning activity. All students need to see instructional presentations, and the arrangement should allow the teacher to be close to all students. Bulletin boards should reflect and add to the learning excitement that is occurring in the classroom. Bulletin boards are used to recognize and display students' work and achievements as well as to provide students with the opportunity to enrich and actively participate in their learning.

Properly designed classroom guidelines provide students with clear expectations. Guidelines are needed for routine activities (procedures) and for general classroom behavior (rules). The teacher can do much to increase the effectiveness of guidelines by (1) analyzing the classroom environment to determine the necessary guidelines needed to protect teaching, learning, safety, and property; (2) communicating the guidelines and the rationales to students; (3) obtaining student commitments to abide by the rules; (4) teaching and evaluating student understanding of the rules; and (5) enforcing each guideline with natural or logical consequences.

The vulnerability index is a tool for preinstructional decisionmaking that enables the teacher to examine four areas that influence classroom behavior—student characteristics, teacher characteristics, teaching/learning activities, and environmental factors. Each area is analyzed to predict the likelihood of disruption in any given classroom activity. When vulnerable areas are identified, the teacher modifies planned learning activities before class to reduce the likelihood of managment problems.

REFERENCES

BROPHY, J. (1988a). Educating teachers about managing classrooms and students. *Teaching and Teacher Education, 4,* 1, 1–18.

BROPHY, J. (1988b). Research on teaching effects: Uses and abuses. *The Elementary School Journal, 89,* 1, 3–21.

CANTER, L. (1989). Assertive discipline—More than names on the board and marbles in a jar. *Phi Delta Kappan, 71,* 1, 57–61.

CLARIZIO, H. F. (1980). *Toward Positive Classroom Discipline,* 3rd ed. New York: Wiley.

CURWIN, R. L., and MENDLER, A. N. (1980). *The Discipline Book: A Complete Guide to School and Classroom Management.* Reston, VA: Reston Publishing Company.

Dayton Public Schools (1973). Corporal punishment: Is it needed? *Schoolday, 5,* 1, 4.

DOYLE, W. (1979). Making managerial decisions in classrooms. In D. L. Duke (Ed.), *Classroom Management.* The 78th Yearbook of the National Society for the Study of Education, Part II. Chicago: University of Chicago Press.

DREIKURS, R. (1964). *Children the Challenge.* New York: Hawthorn Books.

DREIKURS, R., GRUNDWALD, B. B., and PEPPER, F. C. (1982). *Maintaining Sanity in the Classroom, Classroom Management Techniques,* 2nd ed. New York. Harper & Row.

EMMER, E. T., and EVERSTON, C. M. (1981). Synthesis of research on classroom management. *Educational Leadership, 38,* 4, 342–347.

EMMER, E. T., EVERSTON, C. M., SANFORD, J. P., CLEMENTS, B. S., and WORSHAM, M. E. (1989). *Classroom Management for Secondary Teachers,* 2nd ed. Englewood Cliffs, NJ: Prentice-Hall.

EPSTEIN, C. (1979). *Classroom Management and Teaching: Persistent Problems and Rational Solutions.* Reston, VA: Reston Publishing Company.

EVANS, G., and LOVELL, B. (1979). Design modification in an open-plan school. *Journal of Educational Psychology, 71,* 41–49.

EVERSTON, C. M., and EMMER, E. T. (1982). Preventive classroom management. In D. L. Duke (Ed.), *Helping Teachers Manage Classrooms,* pp. 2–31. Alexandria, VA: Association for Supervision and Curriculum Development.

GOOD, T., and BROPHY, J. (1973). *Looking in Classrooms.* New York: Harper & Row.

HEITZMAN, A. J. (1983). Discipline and the use of punishment. *Education, 104,* 1, 17–22.

HOWELL, R. G., JR., and HOWELL, P. L. (1979). *Discipline in the Classroom: Solving the Teaching Puzzle.* Reston, VA: Reston Publishing Company.

JOHNSON, S. M., BOADSTAD, D. D., and LOBITZ, G. K. (1976). Generalization and contrast phenomena in behavior modification with children. In E. J. Mash, L. A. Hamerlynck, and L. C. Handy (Eds.), *Behavior Modification and Families.* New York: Brunner/Mazell.

JONES, V. F., and JONES, L. S. (1981). *Responsible Classroom Discipline: Creating Positive Learning Environments and Solving Problems.* Boston: Allyn & Bacon.

KAZDIN, A. E., and BOOTZIN, R. R. (1972). The token economy: An evaluative review. *Journal of Applied Behavior Analysis, 5,* 343–372.

KOUNIN, J. S. (1970). *Discipline and Group Management in Classrooms.* New York: Holt, Rinehart & Winston.

MADSEN, C. H., BECKER, W., and THOMAS, D. R. (1968). Rules, praise and ignoring: Elements of elementary classroom control. *Journal of Applied Behavior Analysis, 1,* 139–150.

NOLAN, J. F. (1986). Vulnerability index: A planning tool for the prevention of classroom management problems. Paper presented at the Annual Meeting of the American Educational Research Association, San Francisco.

RINNE, C. H. (1984). *Attention: The Fundamentals of Classroom Control.* Columbus, OH: Charles E. Merrill.

SWEENEY, T. J. (1981). *Adlerian Counseling, Proven Concepts and Strategies,* 2nd ed. Muncie, IN: Accelerated Development.

WALKER, H. M. (1979). *The Acting-Out Child: Coping with Classroom Disruption.* Boston: Allyn & Bacon.

EXERCISES

1. For each of the following activities design a seating arrangement accommodating 24 students that maximizes on-task behavior and minimizes disruptions.

    a. Teacher lecture
    b. Small group work (4 students per group)
    c. Open discussion
    d. Individual seat work
    e. Class project to design a bulletin board
    f. Teacher-led group work and simultaneous individual seat work
    g. Student group debate
    h. Teacher demonstration

2. Give examples of how a teacher can use the classroom environment (bulletin boards, shelves, walls, chalkboard, etc.) to create a pleasant atmosphere that increases the likelihood of appropriate student behavior.

3. With your present or future classroom in mind determine the common situation or activities that do or will regularly occur. Design appropriate procedures to accomplish those activities. How would you teach these procedures to the class?

4. a. Considering your own or future classroom, determine what general student behaviors are necessary to ensure that learning and teaching can take place and that both students and property are safe.
    b. State a positive rule for each of these described behaviors.
    c. For each, state a rationale you could communicate to students that is consistent with the definition of a discipline problem and appropriate for the age of the students you do or will teach.
    d. For each determine a natural or logical consequence that occurs when the rule is broken.
    e. How will you communicate these rules to students?
    f. How will you obtain student commitment to follow these rules?

5. Determine a natural, logical, and contrived consequence for each of the following misbehaviors:
    a. Fourth grade student who interrupts small group work
    b. Eleventh-grade student who continually gets out of his seat
    c. Seventh-grade student who makes noises during class
    d. Tenth-grade student who makes noises during class
    e. Twelfth-grade student who refuses to change his seat when requested to do so by the teacher
    f. First-grade student who interrupts reading group to tattle on a student who is not doing his seat work
    g. A group of sixth-grade students who all drop their pencils at a given time throughout the class
    h. Ninth-grade student who threatens to beat up another student after class

    i. Eighth-grade student who continually pushes the chair at the student in front of him

    j. Tenth-grade student who does not wear goggles while operating power equipment

6. Following are examples of some rules developed for an eighth grade science class. Read them and identify and correct any problems in the rule, rationale, or consequences.

	RULE	RATIONALE	CONSEQUENCES
a.	Don't be late to class	Because we have a lot of material to cover and we all need the whole class period	a. Reminder by teacher b. Student required to get a note c. Student writes 100 times "I will not be late"
b.	We all need to work without disrupting others	Because everyone has a right to learn and no one has a right to interfere with the learning of others	a. Reminder by teacher b. Student moved where he cannot disrupt others c. Student removed from class d. Student fails
c.	We all have to raise our hands to answer questions or contribute to a discussion	Because I do not like to be interrupted	a. Student ignored b. Reminder by teacher c. Parents notified
d.	We must use lab equipment properly and safely	Because it is expensive to replace	a. pay for broken equipment b. pay for equipment and additional fine

7. There are four main areas to consider in determining the vulnerability to disruption of any given lesson or activity. Some of these can be controlled or influenced by the teacher; others cannot. Listed are the components of each of the four areas. Classify each component according to the degree of teacher control.

	CONTROLLED BY TEACHER	INFLUENCED BY TEACHER	BEYOND TEACHER CONTROL
a. Student characteristics			
(1) Self-control			
(2) Motivation			
(3) Ability			
(4) Attention span			
b. Teacher characteristics			
(1) Level of preparation			
(2) Energy level			
(3) Relationship with students			
(4) Confidence			
c. Teaching/learning activities			
(1) Monitoring individual behavior			
(2) Student accountability			
(3) Types of activity			
d. Environmental characteristics			
(1) Time of day			
(2) Time of year			
(3) External events			
(4) School events			
(5) Classroom environment			

8. For each component identified as controlled or influenced by the teacher, suggest specific ways in which the teacher can control or influence this component to decrease the vulnerability index.

9. It's Friday, two weeks before Thanksgiving, and the first flurries of snow have begun to fall, with a prediction of five inches by nightfall. As his fifth-graders return from lunch, Mr. Conen readies the room for the first science laboratory activity of the year. The learning objectives call for students to identify and diagram the lines of force in a magnetic field, using iron filings and a bar magnet. Assess the vulnerability of this lesson to disruptive behavior. What modifications can be made to lessen the vulnerability to disruption?

CHAPTER 7

Managing Common Misbehavior Problems:

Nonverbal Interventions

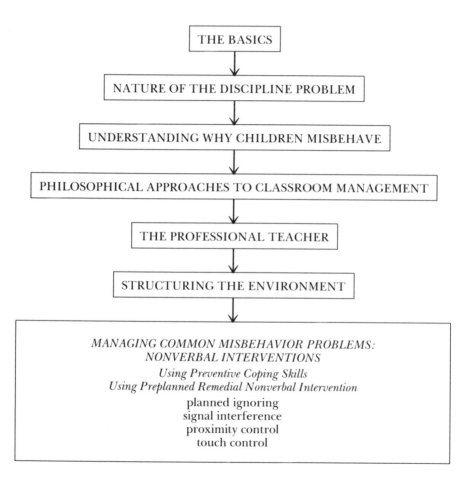

THE BASICS

↓

NATURE OF THE DISCIPLINE PROBLEM

↓

UNDERSTANDING WHY CHILDREN MISBEHAVE

↓

PHILOSOPHICAL APPROACHES TO CLASSROOM MANAGEMENT

↓

THE PROFESSIONAL TEACHER

↓

STRUCTURING THE ENVIRONMENT

↓

*MANAGING COMMON MISBEHAVIOR PROBLEMS:
NONVERBAL INTERVENTIONS*
Using Preventive Coping Skills
Using Preplanned Remedial Nonverbal Intervention
planned ignoring
signal interference
proximity control
touch control

PRINCIPLES OF CLASSROOM MANAGEMENT

24. Classroom management techniques need to be consistent with the goal of helping students become self-directing individuals.
25. Use of a preplanned hierarchy of coping skills improves the teacher's ability to manage misbehavior.

26. The hierarchy of coping skills is structured so that it starts with nonintrusive, nonverbal teacher behaviors, which gives students the opportunity for self-control and causes little if any disruption to the teaching/learning process.

INTRODUCTION

As previously discussed, in most classrooms the majority of student misbehaviors are verbal interruptions, off-task behavior, and disruptive physical movements. These so-called surface behaviors are present in every classroom in every school almost every day. With proper planning, instructional strategies, and environmental structuring, the frequency of surface disruptions is reduced greatly. However, no matter how much time and energy the teacher directs toward prevention, these behaviors do not totally disappear and to some extent are an ever-present, continuing fact of life for all teachers. The successful teacher copes with surface behaviors in a manner that is effective, expedient, and least disruptive to the teaching/learning process.

There are many coping skills teachers use to accomplish this goal. These skills are organized in a decision-making hierarchy of three tiers: (1) nonverbal behaviors, (2) verbal behaviors, and (3) consequences. Each tier in turn consists of the individual coping skills, which are again ordered hierarchically. The dimensions on which these subhierarchies are developed is the degree of intrusiveness and the potential for disruption to the teaching/learning environment. When these coping skills are applied in a preplanned systematic manner, they have been shown to be quite effective in controlling surface behaviors. This chapter presents the first tier in the decision-making hierarchy, nonverbal coping skills. This group of skills is the least intrusive and has the least potential for disrupting the teaching/learning process.

PREREQUISITES TO CONTROL

Teaching and learning are complex processes. Effective teaching and maximum learning occur in classrooms when both teachers and students understand that teaching/learning is not the responsibility of only the teacher but also the student.

The responsibilities of the students are obvious. Students prepare for class, study, ask questions to enhance their understanding, and are on-task. Many of the preventive techniques we have discussed in previous chapters, as well as the control techniques now being discussed, assist students in accepting responsibility for their learning. The concept of shared responsibility for teaching and learning needs to be communicated, demonstrated, and reinforced throughout the school year.

Students more readily accept their responsibilities when it is clear to them that the teacher is fulfilling her responsibilities. These professional responsibilities are the basic minimum competencies that all teachers must possess, and they are considered prerequisites to appropriate classroom management. In other words, teachers must exhibit certain behaviors before they can assume that the cause of behavior problems rests with the students. All too often teachers are quick to place total responsibility for inappropriate behavior on the student without carefully analyzing their own behavior. It is quite common to hear teachers say, "There's nothing I can do; all they want to do is fool around" or "These kids are impossible; why even try!" Such comments clearly indicate that teachers have assigned all blame for student misbehavior to the students themselves.

The teacher behaviors that are prerequisites to appropriate student behavior and have been discussed in previous chapters are these:

1. The teacher is well prepared to teach. Prior to class she has designed specific learning objectives and effective teaching strategies based on accepted principles of learning.
2. The teacher provides clear directions and explanations of the learning material.
3. The teacher ensures that students understand evaluation criteria.
4. The teacher clearly communicates, rationalizes, and consistently enforces behavioral expectations.
5. The teacher demonstrates enthusiasm and encouragement and models the behaviors expected from students.

Once these responsibilities are met, if control techniques are needed, they will have a much better chance of being effective in managing behavior.

SURFACE BEHAVIORS

What are the typical behavior problems teachers must deal with on a day-to-day basis? The most common disruptive behaviors are verbal interruptions (talking, humming, laughing, calling out, whispering), off-task behaviors (daydreaming, sleeping, combing hair, playing with something, doodling), physical movement intended to disrupt (visiting, passing notes, sitting on the desk or on two legs of the chair, throwing paper), and disrespect toward teachers and students (arguing, teasing, vulgarity, talking back) (Huber, 1984; Levin, 1980; Shrigley, 1980; Thomas, Goodall, and Brown, 1983; Weber and Sloan, 1986).

These behaviors are called surface behaviors because they are typically not a result of any deep-seated personal problem but are normal developmental behaviors of children. Even so, they tend to be quite disruptive to both teaching and learning. They are usually readily observable by an experienced teacher.

Surface behaviors are the most common types of disruptive behaviors that teachers must manage on a day-to-day basis. (Laimute E. Druskis)

Some teachers have always been able to manage appropriately, almost intuitively, surface behaviors. Others by experience and hard work have acquired the necessary classroom skills of "overlapping," that is, attending simultaneously to two matters at the same time, and "with-it-ness," the subtle nonverbal communication to students that the teachers are aware of all activities within the classroom (Kounin, 1970). Teachers who do not have these skills have to cope with abnormally high frequencies of surface behaviors, and in some instances, as in the following case, their lack of overlapping and with-it-ness actually causes disruptive behavior.

Case 34: ". . . 3, 2, 1, Blast Off "

Mr. Berk's seventh-grade English class arrives from science, where the concept of propulsion had been illustrated by a piece of tin foil folded around the tip of a match. When tin foil was heated, the match had ignited and accelerated forward.

During the class, Mickey, seated in the back row, decides to try the propulsion experiment. It is not long before many students in the class are aware of Mickey's activity and sneak glances at him.

Mickey is enjoying the attention and continues to propel matches across his desk.

Mr. Berk soon becomes aware that many in the class are not paying attention. Instead of attempting to determine what the distraction is, he reacts impulsively. He sees Terri turn around to look at Mickey and says, "Terri, turn around and pay attention!" Terri immediately fires back "I'm not doing anything." The class begins to laugh, because only Mr. Berk is unaware of the aerospace activity in the back of the room.

It is obvious that with all the activities taking place in a classroom, overlapping is essential. The same is true for with-it-ness. Many teachers attest to the fact that with each new class there are students who test how with-it the teacher really is.

PREVENTIVE COPING SKILLS

Effective classroom managers are experts in the matter-of-fact use of other more specific and more narrow preventive coping skills in addition to overlapping and with-it-ness. They are experts because they have learned to employ these skills with little if any disruption in the teaching/learning process.

The following preventive coping skills are utilized so that the need for more directed control techniques after the fact is less likely to arise.

Changing the pace of classroom activities is necessary when the teacher begins to observe student behaviors that communicate waning interest. Rubbing eyes, yawning, stretching, and staring out the window are clear signs that a change of pace is needed. This is the time for the teacher to restructure the situation and involve students in games, stories, or other favorite activities that require active student participation, to refocus student interests. To reduce the need for on-the-spot change-of-pace activities, lesson plans should provide for a variety of learning experiences that accommodate the attention spans and interests of the students both in time and in type.

Removing seductive objects from students, with the agreement that they will be returned after class, may be done with little, if any, pause in the teaching act. Teachers who find themselves competing with toys, magazines, or combs may simply walk over to the student, collect the object, and quietly inform her that it will be available to her after class.

Interest boosting of a student who shows signs of off-task behavior is easily accomplishd by the teacher. Rather than using other less positive techniques, the teacher chooses to show interest in the student's work, thereby bringing the student back on-task. Interest boosting is often called for when students are required to do individual or small group classwork. It is during these times that the potential for chatter, daydreaming, or other off-task behaviors is high. For example, if the teacher observes a student engaging in activities other than the assigned math problems, it is time for her to boost the interest of the off-task student. One way this can be achieved is to walk over to the student and show interest in her work by asking how she is doing or checking the answers of the completed problems. Asking the student to place correct problems on the board is also effective. Whatever technique is decided on, it must be employed in a matter-of-fact supportive manner to boost the student's interest in the learning activity.

Redirecting the behavior of off-task students often refocuses attention back to the learning activity. Students who are passing notes, talking, or daydreaming may be asked to read, do a problem, or answer a question. It is important when this technique is used to treat the student as if she were paying attention. For instance, if you call on the off-task student to answer a question and the student answers correctly, give positive feedback. On the other hand if she doesn't answer or answers incorrectly, reformulate the question or call on someone else. A teacher who causes the student embar-

A teacher can redirect students to on-task behavior by the use of interest boosting techniques. (Steve Takatsuno)

rassment or ridicule by stating, "You would know where we were if you were paying attention" invites further misbehavior. The "get back on-task" message the teacher is sending is clearly received by the off-task student whether or not she answers the question or finds the proper reading place, without any follow-up, negative comments.

A *non-punitive time out* is in order for students who show signs of encountering a provoking, painful, frustrating, or fatiguing situation. Quietly, the teacher asks the student if she needs a drink or invites her to run an errand or do a chore. This gives the student time to regain her control before reentering the learning environment. Teachers must be alert to these signs so they can act in a timely fashion to help students cope.

Reinforcing appropriate behavior of other students communicates to the off-task student what is expected. A statement such as "I'm glad to see that Joan and Andrea have their books open" serves as a reminder to others of what is expected.

Providing cues to the class is quite effective for obtaining expected behaviors. For example, a teacher who expects students to be in their seats and prepared for class must make sure that the signal that determines the start of class is understood by all. In schools without bells or other indicators, closing the door is an appropriate cue. Similarly, flicking the lights cues a class that the noise has reached unacceptable levels. Using the same cues consistently usually results in quick student response.

The masterful use of preventive coping skills diffuses many surface behaviors, causing minimal disruptions to the teaching act. However no method is 100 percent effective. There will still be classroom situations that induce misbehavior or students who continue to display disruptive behaviors. When such situations occur, more sytematic control is called for.

REMEDIAL COPING SKILLS

Previously attention has been directed at understanding the nature of teaching and discipline and the causes of misbehavior and preventing behavior problems from occurring. An understanding of these concepts is critical for any teacher who wishes to reduce inappropriate behavior to a minimum.

Attention now is directed to strategies to control the inappropriate student behaviors that remain. These behaviors range from mildly off-task to very disruptive. Previous teacher attention in preventing discipline problems probably has produced a classroom with minimal disruptions from most of the students. However, mastering the delivery of the intervention skills discussed now and in Chapters Eight and Nine will likely produce an exceptional classroom, where misbehavior is minimized and teachers are free to teach and children are free to learn.

Teachers must have a basis on which to make decisions concerning common inappropriate behaviors before they are face to face with them in the classroom. To avoid inconsistency and arbitrariness (Canter, 1989), teachers must have a systematic intervention plan of predetermined behaviors that clearly communicates disapproval to the student who calls out, throws paper, walks around, passes notes, or in any way interferes with the teaching or learning act (Canter, 1989; Lasley, 1989). This follows our definition of teaching presented in Chapter One: *the conscious use of predetermined behaviors, which increases the likelihood of changing student behaviors.*

The intervention decision-making approach is a sequence of hierarchically ordered teacher behaviors. This hierarchy is characterized by two main precepts. The first is that students must learn to control their own behavior. Therefore the initial interventions are subtle, nonintrusive, and very student-centered. Although these behaviors communicate disapproval, they are designed to provide students with the greatest opportunity to control their own behavior. If these are not effective in curbing the misbehaviors, the interventions become increasingly more intrusive and teacher-centered; that is, the teacher takes more responsibility for controlling the students' behavior.

The second precept is that control techniques should not in themselves disrupt the teaching and learning act (Brophy, 1988). Early intervention behaviors are almost a private communication between the teacher and the off-task student, alerting the student to her inappropriate behavior but causing little if any noticeable disruption to either teaching or learning. If these nonverbal interventions, the first tier of the decision-making hierarchy, are not successful, they are followed by the second and third tiers: teacher verbal behaviors and consequences. These tiers are increasingly more teacher-centered, more intrusive, and do cause some interruption to the teaching/learning act. (These techniques are discussed in Chapters Eight and Nine.)

The first tier of the hierarchy of coping skills, nonverbal skills, consists of four techniques: planned ignoring, signal interference, proximity control, and touch control. These body language interventions were first identified and labeled by Redl and Wineman (1952). When used randomly, effective control of minor disruptions is not fully achieved. However when consciously employed in a predetermined logical sequence, they serve to curb milder forms of off-task behavior (Shrigley, 1985).

Planned Ignoring

Planned ignoring is based on the reinforcement theory that if you ignore a behavior, it lessens and eventually disappears. As simple as this may sound, it is difficult to ignore a behavior completely. That is why *planned* is stressed. When a student whistles, interrupts the teacher, or calls out, instinctively the teacher turns or looks in the direction of the student, thereby giving the student attention and reinforcing the behavior. In contrast, planned ignoring is intentionally and completely ignoring the behavior. This takes practice.

There are limitations to this planned ignoring. First, according to reinforcement theory, when a behavior has previously been reinforced, removal of the reinforcement causes a short-term increase in the behavior in the hopes of again receiving reinforcement. For this reason there probably will be an increase of the off-task behavior upon initiation of planned ignoring. Therefore this technique is used to control only the behaviors that cause little interference to the teaching/learning act (Brophy, 1988). Second, the disruptive behavior often is being reinforced by the other students who attend to the misbehaving student. If it is, planned ignoring by the teacher has little effect.

Behaviors that usually are managed by planned ignoring are not having materials ready for the start of class, calling out answers rather than raising a hand, mild or infrequent whispering, interrupting the teacher, and daydreaming. Obviously the type of learning activity has much to do with which behaviors can or cannot be ignored. If after a reasonable period of time the off-task behavior is not decreasing or the point is reached where others are beginning to be distracted by it, the teacher has to move quickly and confidently to the next step in the hierarchy.

Signal Interference

Signal interference is any type of nonverbal behavior that communicates to the student without disturbing others, that her behavior is not appropriate. Signal behaviors must be clearly directed at the off-task student. There should be no doubt in the student's mind that the teacher is aware of what is going on and that the student is responsible for the behavior. This intervention sends a single message to the student: "What you are doing is inappropriate. It is now time to get back to work." The teacher's expression should be businesslike. It is ineffective for the teacher to make eye contact with a student and smile. Smiling sends a double message, which confuses students and may be interpreted as a lack of seriousness by the teacher.

Examples of signal interference behaviors are making eye contact with the student who is talking to a neighbor, pointing to a seat when a student is wandering around, head shaking to indicate "no" to a student about to throw a paper airplane, and holding up an open hand to stop a student's calling out. As with coping skills in general, signal interference behaviors may be hierarchically ordered, depending on the type, duration, and frequency of off-task behavior. A simple hand motion may serve to control calling out the first time, whereas direct eye contact with a disapproving look on the teacher's face may be needed the next time the same student calls out.

For disruptive behaviors that continue or for disturbances that more seriously affect others' learning, the teacher quickly and assuredly moves to the next intervention skill in the hierarchy, proximity control.

Proximity Control

Proximity control is any movement toward or taking up a position in the vicinity of the disruptive student. When signal interference doesn't work, or the teacher is unable to gain a student's attention long enough to send a signal because the student is so engrossed in the off-task behavior, proximity control is warranted.

Often just walking toward the student while still conducting the lesson is enough to bring a student back on-task. For students who continue to be off-task, a very effective form of proximity control is for the teacher to conduct the lesson in close proximity to the student's desk. This works extremely well during question-and-answer periods.

Proximity control combined with signal interference results in a very effective nonverbal control technique. It's the rare student who is not brought back on-task by a teacher who makes eye contact and begins walking toward her desk. Like signal interference, proximity control techniques may be hierarchically ordered, from nonchalant movement in the direction of the student to a very obvious standing behind or next to the student during class. If proximity does not bring about the desired behavioral change, the teacher is in a position to implement the next step in the coping skill hierarchy, touch control.

Touch Control

When a teacher takes a child's hand and escorts the child back to her seat and when a teacher places a hand on a student's shoulder, she is using the coping skill of touch control. Touch control is a light, nonaggressive physical contact with the student. Without any verbal exchange, these behaviors communicate to the student that the teacher disapproves of the disruptive behavior. When possible, the touch control also ought to direct the student to the appropriate behavior, such as escorting a student to a seat or moving a student's hand away from a neighbor's desk and back to her own paper.

When using touch control, it is important to be aware of its limitations and possible negative outcomes. Certain students construe any touching by the teacher as an aggressive act and in turn react with aggressive behavior. On one occasion we saw a teacher calmly walk up to a student who was standing at her seat and place her hand on the student's shoulder. The student turned around and confronted the teacher by angrily yelling, "Don't you ever put your hands on me!" To lessen the chance of such an occurrence, teachers need to be sensitive to its use when working with visibly angry or upset students and older students, especially those of the opposite

Touch control is an effective coping skill, but one that can also produce negative outcomes. (Ted Berntsen)

sex. As with all control techniques, the teacher must be cognizant of the situational variables as well as the student characteristics.

EFFECTIVENESS OF NONVERBAL COPING SKILLS

The use of the four nonverbal coping skills is considered effective if any one or any combination in the hierarchy is successful in having the student resume appropriate classroom behavior.

Case 35: Notes vs. Math

As the students finish their math problems, Mr. Rotman asks them to place one of the problems on the board. Out of the corner of his eye, he notices Jerry passing a note to Ben. Mr. Rotman decides to ignore the behavior, waiting to see if it is a matter of a single occurrence. After all the problems are on the board, Mr. Rotman asks the students questions about the solutions. During this questioning period he notices Ben returning a note to Jerry. After a few attempts Mr. Rotman makes eye contact with Jerry while at the same time asks Ben a question about one of the problems. This technique stops the note passing for the remainder of the questioning activity.

The next activity calls for the use of calculators and he asks Jerry to please pass one calculator to each predetermined pair of students. Jerry and Ben are partners, and Mr. Rotman from a distance monitors their behavior. He circulates around the room helping students with the classwork. He makes sure that he stops to look over Jerry and Ben's work, praising them for its accuracy. Throughout the activity both boys are on-task.

Following the group work the students separate their desks and Mr. Rotman begins to review the answers to the problems. He immediately notices that the two boys begin to pass notes again. He is quick to take a position next to the boys, taps Jerry on the shoulder, and holds out his hand for the note. Jerry hands Mr. Rotman the note and he puts it in his pocket. Mr. Rotman stands near the boys for the rest of the period, asking questions of the class and reviewing the problems. Both Ben and Jerry volunteer and participate for the remainder of the class.

Mr. Rotman skillfully used the four nonverbal coping techniques in combination with the preventive coping skills of removing seductive objectives, interest boosting, and redirecting the behavior to manage successfully the note passing between Jerry and Ben. This was accomplished without noticeably disrupting the teaching/learning act. He was able to do this because the coping skills were not randomly and haphazardly applied. Instead Mr. Rotman had a mental flowchart of the hierarchical sequence so that movement from one behavior to the next was accomplished quickly, calmly, and confidently. Teachers cannot expect to do this instantaneously when faced with disruptive behavior in the classroom. They must preplan and practice the behaviors before having to implement them.

Although the coping skills are placed in a hierarchical order, the teacher does not have to apply the skills in a sequential order. Remember the hierarchy is a decision-making model. Therefore depending on the type, frequency, and distracting potential of the behavior, the teacher may decide to bypass the initial coping skills in favor of a later technique. In other words, there are certain behaviors that need immediate attention; they can neither be ignored nor allowed to continue. This is demonstrated in the following case, in which Ms. Niaz decides to bypass planned ignoring and signal interference in favor of proximity control to manage quickly a disruption during a test.

Case 36: Let Your Fingers Do the Walking

Ms. Niaz explains the test-taking procedures and then passes out the tests. She walks around the room, answering questions and keeping students aware of her presence. She notices that Danny is walking his fingers up Tonya's back. Tonya turns around and tells him, "Stop it!" Tonya turns back to her test and once again Danny bothers her. Ms. Niaz immediately walks toward Danny and spends the next ten minutes standing in close proximity to him.

The efficiency of nonverbal coping skills when used in a hierarchical sequence was studied by Shrigley (1985). He found that after a few hours of in-service training, 53 teachers were able to curb 40 percent of 523 off-task surface behaviors. Five percent of the behaviors were corrected by the use of planned ignoring. Signal interference was the most effective technique, rectifying 14 percent of the behaviors. Twelve percent and 9 percent were stopped by proximity and touch control, respectively. Without having to utter a word or causing any interruption to either teaching or learning, teachers were able to control misbehavior.

To manage the remaining 60 percent of unresolved behavior problems, the teachers needed to implement verbal intervention, the group of coping skills covered in the next chapter.

No matter what technique eventually brings the student back on-task, efforts need to be directed toward maintaining the appropriate behavior. This is most easily accomplished by the teacher who reinforces and attends to the student's new behavior. The students must realize that they can obtain the same or even more attention and recognition for appropriate behavior than they did for disruptive behavior. The student who was ignored when calling out answers should immediately be called on when raising her hand. Likewise the student who ceases walking around the room should be told at the end of the period that it was a pleasure having her in the class. These simple efforts of recognizing appropriate behavior are often overlooked by teachers, but they are a necessary supplement for the teacher who wants to maximize the effectiveness of coping skills.

SUMMARY

This chapter stressed the fact that all teachers have to be skillful in managing off-task surface behaviors. Teaching/learning was presented as a joint responsibility of both the teacher and the students. Students are more willing to accept their responsibilities when it is clear to them that the teacher is fulfilling her responsibilities. These responsibilities are being well prepared to teach by developing learning objectives and using effective teaching strategies, providing clear directions and explanations, ensuring that students understand evaluation criteria, communicating and consistently enforcing behavioral expectations, demonstrating enthusiasm and encouragement, and modeling expected behavior. These behaviors are minimum competencies that all teachers must possess and are considered prerequisites to effective classroom management.

Teachers proficient in classroom management are experts in the use of a variety of preventive coping skills. Techniques such as changing the pace, removing seductive objects, interest boosting, redirecting behavior, nonpunitive time out, reinforcing appropriate behavior, and providing cues are employed to bring students back on-task while causing little if any disruption to the teaching/learning process.

A decision-making hierarchy of remedial coping skills, consisting of three tiers, was presented as a means to manage the remaining inappropriate student behavior. The structure of the hierarchy ranges from nonintrusive techniques that cause little disruption to teaching/learning and provide students with the opportunity to control their own behavior to intrusive techniques that potentially disrupt teaching/learning. The first tier of nonverbal intervention consists of four nonverbal behaviors: planned ignoring, signal interference, proximity control, and touch control. When systematically employed, these techniques were shown to be effective in managing surface behaviors.

REFERENCES

Brophy, J. (1988). Educating teachers about managing classrooms and students. *Teaching and Teacher Education, 4*, 1, 1–18.

Canter, L. (1989). Assertive discipline—More than names on the board and marbles in a jar. *Phi Delta Kappan, 71*, 1, 57–61.

Huber, J. D. (1984). Discipline in the middle school—Parent, teacher, and principal concerns. *National Association of Secondary School Principals Bulletin, 68*, 471, 74–79.

Kounin, J. (1970). *Discipline and Group Management in Classrooms.* New York: Holt, Rinehart & Winston.

Lasley, T. J. (1989). A teacher development model for classroom management. *Phi Delta Kappan, 71*, 1, 36–38.

Levin, J. (1980). *Discipline and classroom management survey: Comparison between a suburban and urban school.* Unpublished report, Pennsylvania State University, University Park.

Redl, F., and Wineman, D. (1952). *Controls from Within.* New York: Free Press.

Shrigley, R. L. (1985). Curbing student disruption in the classroom—Teachers need intervention skills. *National Association of Secondary School Principals Bulletin, 69*, 479, 26–32.

Shrigley, R. L. (1980). *The Resolution of 523 Classroom Incidents by 54 Classroom Teachers Using the Six Step Intervention Model.* University Park: Pennsylvania State University, College of Education, Division of Curriculum and Instruction.

Thomas, G. T., Goodall, R., and Brown, L. (1983). Discipline in the classroom: Perceptions of middle grade teachers. *The Clearinghouse, 57*, 3, 139–142.

Weber, T. R., and Sloan, C. A. (1984). How does high school discipline in 1984 compare to previous decades? *The Clearinghouse, 59*, 7, 326–329.

EXERCISES

1. Five teacher behaviors were listed as prerequisites to appropriate student behavior. Should these teacher behaviors be considered prerequisite? Why or why not?

2. Predict what type of student behavior may result if the teacher does not meet each of the five prerequisite teacher behaviors.

3. What, if any, deletions or additions would you make to the five prerequisite teacher behaviors? Explain any modification you suggest.

4. Suggest specific techniques a teacher could use that demonstrates each of the preventive coping skills that follow:
   a. Changing the pace
   b. Interest boosting
   c. Redirecting the behavior
   d. Reinforcing appropriate behavior
   e. Providing cues

5. The hierarchy of coping skills is presented as a decision-making model, not an action model; explain why?

6. Two very effective remedial coping skills are signal interference and proximity control. Suggest specific techniques a teacher could use that would demonstrate their use.

7. What types of student behaviors would cause you to decide to bypass the initial nonverbal coping skills and enter the hierarchy at the proximity or touch control level?

8. Explain why you agree or disagree with the premise that management techniques should be employed in a manner that provides students with the greatest opportunity to control their own behavior.

9. Some teachers consider the hierarchial use of coping skills a waste of time. They say, "Why spend all this time and effort when you can just tell the student to stop messing around and get back to work." Explain why you agree or disagree with this point of view.

CHAPTER 8

Managing Common Misbehavior Problems

Verbal Intervention and Application of Logical Consequences

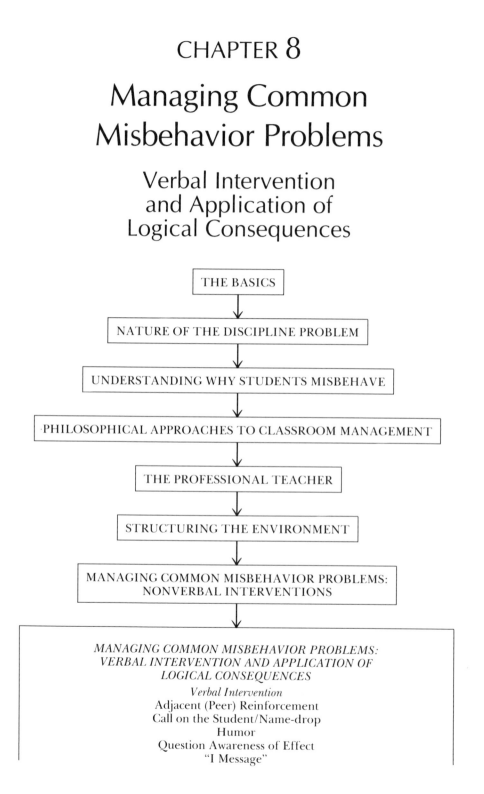

THE BASICS

NATURE OF THE DISCIPLINE PROBLEM

UNDERSTANDING WHY STUDENTS MISBEHAVE

PHILOSOPHICAL APPROACHES TO CLASSROOM MANAGEMENT

THE PROFESSIONAL TEACHER

STRUCTURING THE ENVIRONMENT

MANAGING COMMON MISBEHAVIOR PROBLEMS:
NONVERBAL INTERVENTIONS

*MANAGING COMMON MISBEHAVIOR PROBLEMS:
VERBAL INTERVENTION AND APPLICATION OF
LOGICAL CONSEQUENCES*
Verbal Intervention
Adjacent (Peer) Reinforcement
Call on the Student/Name-drop
Humor
Question Awareness of Effect
"I Message"

> Direct Appeal
> Positive Phrasing
> "Are Not Fors"
> Reminder of Rules
> Glasser's Triplets
> Explicit Redirection
> Canter's "Broken Record"
> *Application of Logical Consequences*

PRINCIPLES OF CLASSROOM MANAGEMENT

27. When nonverbal teacher intervention does not result in appropriate student behavior, the teacher should employ verbal intervention to deal with the misbehavior.

28. Some forms of verbal intervention defuse confrontation and reduce misbehavior, whereas other forms of verbal intervention actually escalate misbehavior and confrontation.

29. When verbal intervention does not lead to appropriate student behavior, the teacher needs to apply logical consequences to the student's misconduct.

INTRODUCTION

Case 37: Blowing His Stack

"You are one of the most obnoxious students I have ever had the misfortune to deal with. How many times have I asked you not to call out answers? If you want to answer a question, raise your hand. It shouldn't tax your tiny brain too much to try and remember that. I'm sick and tired of your mistaken idea that the rules of this classroom apply to everyone but you. It's because of people like you that we need rules in the first place. They apply especially to you. I will not allow you to deprive other students of the chance to answer questions. Anyway, half of your answers are totally off the wall. I'm in charge here, not you. If you don't like it, you can tell your troubles to the principal. Now sit here and be quiet."

When Mr. Hensen finished his lecturette and turned to walk to the front of the room, John (the subject of his tirade) discreetly flipped him the "bird" and laughed with his friends. John spent the rest of the period drawing pictures on the corner of his desk. The other students spent the remainder of the period either in uncomfortable silence or invisible laughter. Mr. Hensen spent the rest of the class trying to calm down and get his mind back on the lesson.

Although it is true that John has caused many problems for Mr. Hensen and for the other students in his class, what did Mr. Hensen accomplish by yelling at John as he did? Other than getting his long-suppressed feelings off his chest, he actually did more harm than good. He disrupted any learning that was taking place. He forced the other students to concentrate on John's behavior rather than on the content of the lesson, and he extended the off-task time by prolonging the reprimand. He reacted negatively and very sarcastically toward John, who already disliked him, and now is no doubt more determined than ever to "get Hensen's goat." Additionally, he probably created some sympathy for John among the other students by obviously overreacting to a very minor incident.

Many teachers find themselves in Mr. Hensen's position at one time or another. They allow many incidents of relatively minor misbehavior to build up over time until one day they just can't take it anymore. So they explode. They let loose their pent-up feelings and make the situation worse rather than better. Teachers can avoid falling into this situation by using the coping skills hierarchy first presented in Chapter Seven to contend with classroom behavior problems. This hierarchy consists of three major tiers of intervention: (1) nonverbal coping skills, (2) verbal intervention, and (3) use of logical consequences. When teachers use this hierarchy to guide their thinking about classroom discipline problems, they are able to cope with misbehavior swiftly and effectively. The first tier of the hierarchy was discussed in detail in Chapter Seven. The second and third tiers of the hierarchy are presented in this chapter.

In the second tier, the teacher must decide which particular verbal intervention technique to use with a student who is misbehaving after determining that nonverbal intervention is not appropriate or after it has been implemented without success. Verbal intervention is one of the most powerful and versatile tools the classroom teacher has for classroom management. When used effectively, verbal intervention makes classroom management relatively easy. When used poorly and thoughtlessly, it may create new management problems, make existing problems worse, and turn temporary problems into chronic ones.

This chapter presents 12 verbal intervention techniques in a systematic, hierarchical format. As in the nonverbal coping skill subhierarchy presented in Chapter Seven, the verbal intervention subhierarchy begins with techniques designed to foster students' control over their own behavior and proceeds to those that foster greater teacher control over student behavior.

The final section of the chapter and the final tier on the management hierarchy concern the use of logical consequences to control student behavior.

CLASSROOM VERBAL INTERVENTION

In explaining the nonverbal coping skills subhierarchy in Chapter Seven, the suggestion was made to deal with misbehavior nonverbally if possible. To reiterate, the advantages of nonverbal intervention are threefold: (1) disruption to the learning process is less likely to occur; (2) hostile confrontation with the student is less apt to happen; and (3) the student is given an opportunity to correct his behavior before being reprimanded in front of peers.

However, nonverbal correction of misbehavior is not always possible. For example, when misbehavior is potentially harmful to any student or potentially disruptive for large numbers of students, it should be stopped quickly, and often verbal intervention is the quickest way to do so. Before discussing specific techniques, there are some general guidelines teachers need to keep in mind when considering verbal intervention:

1. Use nonverbal interventions first whenever appropriate.
2. Keep verbal intervention as private as possible. This minimizes the risk of having the student become defensive and hostile to avoid losing face in front of peers. Brophy (1988) suggests that this is one of the most important general principles for disciplinary intervention.
3. Make the verbal intervention as brief as possible. Your goal is to stop the misbehavior *and* redirect the student to appropriate behavior. Prolonging the verbal interaction simply extends the disruption of learning and enhances the likelihood of a hostile confrontation.
4. As Haim Ginott (1972) suggests, speak to the situation, not the person. In other words, label the behavior as bad or inappropriate, not the person. If a student interrupts a teacher, for example, "Interrupting others is rude" would be a more appropriate response than "You interrupted me. You are rude." Labeling the behavior helps the student to see the distinction between himself and his behavior and also to see that it is possible for the teacher to like him but not his behavior. Labeling the student makes it more likely that the student will feel compelled to defend himself. Also the student might accept the label as part of his self-concept and then match the label with inappropriate behavior in the future. This is exactly what Jimmy Dolan decided to do in the case study that follows.

Case 38: Little Jimmy, the Sneak

Jimmy Dolan is in the sixth grade at Shortfellow School. His teacher, Mr. Gramble, has had a long history of difficulty in dealing with classroom discipline. Jimmy is really a very fine student who rarely misbehaves. One day, however, Mr. Gramble notices Jimmy talking to a neighbor while Mr. Gramble's back is partially turned to the class. (Jimmy was asking Craig Rutler to borrow an eraser to correct a mistake in his homework.) Mr. Gramble turns abruptly and pounces on Jimmy in a flash. "So, you're the one who's been causing all the trouble. You little sneak, and all the time I thought you were one of the few people who never caused trouble in here. Well, Buster, you can bet from now on I'll keep an eagle eye on you. You won't be getting away with any more sneaky behavior in here."

For the next week or so, Jimmy goes back to his typical good behavior; however, every time something goes wrong or someone misbehaves, Mr. Gramble blames Jimmy. After this week of unjust blame, Jimmy decides that he may as well start causing some trouble since he is probably going to get blamed for it anyway. In a very short time, Jimmy truly is a great sneak who causes all sorts of havoc for Mr. Gramble and rarely gets caught in the act.

---

5. A second Ginott suggestion is also important. Set limits on behavior, not feelings. For instance, tell the student, "It is O.K. to be angry but not O.K. to show anger by hitting." "It is O.K. to feel disappointed but not O.K. to show that disappointment by ripping your test paper up in front of this class and throwing it in the basket." We want students to recognize, trust, and understand their feelings. When teachers and parents tell students not to be angry or disappointed, they are telling them to distrust and deny their genuine and often justified feelings. The appropriate message for teachers and parents to communicate is that there are appropriate and inappropriate ways for expressing honest, legitimate feelings. The same principle also applies to teachers.

6. Avoid sarcasm and other verbal behaviors that belittle or demean the student. Using verbal reprimands to belittle students makes them feel insignificant, lowers self-esteem, and creates sympathy among classmates.

7. When verbal intervention is necessary, begin by using a technique that fits the student and the problem situation and is as close as possible to the student-control end of the decision-making hierarchy.

8. If the first verbal intervention does not result in a return to appropriate behavior, use a second technique that is closer to the teacher-control end of the hierarchy.

9. If more than one verbal intervention technique has been used unsuccessfully, it is time to move to the next step of the management hierarchy—application of logical sequences.

Keeping these general guidelines for verbal intervention in mind, let's turn our attention to the hierarchy of verbal intervention. Remember the hierarchy is arranged so that it begins with verbal interventions that foster greatest student control over student behavior and gradually progresses to interventions that foster greatest teacher control over student behavior. It is important to remember, as was suggested in Chapter Seven, that this is a hierarchy of decision making. The teacher uses the hierarchy as a range of options to consider, not a series of techniques to be tried one after another. The teacher should begin the intervention, as we see it, at whatever point on the hierarchy seems most likely to correct the misbehavior and still allow as much student control and responsibility as possible. It is entirely appropriate to begin with a teacher-centered technique whenever the teacher believes that it is important to stop the misbehavior quickly and it appears to the teacher that only a teacher-centered intervention will do so. It is also important to remember that not all of these intervention techniques are appropriate for all types of misbehavior or for all students. For example, Lasley (1989) suggests that teacher-centered interventions are more appropriate for younger, developmentally immature children, and student-centered interventions are more appropriate for older, developmentally mature learners. Therefore, the effective use of this verbal intervention hierarchy requires the teacher to decide which particular intervention techniques are appropriate for his students and for particular types of misbehavior. Teachers must use the various interventions with full awareness of the limitations of each specific technique and of the implicit message about controlling student behavior each one conveys.

The hierarchy of verbal intervention techniques is illustrated in Figure 8-1, followed by an explanation of each technique and an illustration of how

FIGURE 8-1 Hierarchy of Classroom Verbal Intervention Techniques

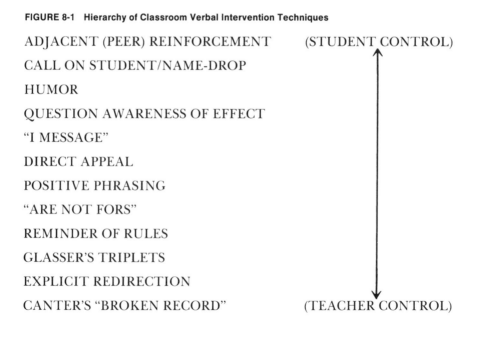

ADJACENT (PEER) REINFORCEMENT   (STUDENT CONTROL)

CALL ON STUDENT/NAME-DROP

HUMOR

QUESTION AWARENESS OF EFFECT

"I MESSAGE"

DIRECT APPEAL

POSITIVE PHRASING

"ARE NOT FORS"

REMINDER OF RULES

GLASSER'S TRIPLETS

EXPLICIT REDIRECTION

CANTER'S "BROKEN RECORD"   (TEACHER CONTROL)

the technique could be used to deal with the case presented in the introduction.

Adjacent (Peer) Reinforcement

This verbal intervention technique is based on the learning principle that behavior which is reinforced is more likely to be repeated. Most often, reinforcement consists of reinforcing a student for his own behavior. Albert Bandura (1977), however, has demonstrated through his work on social learning theory that when peers are reinforced for appropriate behavior, other students are likely to imitate that behavior. The use of peer reinforcement as a verbal intervention technique focuses class attention on appropriate behavior rather than on inappropriate behavior. This intervention technique has been placed first in our hierarchy because it gives the student a chance to control his own behavior without any intervention on the part of the teacher that calls attention to the student or his behavior. As the reader will remember from Chapter Seven, adjacent reinforcement not only stops misbehavior but also can prevent other students from misbehaving.

To use this technique effectively, a teacher does the following. When he notes a disruptive behavior, he simply finds another student who is behaving appropriately and commends that student publicly for the appropriate behavior. Recall Mr. Hensen's anger at John. Mr. Hensen could have handled the problem by saying, "Fred and Bob, I really appreciate your raising your hands to answer questions" or "I am really glad that most of us remember the rule that we must raise our hands before speaking."

This particular model of verbal intervention is more useful at the elementary level than at the secondary level. Younger students are generally more interested in pleasing the teacher and often vie for the teacher's attention. Thus, public praise by the teacher is a powerful reinforcer of appropriate behavior. At the secondary level, peer approval is more highly valued than teacher approval; thus, public praise by the teacher is not a very powerful reinforcer, if a reinforcer at all. For these reasons, it is best to use public praise of individuals sparingly. Public reinforcement of the group as a whole, however, may indeed be an appropriate intervention at the secondary level.

Call on the Student/Name-Drop

When a student is behaving inappropriately, the teacher may redirect the student to appropriate behavior by calling on the student to answer a question, if asking questions is part of the lesson. If questioning is not appropriate, the teacher sometimes can redirect the student's attention by simply inserting the student's name in an example or in the middle of a lecture. Rinne (1984) labels the technique of inserting the student's name within the content of a lecture as "name-dropping." Hearing his name is a good reminder to a student that his attention should be refocused on the lesson. In addition to redirecting students who are overtly disrupting the learning process, this same technique may be used to redirect students who are off-task but are not disrupting the learning of others. (See Chapter Seven).

Calling on a student who is misbehaving is a subtle yet effective technique for recapturing the student's attention without interrupting the flow of the lesson or risking confrontation with the student. Teachers use two different formats for calling on disruptive students. Some teachers state the student's name first and then ask the question; others ask the question and then call on the student. The latter technique invariably results in the student being unable to answer the question because he did not hear it. Often, the teacher follows the period of embarrassed silence with a comment on why the student can't answer and why it is important to pay attention. Although this procedure may satisfy the teacher's need to say, "I gotcha," we believe that it is preferable to call on the student first and then ask the question. Using the name first achieves the goal of redirecting the student's attention without embarrassing him.

In "Blowing His Stack," calling on John to answer or saying John's name would not be appropriate techniques for Mr. Hensen to use in dealing with the situation because the teacher would be rewarding John's calling out by giving him recognition. Although not applicable in this particular instance, calling on the student and name-dropping are appropriate in a wide range of situations with learners of all ages.

Humor

Humor that is directed at the teacher or at the situation rather than at the student can defuse tension in the classroom as well as redirect students to appropriate behavior. The use of humor tends to depersonalize the situation and can be very helpful in establishing positive relationships with students (Saphier and Gower, 1982).

If Mr. Hensen wished to use humor to handle the problem, he would say something like this: "I must be hallucinating or something. I'd swear I heard somebody say something if I didn't know for sure that I haven't called on anyone to answer the question yet." In using humor as a verbal intervention technique, teachers need to be very cautious not to turn humor into sarcasm. There is a fine line between humor and sarcasm. Humor is directed at or makes fun of the teacher or the situation, whereas sarcasm is directed at or makes fun of the student. It is important to keep this distinction in mind when monitoring your own behavior to ensure that what was intended as humor does not turn into sarcasm.

Question Awareness of Effect

Sometimes students who disrupt learning are genuinely not aware of the effect their behavior has on other people. Making them aware of how their behavior affects other people is a powerful technique for getting students to control their behavior. Our research (Levin, Nolan, and Hoffman, 1985) indicates that even students who are chronic discipline problems learn to control their own behavior when they are forced to acknowledge both its positive and negative effects. Therefore, one useful technique for dealing with disruptive behavior is to question students about whether they are conscious of the impact their behavior has on others. Typically, this questioning takes the form of a rhetorical question, which requires no response from the disruptive student.

A teacher who wants to handle Mr. Hensen's problem by questioning the student's awareness of his behavior's effect would say something like this: "John, are you aware that when you call out answers without raising your hand, it robs other students of the chance to answer the question?" This also communicates to other students that the teacher is protecting their right to learn and may build peer support for appropriate behavior. At that point, the teacher continues with the lesson very quickly without giving John an opportunity to respond. In using this intervention, especially with students at the junior high level or above, the teacher must be prepared for the possibility that John will respond to the question. If John does respond and does so in a negative way, the teacher may choose to ignore the answer, thereby sending the message that he will not use class time to discuss the issue; or the teacher may respond, "John, your behavior is having a negative impact on other people, and so I will not permit you to continue calling out answers." This second option sends the message that the teacher is clearly in charge of the classroom and will not tolerate the misbehavior. In dealing with a possible negative response from the student, it is important to remember that the teacher's goal is to stop the misbehavior and redirect the student to appropriate behavior as quickly as possible. Prolonged confrontations frustrate that goal.

Send An "I Message"

Thomas Gordon (1974), the author of *Teacher Effectiveness Training*, developed a useful technique for dealing with misbehavior verbally. He termed the intervention an "I message." The "I message" is a three-part verbal intervention technique that is intended to help the disruptive student recognize the negative impact of his behavior on the teacher. The underlying assumption of the technique, as well as of the previously discussed "questioning awareness of effect," is that once a student recognizes the negative impact of his behavior on others, he will be motivated to stop the misbehavior. The three parts of an "I message" are (1) a simple description of the disruptive behavior, (2) description of its tangible effect on the teacher and/or other students, and (3) a description of the teacher's feelings about the effects of the misbehavior. Just as the teacher expects students to respect the feelings that are expressed in an "I message," the teacher too must be respectful of feelings expressed by students. Also, using "I messages" models for students the important behavior of taking responsibility for and owning one's behavior and feelings. It is hoped that students will learn to use "I messages" as well.

To use an "I message" to stop John from calling out in his class, Mr. Hensen would say, "John, when you call out answers without raising your hand (part I), I can't call on any other student to answer the question (part 2). This disturbs me because I would like to give everyone a chance to answer the questions (part 3)." Teachers who enjoy a positive relationship, which gives them referent power (see Chapter Four), are much more likely to be successful in using "I messages." When students genuinely like the teacher, as in the case with referent power, they are motivated to stop behavior that has a negative impact on the teacher. On the other hand, if the teacher has a poor relationship with students, he should avoid the use of "I messages." Allowing students who dislike you to know that a particular behavior is annoying or disturbing to you may result in an increase in that particular behavior.

Direct Appeal

A second technique that is very useful for instances in which a teacher enjoys a referent or expert power base is direct appeal. Direct appeal means requesting in a courteous way that students stop the disruptive behavior. In Mr. Hensen's situation, he could say, "John, please stop calling out answers so that everyone will have a chance to answer." The statement is not made in any sort of pleading or begging way.

Teachers must not use direct appeal in a classroom in which students seem to doubt the teacher's ability to take command and be in charge of the classroom. In this situation, it may well be perceived as a plea rather than as a straightforward request even if phrased as a polite statement.

Positive Phrasing

Many times parents and teachers fall into the trap of putting far more emphasis on the negative outcomes of misbehavior than on the positive outcomes of appropriate behavior. We tell children and students what will happen if they don't finish their homework rather than telling them what good things will occur if they do finish. This tendency may result, at least in part, from the fact that it is often easier to identify the short-range negative outcomes of misbehavior than it is to predict the short-range positive impact of appropriate behavior. When the positive outcomes of appropriate behavior are easily identifiable, a very useful verbal intervention technique for redirecting students from disruptive to proper behavior is simply to state what the positive outcomes are. This technique has been called positive phrasing by Shrigley (1985) and usually takes the form of "as soon as you do *X* (behave appropriately), we can do *Y* (a positive outcome)."

In using positive phrasing to correct John's calling out, Mr. Hensen would have said, "John, you will be called on as soon as you raise your hand." The long-term advantage of using positive phrasing whenever possible is that students begin to believe that appropriate behavior does indeed lead to positive outcomes. As a result, they will be much more likely to develop internalized control over their behavior.

"Are Not Fors"

Of all the verbal interventions discussed in this chapter, the "are not fors" (Shrigley, 1985) is the most limited in use. It is implemented primarily when elementary or preschool children misuse property or materials and is generally effective in redirecting behavior in a very positive way. For example, if a student is drumming on a desk with a pencil, the teacher may say, "Pencils *aren't for* drumming on desks; pencils *are for* writing." Although the "are not fors" may be effective with certain students or classes above the elementary level, most secondary students perceive this intervention as insulting. The "are not fors" are not an appropriate technique for use by Mr. Hensen since John is a secondary student and is not misusing property or material.

Reminder of the Rules

When the teacher has established a clear set of classroom guidelines or rules early in the year (see Chapter Six) and has received student commitment to the rules, misbehavior frequently may be curbed by merely reminding disruptive students about the rules. This approach is even more effective if past transgressions have been followed by a reminder and then by the application of a negative logical consequence if the misbehavior continued. Notice that we have now moved to a point on the hierarchy of interventions where the teacher is using external rules to control student behavior rather than relying on the student's ability to control his own behavior.

Using this technique, Mr. Hensen might say, "John, the classroom rules state that students must raise their hands before speaking" or "John, calling out answers without raising your hand is against our classroom rules." This is particularly effective for elementary students and for junior high students. The reminder of rules may be used at the senior high level, but many students then resent the feeling that they are being governed by too many rules. It is also important to note that when a reminder of the rules is not sufficient to redirect the misbehavior, application of consequences must follow. If this does not occur, the effectiveness of rule reminders will be greatly diminished in the future because students will not have seen a link between breaking classroom rules and negative consequences.

Glasser's Triplets

In his system for establishing suitable student behavior, which is outlined in *Schools Without Failure* (1969), William Glasser proposes that teachers ask disruptive students three questions in order to direct the students to appropriate behavior: (1) What are you doing? (2) Is it against the rules? (3) What should you be doing? The use of these questions obviously requires a classroom in which the rules have been firmly established in students' minds. To stop John from calling out answers by using Glasser's triplets, Mr. Hensen would simply ask those exact questions. The expectation is that John will answer the questions honestly and will then return to raising his hand to answer future questions. Unfortunately, not all students answer them honestly, and therein lies this intervention's inherent weakness. Asking open-ended questions may result in student responses that are dishonest, improper, or unexpected.

If a student chooses either to answer the questions dishonestly or not to reply at all, the teacher responds by saying (in John's case), "No, John, you were calling out answers. That is against our classroom rules. You must raise your hand to answer questions." To minimize the likelihood of an extended, negative confrontation ensuing from the use of Glasser's triplets, it is suggested that teachers consider using three statements instead of questions from the outset. "John, you are calling out. It is against the rules. You should raise your hand if you want to answer."

Explicit Redirection

Explicit redirection consists of an order to stop the misbehavior *and* return to acceptable behavior. The redirection is made in the form of a teacher command and leaves no room for student rebuttal. If Mr. Hensen had used explicit redirection with John, he would have demanded, "John, stop calling out answers and raise your hand if you want to answer a question." Notice the contrast between this technique and those discussed in the earlier stages of the hierarchy in terms of the amount of responsibility for student behavior that is assumed by the teacher.

The advantages of this technique are its simplicity, clarity, and closed format, which does not allow for student rebuttal. The disadvantage is the teacher is publicly confronting the student, who either behaves or defies the teacher in front of peers. Obviously, if the student chooses to defy the teacher's command, he must be prepared to proceed to the next step in the management hierarchy and enforce the command with appropriate consequences.

Canter's Broken Record

Lee Canter (1978) has developed a strategy for clearly communicating to the student that the teacher will not engage in verbal bantering and intends to make sure that the student resumes appropriate behavior. Canter labeled this method "the broken record" because the teacher's behavior sounds like a broken record to the student. First, the teacher gives the student an explicit redirection statement. If the student doesn't comply or if the student tries to defend or explain his behavior, the teacher repeats the redirection. The teacher may repeat it two or three times if the student continues to argue or fails to comply. Some teachers add the phrase "that's not the point" at the beginning of the first and second repetitions when the student tries to excuse or defend his behavior. The following is an example of this technique as applied by Mr. Hensen.

HENSEN: "John, stop calling out answers and raise your hand if you want to answer questions."
JOHN: "But I really do know the answer."
HENSEN: "That's not the point. Stop calling out answers and raise your hand if you want to answer questions."
JOHN: "You let Mabel call out answers yesterday."
HENSEN: "That's not the point. Stop calling out answers and raise your hand if you want to answer questions."

Return to lesson.

The authors have found the "broken record" to be a very good technique for avoiding verbal battles with students while still insisting that they behave appropriately. If the statement has been repeated three times without any result, it is probably safe to assume that it is time to move to a stronger measure on the teacher's management hierarchy, such as the application of logical consequences.

COMPLY OR FACE THE LOGICAL CONSEQUENCES

Although nonverbal and verbal interventions are often successful in stopping misbehavior, there are some situations in which student misbehavior remains unchecked. Such situations require the use of more overt control on the part of the teacher. The final tier on the decision-making management hierarchy is the use of logical consequences by the teacher to control student behavior.

As the reader will recall from Chapter Six, consequences that result from student behavior may be classified into three types: natural, logical, and contrived (Dreikurs, Grunwald, and Pepper, 1982). Natural consequences result directly from student misbehavior without any intervention by the teacher. The teacher, however, may point out to students the link between their behavior and its consequences. Using natural consequences is a management strategy because the teacher decides to let the natural consequences occur, that is, not to take any action to stop them. Logical consequences require teacher intervention and are related as closely as possible to the student behavior; for example, a student who comes to class five minutes late is required by the teacher to remain five minutes after school to make up the work. Contrived consequences are imposed on the student by the teacher and are either unrelated to student behavior or involve a penalty beyond that which is fitting for the misbehavior. Examples of contrived consequences would include a student who writes on his desk and must write 1,000 times "I will not write on my desk," and a student who comes to class five minutes late one time and is sentenced to two weeks' detention. Since contrived consequences fail to help students see the connection between behavior and its consequences and also place the teacher in the role of punisher, we do not advocate their use, and consequently, contrived consequences are not part of the decision-making management hierarchy.

When students have been given the opportunity to stop misbehaving by means of teacher nonverbal and verbal intervention and have failed to do so, the teacher must take control of the situation and use logical consequences to control student behavior. The teacher applies logical consequences calmly and thoughtfully in a forceful but not punitive manner. Brophy (1988) suggests that the teacher put the emphasis on pressuring the student to change his behavior rather than on exacting retribution. The teacher makes clear to the student that the misbehavior must stop immediately or negative consequences will result. Often, it is effective to give the student a choice of either complying with the request or facing the consequences. For example, if Mr. Hensen was not successful in getting John to stop calling out answers, he would say, "John, you have a choice. Either stop calling out answers immediately and begin raising your hand to answer questions or sit in the back corner away from the group for now, and you and I will have an individual question-and-answer session after school." Phrasing the intervention in this way helps the student to see that he is responsible for the consequences of his own behavior and places the teacher in a neutral rather than punitive role. Students do, in fact, choose how to behave. Teachers can't control student behavior; they can only influence it. (See Chapter Two.)

Once the teacher moves to this final level of the hierarchy, the dialogue is over. Either the student returns to appropriate behavior or the teacher takes action. There are no excuses, no postponements. The teacher has stated his intentions clearly. Consistency is crucial. Thus, it is imperative that the teacher not move to this final tier on the hierarchy unless he is ready to enforce the consequences that have been specified.

The exact consequences to be applied obviously vary with the student misbehavior. However, one principle is always involved in the formulation of consequences: Keep the consequences as directly related to the offense as

A detention to make up the missed work is a logical consequence for some forms of disruptive behavior.

possible. Consistent application of this principle helps students to recognize that their behavior has consequences and helps them learn to control their own behavior in the future by predicting its consequences beforehand.

When faced with a discipline problem, it can be very difficult on the spur of the moment to come up with directly related logical consequences (Canter, 1989). Therefore, teachers should spend time thinking about logical consequences for common types of misbehavior before the misbehavior even occurs. They can begin to do that by developing one or two logical consequences for each of the classroom rules developed in Chapter Six. When misbehavior occurs for which there is no preplanned logical consequence, teachers should ask themselves the following questions to help in coming up with consequences directly related to the misbehavior:

1. What would be the logical result if this misbehavior went unchecked?
2. What are the direct effects of this behavior on the teacher, other students, and the misbehaving student?
3. What can be done to minimize these effects?

The answers to these three questions usually help the teacher to identify the logical consequences to be applied to curb the misbehavior. In the following case, note how Ms. Ramada used the first of the three questions to formulate logical consequences for Doug's behavior.

Case 39: "Doing Nothin' "

Doug is a seventh-grade, learning disabled student who has serious problems in reading and also poses behavioral problems for many teachers. At the beginning of the year, Doug is assigned to Ms. Ramonda's seventh-period remedial reading class. Since Doug hates reading, he is determined to get out of that class and causes all sorts of problems for Ms. Ramonda and the other students. Ms. Ramonda's first reaction is to go to the principal and have Doug removed from her class to protect the other students; however, after talking to Doug's counselor and his resource room teacher, she now believes that it is important that Doug not get his way and that he desperately needs to develop the reading skills that she can teach him.

Ms. Ramonda decides to try to use Doug's personal interests to motivate him to work during reading class, and she asked him, "Doug, what would you like to do?" Doug answers, "Nothin', I don't want to do nothin' in here. Just leave me alone." For the next two days Doug sits in the back of the room during reading period and doodles. Finally, Ms. Ramonda asks herself what the logical result is of granting Doug's request, that is, what the logical result is of doing nothing. She decides that the logical result is boredom and resolves to use that to motivate Doug to work.

On the following day, she announces to Doug that he can do nothing—that he will get his wish. She tells him that from then on he can do nothing as long as he wants to. She also explains that he would no longer need books or papers or pencils since books are for reading, and papers and pencils are for writing, and doing nothing means doing none of those things. He will also not be allowed to talk to her or his friends, she explains, since that too would be doing something and he wants to do nothing. "From now on, Doug, you will be allowed to sit in the back corner of the room and do nothing, just as you wish."

Well, for one full week, Doug sits in the back corner and does nothing. Finally, after five days, he asks Ms. Ramonda if he can do something. She replies that he can do some reading but nothing else. Doug agrees to try some reading. That breaks the ice. Ms. Ramonda carefully selects some low-difficulty, high-interest material for Doug and pulls him gradually more and more into the regular classroom situation.

Certainly most classroom behavior problems do not warrant the drastic measures that Ms. Ramonda took in Doug's case. However, the case does illustrate a successful use of logical consequences to deal effectively with a difficult classroom situation. It must also be pointed out that Ms. Ramonda spoke to the school principal and obtained his approval before allowing

Doug to do nothing. The application of logical consequences in a firm but neutral manner, as was done by Ms. Ramonda, can be a very successful strategy for redirecting students who misbehave to more appropriate behavior while at the same time helping students to recognize the direct connection between behavior and its consequences.

SUMMARY

This chapter has presented the final two tiers of the management hierarchy initially introduced in Chapter Seven: verbal intervention and application of logical consequences. The following guidelines for verbal intervention were developed: (1) use verbal intervention when nonverbal is inappropriate or not effective; (2) keep verbal intervention private if possible; (3) make it as brief as possible; (4) speak to the situation, not the person; (5) set limits on behavior, not feelings; (6) avoid sarcasm; (7) begin with a verbal intervention close to the student-control end of the hierarchy; (8) if necessary, move to a second verbal intervention technique closer to the teacher-control end

FIGURE 8-2 Hierarchy for Management Intervention

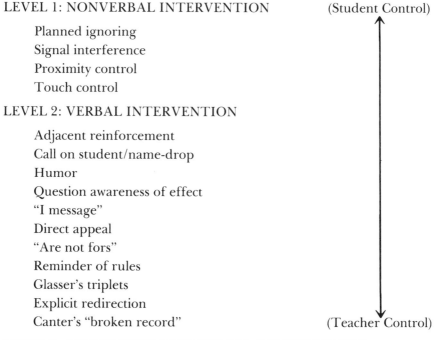

LEVEL 1: NONVERBAL INTERVENTION   (Student Control)

    Planned ignoring
    Signal interference
    Proximity control
    Touch control

LEVEL 2: VERBAL INTERVENTION

    Adjacent reinforcement
    Call on student/name-drop
    Humor
    Question awareness of effect
    "I message"
    Direct appeal
    "Are not fors"
    Reminder of rules
    Glasser's triplets
    Explicit redirection
    Canter's "broken record"   (Teacher Control)

LEVEL 3: APPLICATION OF LOGICAL CONSEQUENCES

of the hierarchy; and (9) if two verbal interventions have been used unsuccessfully, move to the application of consequences.

In addition to these 9 general guidelines, 12 specific intervention techniques were presented in a hierarchical format ranging from techniques that foster greater student control over student behavior to those that foster greater teacher control over student behavior: (1) adjacent reinforcement, (2) call on student/name-drop, (3) humor, (4) question awareness of effect, (5) "I message," (6) direct appeal, (7) positive phrasing, (8) "are not fors," (9) reminder of rules, (10) Glasser's triplets, (11) explicit redirection, and (12) Canter's "broken record."

The final section of the chapter discussed the final tier of the hierarchy: application of logical consequences. Suggestions were made to phrase this intervention in terms of student choice and to relate the consequences as directly as possible to the misbehavior. Finally, three questions were proposed to help teachers formulate logical consequences for student misbehaviors for which the teacher has not already developed a consequence hierarchy.

When taken together with the information presented in Chapter Seven, the ideas presented in this chapter constitute a complete hierarchy which teachers can use to guide their thinking and decision making concerning interventions to cope with classroom misbehavior. The hierarchy is presented in its complete format in Figure 8-2.

REFERENCES

Bandura, A. (1977). *Social Learning Theory*. Englewood Cliffs, NJ: Prentice-Hall.

Brophy, J. (1988). Educating teachers about managing classrooms and students. *Teaching and Teacher Education, 4*, 1, 1–18.

Canter, L. (1978). *Assertive Discipline*. Belmont, CA: Wadsworth.

Canter, L. (1989). Assertive discipline. More than names on the board and marbles in a jar. *Phi Delta Kappan, 71*, 1, 57–61.

Dreikurs, R., Grunwald, B. B., and Pepper, F. C. (1982). *Maintaining Sanity in the Classroom: Classroom Management Techniques*, 2nd ed. New York: Harper & Row.

Ginott, H. (1972). *Between Teacher and Child*. New York: Peter H. Wyden Publishing.

Glasser, W. (1969). *Schools Without Failure*. New York: Harper & Row.

Gordon, T. (1974). *Teacher Effectiveness Training*. New York: Peter H. Wyden Publishing.

Lasley, T. J. (1989). A teacher development model for classroom management. *Phi Delta Kappan, 71*, 1, 30–38.

Levin, J., Nolan, J., and Hoffman, N. (1985). A strategy for the classroom resolution of chronic discipline problems. *National Association of Secondary School Principals' Bulletin, 69*, 7, 11–18.

Rinne, C. (1984). *Attention: The Fundamentals of Classroom Control*. Columbus, OH: Charles E. Merrill.

Saphier, J., and Gower, R. (1982). *The Skillful Teacher*. Carlisle, MA: Research for Better Teaching.

Shrigley, R. (1985). Curbing student disruption in the classroom—Teachers need intervention skills. *National Association of Secondary School Principals' Bulletin, 69*, 7, 26–32.

EXERCISES

1. What types of student misbehavior might lead a teacher to use verbal intervention without first trying nonverbal techniques? Justify your answer.

2. Use each of the verbal intervention techniques presented in this chapter to help redirect the student to appropriate behavior:
    a. Student won't get started on a seatwork assignment.
    b. Student pushes his way to the front of the line.
    c. Student talks to a friend sitting on the other side of the room.
    d. Student lies about a forgotten homework assignment.

3. Choose any three sequential verbal intervention techniques from the hierarchy and justify the placement of the three in that order in terms of teacher vs. student control over behavior.

4. Under what circumstances, if any, would it be appropriate for a teacher to move directly to the third tier of the hierarchy: application of logical consequences? Justify your answer.

5. Why is the application of logical consequences more teacher-centered in terms of control than explicit redirection or Canter's broken record?

6. Develop logical consequences for each of the following misbehaviors:
    a. Student interrupts while teacher is talking to small group of students.
    b. Student steals money from another student's desk.
    c. Student copies a homework assignment from someone else.
    d. Student squirts a water pistol during class.
    e. Student throws spitballs at the blackboard.
    f. Student physically intimidates other students.
    g. Graffiti is found on the restroom wall.

7. List any classroom misbehaviors that do not have logical consequences. What can be done about these misbehaviors in order to employ the principles of the consequence model?

CHAPTER 9

Classroom Interventions for Chronic Problems

```
┌─────────────────────────────┐
│         THE BASICS          │
└─────────────────────────────┘
              ↓
┌─────────────────────────────────────┐
│ NATURE OF THE DISCIPLINE PROBLEM    │
└─────────────────────────────────────┘
              ↓
┌──────────────────────────────────────────┐
│ UNDERSTANDING WHY STUDENTS MISBEHAVE     │
└──────────────────────────────────────────┘
              ↓
┌────────────────────────────────────────────────────────┐
│ PHILOSOPHICAL APPROACHES TO CLASSROOM MANAGEMENT       │
└────────────────────────────────────────────────────────┘
              ↓
┌────────────────────────────────────┐
│     THE PROFESSIONAL TEACHER       │
└────────────────────────────────────┘
              ↓
┌────────────────────────────────────┐
│  STRUCTURING THE ENVIRONMENT       │
└────────────────────────────────────┘
              ↓
┌────────────────────────────────────────────────────┐
│ MANAGING COMMON MISBEHAVIOR PROBLEMS:              │
│ NONVERBAL INTERVENTION                             │
└────────────────────────────────────────────────────┘
              ↓
┌────────────────────────────────────────────────────┐
│ MANAGING COMMON MISBEHAVIOR PROBLEMS:              │
│ VERBAL INTERVENTION AND                            │
│ APPLICATION OF LOGICAL CONSEQUENCES                │
└────────────────────────────────────────────────────┘
              ↓
┌────────────────────────────────────────────────────────┐
│ CLASSROOM INTERVENTIONS FOR CHRONIC PROBLEMS          │
│ Behavior Contracting                                  │
│ Anecdotal Record Keeping                              │
└────────────────────────────────────────────────────────┘
```

PRINCIPLES OF CLASSROOM MANAGEMENT

30. When dealing with students who pose chronic discipline problems, teachers should employ strategies to resolve the problem within the classroom before seeking outside assistance.

31. When teachers employ effective communication skills in private conferences with students who pose chronic discipline problems, such conferences are more likely to be productive in resolving the problem.

32. Techniques requiring students to recognize their own inappropriate behavior and its effect on themselves and others maximize the likelihood of appropriate behavior.

33. Techniques that require students to be accountable for controlling their own behavior on a daily basis maximize the likelihood of appropriate behavior.

34. Management techniques that call for gradual but consistent behavioral improvement by students who pose chronic discipline problems maximize the likelihood of long-term improvement.

INTRODUCTION

The vast majority of the discipline problems teachers face are surface-level disruptions such as short, infrequent periods of talking. As suggested in Chapters Seven and Eight, most of these surface-level disruptions can be handled quickly and painlessly by use of a preplanned hierarchy of nonverbal and verbal intervention. In fact research, as well as our own experience, indicates that the overwhelming majority of discipline problems (somewhere in the neighborhood of 97 percent) can either be prevented or redirected to positive behavior by use of the various techniques detailed in Chapters One through Eight (Shrigley, 1980).

Unfortunately, some students pose classroom discipline problems of a more chronic nature. These students continually misbehave even after all the preventative and coping techniques have been appropriately employed. They disrupt learning, interfere with the work of others, challenge teacher authority, and often try to entice others to misbehave on a fairly consistent basis. These are the students who prompt teachers to make such remarks as "If I could only get rid of that—Sammy, third period would be a pleasure to teach." "Everytime I look at that smirk on Jody's face, I'd like to wring her little neck." "If that—Greg weren't in this class, I would certainly have a lot more time to spend on helping the other students learn." The student described in the case study that follows is a good example.

Case 40: "I Just Dropped My Book"

Jodi entered Mr. Voman's guidance office hesitatingly, sat down, and looked at Mr. Voman with a blank look on her face.

MR. VOMAN: "Well, Jodi, what are you doing here?"
JODI: "Ms. Kozin sent me out of class and told me not to ever come back. She told me to come see you."

MR. VOMAN:	"Why did she send you out of class?"
JODI:	"I don't know. I just dropped my book on the floor accidentally!"
MR. VOMAN:	"Now, come on Jodi. Ms. Kozin wouldn't put you out of class just for that. Come on now. Tell me the truth. What did you do?"
JODI:	"Honest, Mr. Voman, you can ask the other kids. All I did was drop my book."
MR. VOMAN:	"Jodi, I'm going to go and talk to Ms. Kozin about this. If you're lying to me, you're in big trouble. Wait here until I get back."
JODI:	"O.K., Mr. Voman, I'll wait here and you'll see that I'm not lying."

Mr. Voman did talk to Ms. Kozin and found out that Jodi was telling the truth. All Jodi had done on this particular day was drop her large textbook on the floor with a resounding thud during a lecture. However, the book-dropping incident was simply the straw that broke the camel's back. Jodi had been a constant nuisance to Ms. Kozin for the past month. She continually talked during lectures; forgot to bring pencils, books, and paper; refused to complete homework; didn't even attempt quizzes or tests; and reacted rudely whenever Ms. Kozin reprimanded her. Ms. Kozin had tried nonverbal reprimands, verbal reprimands, time out, detention, and notes to parents. By this point, she was totally fed up with Jodi and the dropped book was more than she could take.

Many students like Jodi, though not all, have problems that extend beyond school. Some have very poor home lives with few, if any, positive adult role models. Some have no one who really cares about them or expresses an interest in what they are doing. Lastly, some simply view themselves as losers who couldn't succeed in school even if they tried. As a result, these students act out their frustrations in class and make life miserable for teachers and for the other students as well.

No matter how understandable these students' problems might be, and no matter how sorry teachers might feel for them, the bottom line is that these students must learn to control their own behavior. Otherwise, they are doomed to a life of continued failure and unhappiness. Notwithstanding our great concern for the future of the disruptive student, there is another factor, perhaps even more important, that must be considered. The classroom teacher has a major responsibility to the other students in the class. Chronic misbehavior must not be allowed to continue because it deprives the other students of their right to learn.

In attempting to deal with these chronically disruptive students, classroom teachers often fall into a two-step trap. First, they fulfill that natural, fully understandable, human urge to "get even." They scream, punish, and retaliate. When this retaliation does not work, since the chronically disruptive student often loves to see the teacher explode, the teacher feels helpless and seeks outside assistance; that is, she turns the student over to somebody else. Often, these students are removed from the classroom for a period of time by being sent to an administrator or counselor and sentenced to some form of in-school or out-of-school suspension.

Because outside referral removes the disruptive student from the class, obviously the disruptive behavior ceases. However, this is usually a short-term solution because the student soon returns and once again disrupts the classroom after a brief period of improvement. The severity and frequency of the misbehavior after this return to the classroom often increase. Two of the hypothesized reasons for this increased misbehavior are that the student views the referral either as a further punishment or as a victory over the teacher. When viewed as a punishment, many disruptive students seek to retaliate as soon as they return to the classroom. When viewed as a victory, such students often feel compelled to demonstrate even more forcefully, to both the teacher and the other students, their perceived superiority over the teacher.

The advisability of dealing with chronic discipline problems within the classroom was pointed out by Porter and Brophy (1988) in a research synthesis on effective teaching. "In a study of teacher's strategies for coping with students who presented sustained problems in personal adjustment or behavior, teachers who were identified as most effective in coping with such problems viewed them as something to be corrected rather than merely endured. Furthermore, although they might seek help from school administrators or mental health professionals, such teachers would build personal relationships and work with their problem students, relying on instruction, socialization, cognitive strategy training and other long-term solutions. In contrast, less effective teachers would try to turn over the responsibility to someone else (such as the principal, school social worker, or counselor)" (p. 78).

Removing chronically disruptive students from the classroom or seeking outside assistance for them should be done only as a last resort. Contrary to popular belief, chronic behavior problems often can be managed successfully within the confines of the regular classroom, with a minimum of additional effort by the teacher. When chronic discipline problems are dealt with by the classroom teacher, the disruptive student, the other students, and the teacher all benefit. The disruptive student benefits by learning to behave appropriately without loss of instructional time and without development of negative attitudes, which are often evident in students who have been excluded from the classroom. The teacher benefits by gaining additional confidence in her ability to handle successfully all types of discipline problems and by the improved behavior of the formerly disruptive student. Finally, the other students in the class benefit by being able to concentrate their attention once again on learning tasks rather than having to be exposed to periodic misbehavior by the chronically disruptive student.

The purpose of this chapter is to discuss two interventions teachers can use to deal with students who pose chronic behavior problems in the classroom: behavior contracting and anecdotal record keeping. It is important that teachers understand under what conditions these interventions are appropriate. Each of them requires the teacher to hold private conferences with the student who is a chronic behavior problem. During these private conferences, the teacher must use effective communication skills. Therefore, this chapter is divided into four major parts: (1) a discussion of the assumptions underlying the use of behavior contracting and anecdotal record keeping; (2) a discussion of communication skills, which are essential in using behavior contracting and anecdotal record keeping effectively; (3) a description of the procedures employed in using behavior contracting; and (4) a description of the procedures employed in using anecdotal record keeping.

ASSUMPTIONS UNDERLYING THE USE OF BEHAVIOR CONTRACTING AND ANECDOTAL RECORD KEEPING

Before a teacher begins to use either behavior contracting or anecdotal record keeping, it is important for her to be aware of the assumptions that underlie their use. Lack of knowledge of these underlying assumptions may lead a teacher to employ these interventions ineffectively or inappropriately in a given situation. These assumptions are as follows:

1. The teacher's major responsibility is not to solve the chronically disruptive student's underlying problems but rather to control the behavior of the student in the classroom. The student's underlying problems are often far beyond the teacher's control and expertise and simply may not be amenable to solution.

2. The number of students who should be classified as chronic discipline problems in any particular class is small.

3. The teacher is well prepared for each class and is able to structure and present material in a way that is interesting and motivating for students (see Chapter Five).

4. The teacher uses teaching techniques based on generally accepted principles of learning and research on effective teaching (see Chapter Five).

5. The teacher has clear expectations for student behavior, has communicated these expectations to students, and enforces these expectations consistently (see Chapter Six).

6. The teacher controls commonplace, less serious disruptions by using the preplanned hierarchical system of nonverbal and verbal intervention and by applying logical consequences to student misbehavior (see Chapters Seven and Eight).

7. The teacher is able to use these techniques with a minimum of additional effort and no further training other than reading this chapter and completing the exercises at the end.

If these assumptions are incorrect or the teacher does not agree with them, the use of behavior contracting and/or anecdotal record keeping is not advised. On the other hand, if the assumptions are correct, the teacher should consider the use of these interventions to deal with chronically disruptive students.

EFFECTIVE COMMUNICATION SKILLS
FOR PRIVATE CONFERENCES

An important component of both behavior contracting and anecdotal record keeping is a face-to-face conference between teacher and student. If such conferences are going to be productive, it is important that the teacher use positive communication skills. Positive communication skills for private conferences can be divided into two categories: (1) receiving skills, which ensure that the teacher receives the student's messages accurately, and (2) sending skills, which allow the teacher to communicate her feelings and ideas accurately to the student. In addition to conferences with students, receiving and sending skills are also important for conferences with parents, counselors, administrators, and people from outside referral agencies.

Receiving Skills

During private conferences, the teacher needs to be aware of the student's perception of the problem and point of view in order to focus the intervention on the actual problem. For example, suppose the student's chronic misbehavior is motivated by the student's belief that she doesn't have the ability to do the assigned work. Solutions targeted solely at the misbehavior, which ignore the student's underlying feeling of inability to succeed, are not likely to be successful in the long run. Therefore, it is important during conferences to make sure the teacher is receiving the message that the student is sending to ensure that the teacher understands all facets of the problem and the student's perspective. The following receiving skills are very useful:

1. *Use silence and nonverbal attending cues.* Allow the student sufficient time to express her ideas and feelings and employ nonverbal cues such as eye contact, facial expressions, head nodding, and body posture (for example, leaning toward the student). This communicates to the student that you are interested in and listening to what she is saying. Most important, make sure these cues are sincere, that is, that you really are listening carefully to the student.

2. *Probe.* Ask relevant and pertinent questions to elicit extended information about a given topic, for clarification of ideas, and for justification for a given idea. Examples are "Can you tell me more about the problem with Jerry?" "What makes you say that I don't like you?" "I'm not sure I understand what you mean by hitting on you; can you explain what that means?"

3. *Check perceptions.* Paraphrase or summarize what the student has said using slightly different words. This acts as a check on whether you have understood the student correctly or not. This is not a simple verbatim repetition of what the student says. It is an attempt by the teacher to capture the student's message as accurately as possible in the teacher's words. Generally a perception check ends by giving the student an opportunity to affirm or negate the teacher's perception, for example, "So, as I understand it, you think that I'm picking on you when I give you detention for not completing your homework; is that right?" and "You're saying that you never really wanted to be in the gifted program anyway, and so you don't care whether you are removed from the program. Do I have that right?"

4. *Check feelings.* Feeling checks refer to teacher attempts to reach student emotions through questions and statements. In doing feeling checks, use nonverbal cues (for example, facial expression) and paralingual cues (voice volume, rate, and pitch) to go beyond the surface-level statements and understand the emotions behind the words. For instance, "You are really proud of what you're doing in basketball aren't you?" or "You look really angry when you talk about being placed in the lower section. Are you angry?"

Sending Skills

In addition to gaining an understanding of the problem from the student's vantage point, the teacher uses an individual conference with a student who poses a chronic discipline problem to make certain that the student understands the problem from the teacher's point of view. Using sending skills to communicate the teacher's thoughts and ideas clearly is a first step toward helping the student gain that insight. Ginott (1972) and Jones (1980) gave the following guidelines for sending accurate messages:

1. *Deal in the here and now.* Don't dwell on past problems and situations. Communicate your thoughts about the present situation and the immediate future. It is certainly appropriate to talk about the past behavior, which has created the need for the private conference; however, there is nothing to be gained by reciting a litany of all of the student's past sins and transgressions.

2. *Make eye contact and use congruent nonverbal behaviors.* Avoiding eye contact when confronting a student about misbehavior gives the student the impression that you are uncomfortable about the confrontation. In contrast, maintaining eye contact helps to let the student know that you are confident and comfortable in dealing with problems. In addition to eye contact, other nonverbal cues should match the verbal messages; for example, smiling when telling the student how disappointed you are in the student's behavior is clearly inappropriate. Research indicates that when verbal and nonverbal behavior are not congruent, students believe the nonverbal messages (Wolfolk and Brooks, 1983).

3. *Make statements rather than ask questions.* Asking questions is very appropriate for eliciting information that the student has and the teacher does not have. However, when the teacher has specific information or behaviors to discuss, it is preferable to lay the specific facts out on the table rather than to try to elicit the information from the student by playing "guess what's on my mind."

4. *Use "I"—take responsibility for your feelings.* You have a right to your feelings. It is appropriate sometimes to be annoyed at students and also appropriate to be

proud of students. Sometimes we try to disown our feelings and act as if we were robots. Students must know that we, too, are people who have legitimate feelings and that our feelings must be considered in determining the effects of the student's behavior on others.

5. *Be brief.* Get to the point quickly. Let the student know what the problem is as you see it and what you propose to do about it. Once you have done this, stop. Don't belabor the issue with unnecessary lectures and harangues.

6. *Talk directly to the student, not about her.* Even if other people are present, talk directly to the student rather than describing the student's behavior to parents or counselors. Use "you" and specifically describe the problem to the student. This behavior sends the student the powerful message that she, not her parents or anyone else, is directly responsible for her own behavior.

7. *Give directions to help the student correct the problem.* Don't stop at identifying the problem behavior. Be very specific in setting forth exactly what behaviors must be replaced and identifying appropriate behaviors to replace them.

8. *Check student understanding of your message.* Once you have communicated clearly what the specific problem is and what steps you suggest for solving the problem, it is important to ask a question to check whether the student has received the message correctly or not. This question often takes the form of asking the student for a summary of the discussion during the conference. If the student's summary indicates that she has missed the message, the teacher has an opportunity to restate the main idea once again or to rephrase it in a slightly different way to try to make certain that the student understands it correctly this time.

Keeping these guidelines for effective communication in mind, let's turn our attention to the two specific classroom interventions for dealing with chronic misbehavior.

BEHAVIOR CONTRACTING

The first technique to consider is behavioral contracting. This procedure is grounded in the theoretical principles of operant conditioning, which state that a behavior that is reinforced is likely to be repeated and that a behavior that is not reinforced will soon disappear.

A behavioral contract is a written agreement between the teacher and student that commits the student to behave more appropriately and provides a specified reward for meeting the commitment. The contract details the expected behavior, a time period during which this behavior must be exhibited by the student, and the reward that will be provided. The purposes of the contract are to control behavior that is not controlled effectively by normal classroom procedures, to encourage self-discipline on the part of the student, and to foster the student's sense of commitment to appropriate classroom behavior. Although behavior contracting can be used with students at any grade level, it often is more appropriate and effective with elementary and middle school students since older students often resent

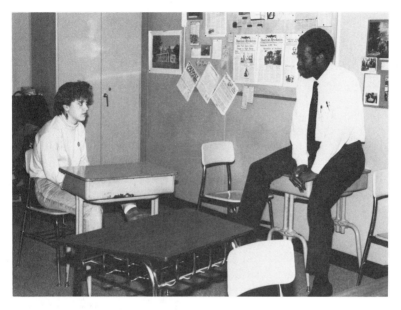

A private conference in which appropriate sending and receiving skills are used is the first step in setting up a behavioral contract or anecdotal record system.

obvious attempts to manipulate their behavior. This procedure also is used very frequently and quite effectively in special education classes.

Because an integral part of behavior contracting is the use of rewards, often extrinsic, concrete rewards, some teachers may be philosophically opposed to this method. Some teachers feel that students should not be rewarded for behavior that is normally expected of all students. Since this technique has been shown to be effective and is one of the last possible strategies that can be used within the classroom, these teachers may wish to rethink their position. The improvements in their classroom learning environment may outweigh their philosophical objections. However, if strong philosophical objections still remain, the teacher should not use behavior contracting because the likelihood of its successful use is diminished if one does not believe in its philosophical underpinnings. (See Chapter Four.)

If you, the teacher, decide to use behavior contracting, remember that it is unlikely that one behavioral contract will be sufficient to turn a chronically disruptive student into the epitome of model behavior. Drastic changes in behavior usually do not occur overnight. The normal course of events requires a series of behavioral contracts, which result in steady, gradual improvement in the student's behavior. By using a series of short-term behavioral contracts rather than one long-term contract, the wise teacher allows the student to see the behavior changes as manageable and to receive small rewards after short intervals of improvement. In other words, a series of contracts provides the student with the opportunity to be successful. Manageable changes in behavior, shorter time intervals, and frequent opportunities for success make it much more likely that the student will be motivated to improve continuously over a longer period of time.

In designing the series of contracts, it is necessary to keep the following three principles in mind. First, design the contracts to require specific, gradual improvements in behavior. For example, if a student normally disrupts learning six times a period, set the initial goal at four disruptions or fewer per day, and then over time increase the goal gradually until it is set eventually at zero disruptions per day. Second, gradually lengthen the time period during which the contract must be observed in order to gain the reward. For instance, the set time is one day for the first contract, a few days for the second contract, a week for the third contract, and so on. Third, move little by little from more tangible, extrinsic rewards to less tangible, more intrinsic rewards. Thus, a pencil or other supplies are the rewards under the first few contracts, and free time for pleasure reading is the reward under a later contract. Using these three principles takes advantage of the behavior modification technique called behavior shaping and step by step moves control over the student's behavior from the teacher to the student, where it rightfully belongs.

Keeping these principles in mind, the teacher implements behavior contracting by observing the following procedures. The first step is to identify the chronically disruptive students for whom this technique is necessary. Chronically disruptive students are those who are still seriously and frequently disrupting the learning process, even after the teacher has employed the preplanned management intervention hierarchy. It is assumed that the number of chronically disruptive students in any particular class is small (one to three students); therefore, all such students can be involved in behavior contracting simultaneously. If this is not the case, the teacher needs to reconsider whether her teaching behavior meets the underlying assumptions. If, after reconsideration, the teacher still believes that her teaching behavior meets these assumptions but she finds herself with a large number of chronic discipline problems, it is advisable for her to select a few particular students with the idea that the correction of these students' behavior will have a ripple effect, producing changes in other students as well (Kounin, 1970).

When the number of chronically disruptive students is large, two types of students are usually selected for behavior contracting, those viewed as having the greatest potential to improve their behavior and those who are causing the most disruptions in the classroom. There are, however, pitfalls in choosing either. Usually those students with the greatest likelihood for improvement are those with the least severely disruptive behavior. Thus, if they are chosen, the level of disruptive behavior may still remain high. Nevertheless, once the contract produces improved behavior in these students, the teacher may then turn her attention fully to the more severely disruptive students. Some positive rippling effect may also occur.

If, on the other hand, the most disruptive students are chosen, the process may require an extremely long time to produce noticeable results in the classroom. In addition, the ripple effect may not be as effective in the early stages of the contracting process because there will be many contracts, each requiring very small, almost unnoticeable changes in behavior to ensure ultimate success.

At the present time, there is no definite research that helps teachers decide which students or mix of students should be chosen. Thus, if teachers have more than the usual few chronically disruptive students in the classroom, the teachers must weigh these considerations in reference to their particular situation and use their own judgment about which type of student to choose.

Once a student has been identified, the teacher makes a record of both the student's past misbehaviors and the teacher's management techniques that were used to try to ameliorate these misbehaviors. The teacher should use all available evidence, including documents and personal recollections, trying to be as accurate and neutral as possible. This record helps the teacher decide what specific behaviors must be changed and how much change seems manageable for the student at one time. In addition, it ensures that all appropriate management techniques have been used before the implementation of the behavior contract process.

After this record is compiled, the teacher holds a private conference with the student. During this conference, she employs the receiving and sending skills that were described previously. It is best to begin this conference on a positive note. The teacher communicates to the student that the student has the potential to do well and to succeed in the classroom if she can learn to behave appropriately, thus employing the concept of encouragement (Dreikurs, Grunwald, and Pepper, 1982). The teacher attempts to get the student to acknowledge that her behavior has been inappropriate and to recognize its negative impact on everyone in the classroom. Stressing the effect of the student's behavior on others promotes the development of higher moral reasoning (Tanner, 1978). The teacher uses questions similar to these. "What have you been doing in class?" "How is that affecting your chances of success?" "How would you like it if other students treated you like that?" "How would you like it if you were in a class you really liked but never got a chance to learn because other students were always causing trouble?" Such questions often help the student recognize that the behavior has been unacceptable. Thereafter, the teacher informs the student that such behavior, no matter what the explanation for it, is unacceptable and must change. This is followed by a statement such as "I'd like to work out a plan with you that will help you to behave more appropriately in class."

The teacher clearly states how the plan works. The student commits herself to improvements in classroom behavior for a specified period of time; and if this commitment is kept, some positive consequences or reward results. If the student refuses to make this commitment, behavior contracting cannot be used because a contract is an agreement between two people.

Specific rewards that are often used include free time for the student to pursue activities of special interest; a letter, note, or phone call to parents describing the improvements in behavior; or supplies, such as posters, pencils, and stickers, from the school bookstore. The most important consideration in deciding on what particular reward to use is whether it is perceived as motivating by the student. For that reason, it is often a good idea to allow the student to suggest possible rewards or at least to discuss rewards jointly with the student. If the student's parents are cooperative, it is sometimes possible to contact them and ask them to provide a reward at home that is more meaningful to the student. The teacher now draws up the contract, setting forth clearly and simply the specific improvements in behavior, the time period, and the reward. Both the teacher and student sign the contract, and each receive a copy. In the case of younger students, it is often a good idea to send a copy of the behavioral contract home to parents as well.

The conference ends as it began, on a positive note. The teacher tells the student that she is looking forward to positive changes in the student's behavior beginning right away.

Here is an example of a behavior contract and a behavior contract checklist which may be used by teachers to evaluate the quality of behavior contracts that they draw up. The sample contract is the third in a series between Jessica and her fifth-grade teacher, Ms. Jones. Before the behavior contract intervention, Jessica spent the vast majority of each day's 40-minute social studies period wandering around the room. The first two contracts resulted in her being able to remain seated for about half the period.

THIRD CONTRACT BETWEEN JESSICA AND MS. JONES

1. *Expected Behavior*
   Jessica remains in her seat for the first 30 minutes of each social studies period.

2. *Time Period*
   Monday, February 27, to Friday, March 3, 1989.

3. *Reward*
   If Jessica remains in her seat for the first 30 minutes of each social studies period, she
   a. Can choose the class' outdoor game on Friday afternoon, March 3.
   b. Ms. Jones will telephone her parents to tell them of the improvement in Jessica's behavior on Friday afternoon, March 3.

4. *Evaluation*
   a. After each social studies period, Ms. Jones records whether Jessica did or did not get out of her seat during the first 30 minutes.
   b. Jessica and Ms. Jones will meet on Friday, March 3, at 12:30 P.M. to determine whether the contract has been performed and write next week's fourth contract.

Student _____

Teacher _____

Date _____

BEHAVIOR CONTRACT CHECKLIST

1. Is the expected behavior described specifically?	__ Yes	__ No
2. Is the time period specified clearly?	__ Yes	__ No
3. Has the reward been specified clearly?	__ Yes	__ No
4. Is the reward motivating to the student?	__ Yes	__ No
5. Is the evaluation procedure specified?	__ Yes	__ No
6. Has a date been set to meet to review the contract?	__ Yes	__ No
7. Has the student understood, agreed to, and signed the contract?	__ Yes	__ No
8. Has the teacher signed the contract?	__ Yes	__ No
9. Do both the teacher and student have copies?	__ Yes	__ No
10. Did the student's parents get a copy of the contract?	__ Yes	__ No

Once the contract is made, the teacher simply records the behavior of the student each day in regard to the terms specified in the contract. Then the teacher uses this record to conduct the conference with the student at the end of the contract period.

If the student has kept her commitment, the teacher provides the reward. If the student's behavior is in need of further improvement, the teacher draws up a new contract, which specifies increased improvement over a longer time period. If at the end of the contract, the student's behavior has improved sufficiently to conform to final expectations, the teacher informs the student that it is no longer necessary to go to such unusual measures to help her learn to behave. If possible, the teacher points out to the student the direct relationship between the improved behavior and the student's academic success in the classroom. Additionally, the teacher makes clear to the student that since the student is now able to control her own behavior, the teacher expects continued acceptable behavior and success from the student. Most importantly, the teacher must not stop giving the student attention after the contract has ended. It is imperative to continue to find ways to give the student some attention when she is behaving appropriately. This consistent attention helps the student to recognize that positive behavior results in positive consequences and usually helps maintain appropriate behavior over a long period of time.

If at the end of the contract period the student has not kept the commitment, the teacher accepts no excuses. The teacher assumes a neutral role by explaining to the student that the reward cannot be given because her behavior did not live up to the behavior that was agreed on in the contract. The teacher points out to the student that the lack of reward is simply a logical consequence of her behavior. This helps the student to see the cause-and-effect relationship between behavior and its consequences. If a student learns only this, she has learned an extremely valuable lesson.

At this point, the teacher must make a professional decision concerning whether or not it is worth trying a new contract with this student. If the teacher believes that the student really did try to live up to the contract, it is often worth trying a new contract that calls for a little less drastic improvement or calls for improvement over a slightly shorter time frame.

If the student has not made a sincere effort to improve, obviously the contracting is not working. It is time to try another option. By using the behavior contract, even if it does not work, nothing is lost except a little bit of time, and the teacher has accumulated additional documentation, which will be helpful if it is later necessary to seek outside assistance.

ANECDOTAL RECORD KEEPING

If the teacher either has tried behavioral contracting unsuccessfully or has decided not to try behavioral contracting because of philosophical objections or the student's refusal to make the required commitment, she still has another classroom option, called anecdotal record keeping, for remediating chronic behavioral problems. This method has been used successfully by student teachers and veteran teachers alike to handle a variety of chronic discipline problems at a variety of grade levels (Levin, Nolan, and Hoffman, 1985). It is based on the principles of Adlerian psychology, which state that changes in behavior can be facilitated by making people more aware of their behavior and its consequences for themselves and others (Sweeny, 1981). Anecdotal record keeping is an interactionalist approach to controlling classroom behaviors (see Chapter Four).

This technique can be used with a minimum of effort and no additional training. The teacher merely records the classroom behavior, both positive and negative, of chronically disruptive students over a period of a few weeks. Although it is preferable to have the student's cooperation, anecdotal record keeping can still be employed without it. In contrast to behavior contracting, which is often more effective at the elementary level, anecdotal record keeping is most appropriate in dealing with middle and secondary students who are chronic discipline problems since students at these levels have better developed self-monitoring strategies.

As was the case for behavioral contracting, the teacher begins by documenting the behaviors of the disruptive student and the measures that have been taken to improve that behavior. Once again, this documentation forms the basis for a private conference with the student, which formally begins the process. As was true for behavioral contracting, the teacher employs positive receiving and sending skills during this conference.

The important guidelines for conducting this initial conference for anecdotal record keeping are similar to those for behavioral contracting.

1. The teacher begins on a positive note.
2. The teacher helps the student recognize the past behavior and its negative impact, showing the student the record of past behaviors and discussing it if necessary.
3. The teacher explains that this behavior is unacceptable and must change.
4. The teacher tells the student that she will keep a record of the student's behavior on a daily basis, including both positive behaviors and misbehaviors, and that the student will be required to sign the record at the end of class each day.
5. The teacher records the student's home phone number on the top of the record and indicates that she will contact the parents to inform them of either improvements in the student's behavior or continued unacceptable behavior. (This option may not be useful for senior high students since parents are often not so influential at this age.)
6. The teacher is positive and emphasizes expectations of improvement in behavior.
7. The conference is recorded on the anecdotal record.
8. A verbal commitment for improved behavior from the student is sought. This commitment, or the refusal to give it, is noted on the anecdotal record.
9. The student signs the anecdotal record at the end of the conference. If the student refuses to sign, this is recorded.

After the initial conference, the teacher keeps the anecdotal record, each day highlighting positive behaviors and documenting negative behaviors, as well as any corrective measures taken. Keeping this systematic record enables the teacher to focus on the behavior (the deed) rather than on the student (the doer) (Ginott, 1972). The teacher reinforces the student for improved behaviors and, if possible, clarifies the connection between improved behaviors and academic achievement. Thus, the teacher "catches the student being good" (Canter, 1989; Jones, 1980) and also demonstrates the concept of encouragement (Dreikurs, Grunwald, and Pepper, 1982). It is important to be consistent in recording behaviors, sharing the record with the student, and obtaining the student's signature on a daily basis. This illustrates the concept of student accountability (Brophy, 1988). If the student refuses to sign the record on any day, this is simply recorded on the record.

Teachers often anticipate that such a technique will consume a lot of instructional time; however, this is not the case. If the documentation occurs in the last few minutes of class, perhaps when students are doing homework or getting ready for the next class, the two or three minutes required compare very favorably to the enormous amount of time that can be wasted by unresolved chronic discipline problems. Thus, this technique actually helps to conserve time by making more efficient use of classroom time.

Following is an actual anecdotal record used with one tenth-grade student over a three-week period. This technique succeeded after the management hierarchy had been utilized with little resultant improvement in the student's behavior. Note that the teacher highlighted positive behaviors to "catch the student being good."

In studying the use of anecdotal record keeping, Levin, Nolan, and Hoffman (1985) requested teachers to keep a log of their views of the effectiveness of the procedure. Here are three representative logs by secondary teachers.

Teacher's Log—Eleventh-Grade English

About a week and a half ago, I implemented the anecdotal record in one of my classes. Two male students were the subjects. The improvement shown by one of these students is very impressive.

On the first day that I held a conference with the student, I explained the procedure, showed him my records for the day, and asked for his signature. He scribbled his name and looked at me as if to say, "What a joke." On the second day, his behavior in class was negative again. This time, when I spoke to him and told him that one more day of disruptive behavior would result in a phone call to his parents, he looked at me as if to say, "This joke isn't so funny anymore." From that moment on, there was a marked improvement in his behavior. He was quiet and attentive in class. After class, he would come up to me and ask me where he was supposed to sign his name for the day. And he "beamed" from my remarks about how well behaved he was that day. Only one time after that did I have to speak to him for negative behavior. I caught him throwing a piece of paper. As soon as he saw me looking at him, he said, "Are you going to write that down in your report?" Then, after class, he came up to me with a worried expression on his face and asked, "Are you going to call my parents?" I didn't because of the previous days of model behavior.

I must say that I was skeptical about beginning this type of record on the students. It seemed like such a lengthy and time-consuming process. But I'll

Anecdotal Record

Student's Name ___Rhonda___

Home Phone _____

Date	Student Behavior	Teacher Action	Student Signature
4/15	Talking with Van Out of seat 3 times Refused to answer question	Verbal reprimand Told her to get back Went on	
4/16	Had private conference *Rhonda agreed to improve*	Explained anecdotal record Was supportive	
4/17	*Stayed on-task in lab*	Positive feedback	
4/20	Late for class *Worked quietly*	Verbal reminder Positive feedback	
4/21	*Worked quietly* Wrestling with Jill	Positive feedback Verbal reprimand	
4/22	*No disruptions* *Volunteered to answer*	Positive feedback Called on her 3 times	
4/23	Late for class Left without signing	Detention after school Recorded it on record	
4/24	Missed detention	Two days' detention	
4/27	*Stayed on-task all class*	Positive feedback	
4/28	*Listened attentively to film*	Positive feedback	
4/29	*Worked at assignment well*	Positive feedback	
4/30	*Participated in class* *No disruptions* Left without signing	Called on her twice Positive feedback Recorded it	
5/1	Conference to discontinue anecdotal records		

say what I'm feeling now. If the anecdotal record can give positive results more times than not, I'll keep on using it. If you can get one student under control, who is to say you can't get five or ten students under control? It truly is a worthwhile procedure to consider.

Teacher's Log—Tenth-Grade Science

DAY 1

As a third or fourth alternative, I used an anecdotal record to help control the discipline problems incurred in my second-period class. Previously, I had used direct requests or statements (for example, "What are you doing? What should you be doing?" "Your talking is interfering with other students' right to learn," et cetera). The anecdotal record involved having one-to-one conferences with the four students. The conferences were aimed at reviewing the students' classroom attitudes and securing commitments from them for improved behavior. It was fairly successful, as I received a commitment from the four involved; and they, in turn, let the rest of the class in on the deal. In choosing the four students, I tried to pick a student from each trouble pair. Hopefully, this will eliminate misbehavior for both.

DAY 2

The progress in my class with the anecdotal records was excellent today, as I expected. The four students were exceptionally well behaved. I will be sure to keep extra-close tabs on their progress the next few days to prevent them from reverting back to old ways.

DAY 3

My second-period class was again very well behaved. I did, however, need to put a few negative remarks (for example, talking during film) on the anecdotal records. I will continue to keep close tabs on the situation.

DAY 4

My second-period class (anecdotal records) is quickly becoming one of my best. We are covering more material, getting more class participation, and having less extraneous talking. I did need to make a couple of negative remarks on the record; but on seeing them, the students should, hopefully, maintain a positive attitude and appropriate behavior.

Teacher's Log—Eighth-Grade Science

DAY 1

I discovered a method with which to deal with some major discipline problems in one of my classes. It uses an anecdotal record, which is a record of student actions and student behaviors. I think it will probably work because it holds the student accountable for her behaviors. If something must be done, the student has nobody to blame but herself.

DAY 2

Today, I set up private conferences with anecdotal record students. I wonder if they'll show up—and if they do, how will they respond?

DAY 3

Two students (of three) showed up for their anecdotal record conferences. The third is absent. Both students were very cooperative and made a commitment to better behavior. One student even made the comment that she thought this idea was a good one for her. The way things look, this will work out fairly well. We'll see. . . .

DAY 8

One of the students on anecdotal record has improved in behavior so much that I informed her that if her good behavior kept improving, I'd take her off the record next Wednesday. I think it will be interesting to see how her behavior will be; will it keep improving or will it backtrack again?

Implementing any new strategy may be difficult, and this is no exception. The teacher must expect that some students will act in a very hostile manner when the procedure is introduced. Some may adamantly refuse to sign the record; others may scribble an unrecognizable signature. The teacher must remain calm and positive and simply record such behaviors. This communicates to the student that the student is solely responsible for her behavior and that the teacher is merely an impartial recorder of the behavior. Student behavior will usually improve, given time. Since improved behaviors become a part of the record, the anecdotal record reinforces the improvement and becomes the basis for a cycle of improvement.

When the student's behavior has improved to an acceptable level, the teacher informs the student of her progress and that it will no longer be necessary to keep the anecdotal record. It is important, as suggested earlier, that teachers connect the improved behavior to academic success and improved grades if possible. Also, it must be made clear to the student that her fine behavior is expected to continue. The teacher must continue to give the student attention when she is behaving appropriately because this continued attention is a key link in the chain of behaviors that turns disruptive students into students who behave appropriately. If the student's behavior shows no improvement, it is time to discontinue the process.

This teacher decision concerning when to stop using the anecdotal record is a difficult one. Although there are no rules, there are some helpful guidelines. If the student has displayed acceptable behavior for a few days to a week, the record may be discontinued. If the student's behavior is disruptive continuously or intermittently, the teacher must make the decision whether or not, under the specific circumstances, it is worthwhile to continue the recording for a little longer. Within a week, if the behavior has not decreased substantially, the record keeping should be discontinued and the student told why. If the conduct is somewhat reduced to an intermittent level, it may be advisable to have a second conference with the student to determine whether it is advisable to continue.

If the decision is made to discontinue the record keeping because it has had no effect on the student's behavior, the teacher has one final alternative in which the teacher will still be primarily involved. This is the exclusion of the student from the classroom until she makes a written commitment to improve her behavior.

Prior to exclusion, the student is informed that she is no longer welcome in the class because of her disruptive behavior, which is interfering with the teacher's right to teach and the students' right to learn. The student is then told that she should report to a specified location in the school where appropriate classroom assignments involving reading and writing will be given. The student is also informed that she will be held accountable for the completion of all assignments in an acceptable and timely manner, the same as required in the regular classroom. The teacher stresses that the student may return to the classroom at any time by giving a written commitment to improve her behavior so that the student no longer interferes with the learning/teaching rights of others. This written commitment must be in the student's own words. It specifically informs the teacher of the changed behavior that will be evident when the student returns to the classroom. This exclusion to another setting within the school presupposes that the administration is supportive of such a technique and has made appropriate arrangements for the setting.

Our experience shows that those few students who have been excluded from the classroom and have then made the written commitment and returned to the classroom and remained in the classroom with acceptable behavior. Exclusion finally demonstrates to the student that her behavior will no longer be tolerated and that the entire responsibility for the student's behavior is on the student and only the student.

If a student does not make the written commitment within a reasonable period of time, usually no more than a few days, outside assistance (in the form of parents, counselor, principal, or outside agency) must be sought (see Chapter Ten). If it is necessary to seek outside assistance, the anecdotal record keeping provides the documented evidence needed to make an appropriate referral.

SUMMARY

This chapter has discussed intervention techniques that can be employed within the regular classroom to deal with students who pose chronic discipline problems. Two primary intervention strategies, behavior contracting and anecdotal record keeping, were described in detail. Procedures for when, how, and with which students to employ these techniques were detailed. The advantages of resolving chronic problems within the classroom were identified along with assumptions for the effective use of behavior contracts and anecdotal records. Communication skills for effective private conferences were categorized into two groups, receiving skills and sending skills. Finally, the technique of exclusion from the classroom, a interim step between in-classroom teacher management and outside referral, was presented.

REFERENCES

BROPHY, J. (1988). Educating teachers about managing classrooms and students. *Teaching and Teacher Education, 4,* 1, 1–18.

CANTER, L. (1989). Assertive discipline: More than names on the board and marbles in the jar. *Phi Delta Kappan, 71,* 1, 57–61.

DREIKURS, R., GRUNWALD, B. B., and PEPPER, F. C. (1982). *Maintaining Sanity in the Classroom: Classroom Management Techniques,* 2nd ed. New York: Harper & Row.

GINOTT, H. G. (1972). *Teacher and Child.* New York: Macmillan.

GLASSER, W. (1969). *Schools Without Failure.* New York: Harper & Row.

JONES, V. F. (1980). *Adolescents with Behavior Problems.* Boston: Allyn & Bacon.

KOUNIN, J. S. (1970). *Discipline and Group Management in Classrooms.* New York: Holt, Rinehart & Winston.

LEVIN, J., NOLAN, J., and HOFFMAN, N. (1985). A strategy for the classroom resolution of chronic discipline problems. *National Association of Secondary School Principals; Bulletin, 69,* 479, 11–18.

PORTER, A. C., and BROPHY, J. (1988). Synthesis of research on good teaching: Insights from the work of the IRT. *Educational Ledership, 45,* 8, 74–83.

SHRIGLEY, R. L. (1980). *The Resolution of 523 Classroom Incidents by 54 Classroom Teachers Using the Six Step Intervention Model.* University Park: Pennsylvania State University, College of Education, Division of Curriculum and Instruction.

SWEENY, T. J. (1981). *Adlerian Counseling: Proven Concepts and Strategies.* Muncie, IN: Accelerated Development.

TANNER, L. N. (1978). *Classroom Discipline for Effective Teaching and Learning.* New York: Holt, Rinehart & Winston.

WOOLFOLK, A., & BROOKS, D. (1983). Nonverbal communication in teaching. In E. W. Gordon, Ed., *Review of Research in Education,* 10. Washington, DC: American Educational Research Association.

EXERCISES

1. Several assumptions underlying the use of behavior contracting and anecdotal record keeping were identified in this chapter. Examine assumptions 3 through 6, and explain why each of these is important.

2. Do you agree that the teacher's major responsibility is not to solve underlying problems but rather to control the chronically disruptive student's behavior in the classroom? Justify your answer.

3. Form a triad with two other classmates. Designate a letter (A, B, or C) for each of you. Role-play three conferences between a teacher and a chronically disruptive student. For each role play, the teacher will create the scenario that has led to the need for this conference. During each conference, the person who plays the role of teacher should practice using effective receiving and sending skills. The process observer will give feedback to the teacher on the use of effective communication. Divide the roles for the three conferences according to the following format:

	PERSON A	PERSON B	PERSON C
Conference 1	Teacher	Student	Process observer
Conference 2	Process observer	Teacher	Student
Conference 3	Student	Process observer	Teacher

4. Should chronically disruptive students receive special rewards for behaviors that are typically expected of other students? Justify your answer.

5. Make a list of rewards under the regular classroom teacher's control that could be used in behavior contracts for students at each of the following levels: (a) elementary, (b) middle or junior high, (c) senior high.

6. Design an initial behavior contract for the following situation: Jonathan, a sixth-grade, middle school student who loves sports, has refused to do homework for the last three weeks, has started fights on three different occasions during the past three weeks, and has disrupted class two or three times each day during the past three weeks.

7. We classify anecdotal record keeping as an interactionalist approach to classroom management. Do you agree? If so, what makes it an interactionalist approach? If not, how should it be classified?

8. Examine the sample anecdotal record included in the chapter. Explain whether you concur with the following decisions made by the teacher: (a) to continue the intervention after 4/23 and 4/24; (b) to stop the record after 4/30. Justify your decisions.

9. What types of misbehavior constitute sufficient grounds for exclusion from the classroom? Justify your answers.

CHAPTER 10
Seeking Outside Assistance

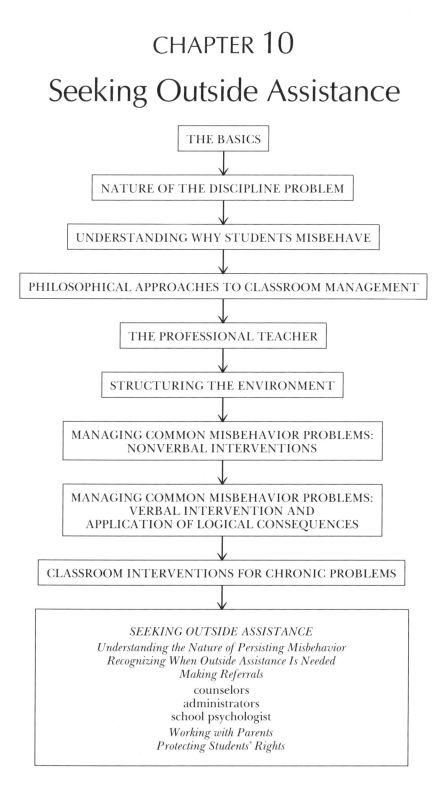

THE BASICS

NATURE OF THE DISCIPLINE PROBLEM

UNDERSTANDING WHY STUDENTS MISBEHAVE

PHILOSOPHICAL APPROACHES TO CLASSROOM MANAGEMENT

THE PROFESSIONAL TEACHER

STRUCTURING THE ENVIRONMENT

MANAGING COMMON MISBEHAVIOR PROBLEMS:
NONVERBAL INTERVENTIONS

MANAGING COMMON MISBEHAVIOR PROBLEMS:
VERBAL INTERVENTION AND
APPLICATION OF LOGICAL CONSEQUENCES

CLASSROOM INTERVENTIONS FOR CHRONIC PROBLEMS

SEEKING OUTSIDE ASSISTANCE
Understanding the Nature of Persisting Misbehavior
Recognizing When Outside Assistance Is Needed
Making Referrals
counselors
administrators
school psychologist
Working with Parents
Protecting Students' Rights

PRINCIPLES OF CLASSROOM MANAGEMENT

35. Professional teachers recognize that some chronic misbehavior problems are not responsive to treatment within the classroom or are beyond their expertise and necessitate specialized outside assistance.

36. When outside assistance must be sought to manage adequately and appropriately a chronic misbehavior problem, a multidisciplinary team is the most effective approach.

37. Parental support and cooperation with the school is critical when attempting to manage a chronic misbehaving student. Careful planning and skilled conferencing techniques are essential in developing a positive home-school working relationship.

INTRODUCTION

Even when teachers employ all of the strategies suggested in this text to prevent, manage, and solve discipline problems, there are some students who simply cannot be managed effectively in the classroom without some type of specialized outside assistance or intervention. Problems of misbehavior in some cases remain unresponsive to the most skilled and diligent classroom management principles or approaches. Students with unmanageable discipline problems are draining on both the teacher and classmates. They are a negative influence, which distracts from the overall positive educational climate of the classroom environment. Such students are a continual source of frustration to the teacher and cause the teacher to question his professional competence. It is very important for teachers to acknowledge that there are certain circumstances under which teachers, without experiencing any sense of doubt in their own competence of effectiveness, should and must seek outside support and expertise. In fact, the mark of a skilled professional is to recognize the limits of his expertise and to make the necessary and appropriate consultation and referrals without a sense of professional inadequacy.

Sometimes the first referral is a teacher-initiated contact with the parents through written correspondence or a phone conversation. Teachers should make this contact when (1) the misbehavior is a minor surface behavior that continues after the teacher employs the strategies discussed in this text and (2) the teacher is confident that parental input is all that is needed to assist the teacher in managing the misbehavior. The contact should be made only after the student has been notified that if improvement is not forthcoming his parents will be informed of his behavior because the primary responsibility for controlling his behavior rests with the student, not his parents. Often this in itself will bring the desired change. If not, parental contact is made and usually results in negative consequences at home, which are enough to motivate a change in school behavior.

At other times student behavior is such that the teacher decides that parental contact would not be sufficient to remedy the problem and he needs outside expertise to understand and cope with the disruptive student. In such cases parental contact comes after consultation with other professional staff members. Such consultation ensures that parents will be provided with an adequate description of the problem, an explanation of the intervention strategies attempted, and a comprehensive proposed plan of action.

Although parental contact may or may not be the first step in seeking outside assistance, it is critical that when this contact is made, it sets the stage for a cooperative home-school relationship. For this to occur, often it is necessary to overcome negative, defensive parental perceptions and attitudes toward the school and/or the teacher. Thus, such contacts must be preceded by careful planning and preparation. In addition to the parents, a consultative team that may include counselors, administrators, school psychologists, learning specialists, and school social workers many times is called on to bring specialized expertise to bear on understanding and working with both the student who is displaying unremitting misbehavior and his family. In some cases referrals outside the school may be necessary.

This chapter discusses the nature of persisting misbehavior, when a teacher needs to seek outside assistance, preparing for and conducting parent conferences, and the roles of other school staff members. The final section details behaviors that may not be disruptive but which teachers must be aware of because they may be symptomatic of other serious problems that require outside referrals.

THE NATURE OF PERSISTING MISBEHAVIOR

Chapter Three, which dealt exclusively with why children misbehave, concluded for the most part that much of the daily disruptive behavior observed in children is a normal reaction to society in general and to recent societal changes in particular, as well as characteristics of developmental stages that all children go through. Obviously some children display disruptive behavior that is more frequent or more deviant than that exhibited by others, but again most of this is viewed as being within the range of normal childhood and adolescent behavior and usually is effectively managed through the techniques and strategies suggested in this text. However there are some students that still display behaviors that have resisted all attempts at modification.

These students often are reacting to negative influences within their environment. These influences at times are quite obvious and identifiable, while at other times are rather subtle. When trying to understand a long-term pattern of misbehavior, environmental influences must be viewed in a summative manner. Long-term behavior is not understood by examining one or two snapshots of specific environmental influences; instead a history of influences must be considered.

One concept that is especially helpful in understanding historical influences is the success-failure ratio. This is the ratio of how much success a student experiences in his daily life to how much failure he experiences. It may be stated with a reasonable degree of confidence that most students exhibit adaptive, productive behavior and feel good about themselves when they are successful. In contrast, when students do not meet with a reasonable degree of success, they become frustrated and discouraged and their behavior becomes maladaptive and destructive (Glasser, 1969). Despite the hard, resistant, and defiant facade so characteristic of the student with chronic behavior difficulties, further study of the student often reveals a very damaged and vulnerable inner core. These students often are encased in a negative and failure-oriented system of experiences, beliefs, and expectations, which remains highly resistant to normal classroom influences. More particularly, they are no longer responsive to normal classroom rewards and reinforcements intended to increase the success-failure ratio. What are the influences that cause students to have a low success-failure ratio?

Failure in the Classroom Environment

There are students who simply are not or cannot find a way to be successful at school in academic, social, and/or extracurricular activities. For such students, school is a daily source of failure, which causes a significant reduction in their overall success-failure ratio. Success in school and behavior are so interrelated that it has been concluded that "most misbehaving students do not feel successful in school" (Wolfgang and Glickman, 1980, p. 112).

In some cases, careful observation and evaluation uncover a previously undiagnosed learning disability, which sometimes becomes more apparent as the child moves toward higher grade levels, where the conceptual demands of the curriculum are increased. Such students are not involved or interested in what they learn, and their misbehavior serves as a protection from further hurt and feelings of inadequacy (Wolfgang and Glickman, 1980). In other cases a student may possess personality traits that cause classmates to pick on or ignore him.

The behavioral difficulties that these students display may be understood as an expression of the child's frustration and discouragement, which many times escalate into the observable behaviors of anger and retaliation. For these students, reward and gratification stem more from their success at focusing attention on themselves than from meeting appropriate behavioral and instructional objectives.

Failure Outside the Classroom Environment

Some students exhibit extreme behaviors in response to their teachers, classroom expectations, or academic pressures that seem to have little to do with the day-to-day realities of the class environment. Extreme apprehension, distrust, disappointment, hurt, anger, or outrage are triggered under the most benign circumstances or the slightest provocation. It is not unusual for a teacher to find such a student reacting to him as if he were an abusive or rejecting parent, other adult, or peer.

These distorted emotional responses are reactions that often have been shaped outside the classroom and reflect problems that exist within the home and family or long-standing problems with peers. This conclusion is somewhat substantiated by studies that concluded that 50 percent of children who experience behavior problems at school also experience them at home (Johnson, Bolstad, and Lobitz, 1976; Patterson, 1974). Some students with long-standing interpersonal relationship difficulties find the normal social pressures of the classroom just too much to tolerate. As with failure within the classroom, failure outside the classroom also lowers a student's perceived success-failure ratio.

In some instances initial failure outside the classroom may actually lower the student's perceived success-failure ratio more than initial failure within the classroom. This is so because the student not only experiences difficulties outside the classroom but also the resultant distorted, inappropriate classroom behaviors cause additional experiences of failure within the classroom.

Failure as a Result of Primary Mode of Conduct

For some students, misbehavior seems to be the natural state of affairs. Their behavior seems not to be a reaction to any apparent environmental influence but rather an expression of their own internal tension, restlessness, and discomfort. These students' difficulties emerge during the preschool and kindergarten years. They are seen by their teachers as immature, emotionally volatile, inattentive, demanding, overly aggressive, and self-centered. They are usually quick to react with anger to any sort of stress or frustration. This pattern, although difficult and frustrating, too often is explained simplistically as the natural expression of the "difficult child" temperament. For some there is a significant improvement with age; for others, the problems intensify with the passage of time, as negative reactions to home and school further reduce the success-failure ratio.

WHEN OUTSIDE ASSISTANCE IS NEEDED

How does a teacher decide at what point he should seek outside consultation or referral? Although there are no rules, two general guidelines can assist with the decision. First, referral is warranted when a teacher recognizes that a developing problem is beyond his professional expertise. When a true professional recognizes this, he then takes the necessary actions to identify and contact alternative sources of specialized professional assistance. Second, the more deviant, disruptive, or frequent the behavior, the more imperative it is to make referrals. Specifically this means referral is necessary

1. When a misbehaving student does not improve even after the hierarchical interventions described in this text have been exhausted
2. When the hierarchical approach has resulted in improvement, but the student continues to manifest problems that disrupt either teaching or learning

Finally there are students who were never discipline problems but show signs that may be symptoms of serious problems needing the attention of professionals with specialized training. Symptoms of social difficulty, illness, anxiety, depression, learning difficulty, abuse, substance abuse, suicide, and family discord become apparent to the knowledgeable and sensitive teacher. A more detailed discussion of these symptoms is included in a later section of this chapter.

THE REFERRAL PROCESS

This text has continually stressed that except for very serious problems, teachers should attempt to manage student misbehavior within the classroom before seeking outside assistance. When assistance is warranted, it is essential that the school have a referral system already established so that a teacher has ready access to a network of school support personnel who are trained to cope with children with unremitting problematic classroom behavior. Most often the first referral is to a counselor and/or an administrator (typically a principal in elementary school and an assistant principal at the secondary level).

Contact with the counselor and/or the appropriate administrator helps ensure that parents are not called on prematurely in the referral process before the school has explored all the possible interventions at its disposal. Except for serious problems, parents should be contacted only when it is apparent that the school has no other alternatives (Jones and Jones, 1981).

If it becomes necessary for parents to be called on, in most cases they will be much more responsive and cooperative if they see a history of teacher and school interventions. Working closely with parents of chronically misbehaving students is so critical that this area will be dealt with in depth later in this chapter, but first, what role does the administrator or counselor play?

The Role of the Counselor

In schools where there is a counselor on the professional staff, once the decision is made to seek outside assistance, the teacher contacts the student's counselor immediately. Teachers need to be prepared to present documented data on the student's misbehavior and all approaches attempted so far by the teacher to manage the disruptive behavior. Anecdotal records and behavior contracts discussed in Chapter Nine are excellent sources for this information.

In difficult situations, many times a teacher tends to become blinded and sometimes stuck, repetitively applying strategies that do not work. The counselor as an outside observer is quite useful, such as a coach observing an athlete, and is in a position as a neutral onlooker with a fresh view to see flaws and make suggestions regarding possible modifications. The counselor may want to explore further the student's behavior, the teacher's style, the nature of the teacher-student interaction, and the learning environment by visiting the classroom or by scheduling further conferences with the student and/or teacher, either alone or together. The counselor then is able to play an active role in providing objective feedback and offering suggestions for new approaches and/or working closely with the student to develop more acceptable behaviors.

The counselor also helps in improving the strained teacher-student relationship by assisting both the teacher and the student simultaneously. He provides support to the teacher as the teacher copes with the stress of managing a chronically disruptive child and is also available to the student to discuss classroom problems that arise from behavior, academics, or social interactions. By having a thorough understanding of the viewpoints of both the teacher and student, the counselor is able to act as an intermediary.

Often problems are adequately handled at the counselor level. However in those cases in which this is not sufficient, additional consultants are called on. Typically they may include an administrator, parents, or school psychologist.

The Role of the Administrator

In many cases of chronic misbehavior, certain in-school strategies or decisions that must be made require the authoritative and administrative power of the principal or assistant principal. For example, the decision to remove a student from a classroom for an extended period of time, to change a student's teacher, and in-school or out-of-school suspensions all include additional space and/or personnel, which must be approved and supported by an administrator. Also if the decision involves referral to a learning specialist or the school psychologist, an administrator's approval is often necessary.

For very deviant behavior, action at the school district level, such as placement into specialized educational settings outside the school or expulsion, may be required. In such instances the administrator will be required by the district to be thoroughly familiar with the student's history and be expected to provide testimony at any hearings that may be held.

The Role of the School Psychologist

If there are indications that a student's conduct problems are rooted in deeper and more pervasive personality disturbances or family problems, the clinical resources of the school psychologist should be sought. The initial role of the school psychologist is one of more intensive evaluation and diagnostic study. Although the school psychologist will apply independent observational, interview, and testing techniques, these are really an extension of the rich day-to-day data that have already been accumulated by the classroom teacher, counselor, and administrator. The results of these additional evaluative studies may lead to recommendations for further study, specialized programming, or referral to outside resources.

The Consultation Team

At this point in the referral process there are a number of professionals involved, including the teacher, the counselor, an administrator, and possibly a learning specialist or school psychologist. It is most useful to view this as a consultative team approach. Although a team approach is not formalized in many schools, some type of team work is usually necessary in dealing with difficult students. A team approach is quite effective in delineating responsibilities and keeping the lines of communication open and clearly defined. The team approach facilitates group problem solving, offers a multidisciplinary perspective, and reduces the possibility that any one individual will become overburdened with a sense of responsibility for "the problem." As with any team, a leader is needed to coordinate the team's efforts. The counselor, being thoroughly familiar with the student and having quick access to all members of the team, is in a good position to act as a coordinator.

Many school districts have realized that teachers cannot be expected to possess the expertise necessary to deal effectively with all the learning and behavior problems that are found in today's classrooms. To provide support in modifying these problems many districts have implemented school-based consultation teams that follow systematic models of assistance and/or intervention. These consultative teams are often referred to as Intervention Assistance Teams, Motivational Resource Teams, and so on. Many districts in the State of Ohio have implemented such an approach by providing school staffs with in-service training on Intervention Assistant Team models and then allowing each school to develop a model to meet the unique needs of the school (Champaign Co. and Holmes, Co.).

WORKING WITH PARENTS

When it is apparent that the teacher and school have explored all the interventions at their disposal, parents should be contacted. It is essential to have the support and cooperation of parents in working effectively with a chronically misbehaving student. Often however, parental contacts are characterized by negative reactions and defensiveness on the part of both parents and the teacher. It is imperative that the negativity is minimized and the positive support and cooperation are maximized. This takes careful planning and much skill in interpersonal interaction and conferencing techniques on the part of the consultative team members (Canter, 1989).

When Parents Should Be Contacted

Parents need to be contacted under the following conditions:

1. When the student displays unremitting misbehavior after the teacher and the school have employed all available interventions
2. When the consultative team decides that the student needs a change in teacher or schedule
3. When the consultative team decides that the student should be removed from a class for an extended period of time or from school for even one day
4. When the consultative team decides that the student needs to be tested for learning, emotional, or physical difficulties
5. When the consultative team decides that outside specialists such as psychiatrists, physicians, and social workers, are required

The Importance of Working with Parents

Whether a student is disruptive or not, all parents have the right to be informed of their child's school progress, both behaviorally and academically. In addition, parental support of school has a major impact on a child's positive attitude toward school (Jones, 1980). When the student's parents feel good about the teacher and school, it is more likely that the student will receive encouragement and be reinforced for appropriate school behavior (Jones and Jones, 1981). Parents can be one of the teacher's strongest allies. Thus, parental support and cooperation must be cultivated by the teacher and other school staff members. To this end schoolwide programs such as parent visitation, back-to-school nights, parent-teacher organizations, parent advisory boards, and volunteer programs have been instituted. Individual teachers complement these efforts by communicating positive aspects of children's schooling to their parents through notes and phone calls, inviting parents to call when they have any questions, and requiring students to take home graded assignments and tests.

When the school has exhausted its alternatives in attempting to manage a chronically misbehaving student, it is essential that parents be contacted and made members of the consulting team. There are a number of reasons for involving parents. With few exceptions, parents care greatly about their children and parents exert much influence on their children. When parents communicate to students the seriousness of the problems that are occurring in school, while at the same time valuing both the importance of education and the school's efforts, the likelihood of a successful resolution is increased. Also many children, especially adolescents, are no longer motivated or responsive to the reinforcements and rewards a school can provide. Parents, on the other hand, provide a wider variety of more attractive rewards. A system of home rewards contingent on school behavior is an effective means for modifying classroom behavior (Ayllon, Garber, and Pisor 1975). Such a system is illustrated in Case 41.

Case 41: In Order to Drive You Must Speak Spanish

Dawn is 15 years old. Her grades have gone from B's to D's in a couple of subjects. The decline in academic performance results from inattentiveness and poor study habits. After the teacher and counselor speak to Dawn without any noticeable improvement her parents are called.

Dawn explains that she doesn't like Spanish or social studies and doesn't see why she needs these subjects anyway. Her teachers try to explain why these subjects are important, especially in today's world. Finally her parents intervene and point out to Dawn that she has scheduled driver's education for the spring semester. They explain that if she expects to be able to drive she must demonstrate responsibility and discipline and one way to do so is to do well in all school subjects. They finally decide that unless her grades improve she will not be allowed to take Driver's Education nor obtain her learner's permit.

Her teachers and parents keep in contact, and by the end of the fall semester her grades are again B's.

Parents thus represent an interested party that can provide an inexpensive continuous treatment resource augmenting school efforts. The school's positive working relationship with parents often is the most critical component for effectively managing a disruptive student. However this is not automatically forthcoming. Much effort and planning goes into developing a productive relationship between home and school.

Understanding Parents

As stated previously many parents have negative feelings toward their child's teachers and school. Similarly many teachers and other school personnel feel uncomfortable contacting parents; they state that it is one of the least desirable and difficult aspects of their work. Educators complain that parent contacts often necessitate using considerable time, usually before or after school, which could be put to better use. Teachers also complain that they are often intimidated by parents because of the low status teachers have in many communities; the perception of many parents that the teacher should be able to do his job and maintain discipline; and the fact that education is funded by tax dollars, and so parents believe that they should be able to judge and monitor teacher performance. However, since teachers and other school staff are professionals, they must not allow these feelings to influence their behavior to the point where it jeopardizes gaining the support and cooperation of parents.

Unfortunately many parental contacts do result in increased distrust, apprehension, and dissatisfaction for both parents and teachers and cause further deterioration in efforts to assist the disruptive student. The members of the consultative team must therefore create an atmosphere that facilitates a change of negative parental perceptions and assumptions into positive ones. This is more easily accomplished when the consultative team members better understand the parents' perspectives.

It is well accepted that many children who chronically misbehave in school display similar behaviors at home. Parents of those students often have been frustrated by their own failures in managing their child. Since parents consider children to be extensions of themselves and products of their parenting, they are not anxious to have reminders of how inadequate they have been in raising their child. Sometimes they have experienced a long history of negative feedback from teachers, counselors, and administrators, and they are quite wary of any sort of school contact. These school contacts may very well have created a feeling of powerlessness and humiliation because some parents feel everyone is blaming them for their child's misbehavior. These parents react by withdrawing, resisting, or angrily counterattacking and blaming the school for their child's problems.

Under such circumstances the school-parent communication system becomes distorted and tense, increasing the parents' sense of alienation from the school. This alienation is passed onto the child, lessening the possibility of the school working with the parents to find an acceptable means to redirect the student toward acceptable behavior. Under such circumstances the teachers and school staff wait for the student to move through the grades or drop out, while the parents move back and forth between feeling that "no news is good news" and frustration and anger with the school's ineffectiveness in working with their child. This understandable standstill doesn't have to develop. Through careful planning and the use of proper conferencing skills, the school consultative team can do much toward gaining the needed support and cooperation from parents.

Conducting Parent Conferences

When the consultative team determines that conditions exist that warrant parental involvement, the counselor, who is the coordinator, usually makes the first contact. The counselor normally expects some degree of defensiveness on the part of the parent, especially if the student has had a history of school misbehavior. This attitude is understood and not taken personally. The tone of this initial contact is extremely important in developing a cooperative working relationship. The cause of the school's concern is stated clearly and honestly. The climate of the conversation is "How can we work as a team to best meet your child's needs?" rather than "Here we go again!" or "We've done everything we can; now it's up to you."

Once a conference has been scheduled, it is important to ensure that the experience will be positive so that the parents will return and work with, not against, the school personnel. The first decision to be made is, who will attend the conference? Should all the members of the consultative team be in attendance? Should the student be at the conference? The answers depend on the particular problem, the amount of expertise that must be present to explain the situation clearly, the approaches that have been tried, and who should be available to answer any questions that may arise. In addition, it must be kept in mind that the conference must be conducted in a manner that is least threatening to the parents; this often equates to fewer people. In most circumstances, the initial conference is adequately conducted by the counselor or administrator and the teacher. Students are usually in attendance at the initial meeting unless the problem includes discussing behavior or other signs that indicate serious health, emotional, or legal problems.

At the conference, the counselor, who is the coordinator, begins by introducing all in attendance, thanking the parents for their willingness to attend, and outlining the goal of the conference. Throughout the conference the counselor ensures that everyone has an equal chance to express his viewpoint. The counselor also looks for any signs that indicate that the conference is deteriorating into a debate or blaming session and acts rapidly to defuse the situation if it arises by redirecting the conference back to the major purpose of how best to meet the student's needs.

Appropriate interpersonal and conferencing skills must be familiar to and practiced by all professionals in attendance. Some of these skills are to be friendly, to be supportive, and to use active listening, which includes paraphrasing to ensure proper understanding by all included (See Chapter Nine). The teacher should be prepared to have some positive things to say about the student. Information should be elicited through the use of questions rather than directive statements aimed at the student or parents.

It is essential that neither the child nor the parents be attacked, disparaged, or blamed. However, parents and the student may do just such things to the teacher or other school officials. If this occurs, some educators naturally feel a need to defend their competence. It is important to remember one need not defend one's professional competence with words, but with behavior.

One of the best means to demonstrate professional competence is through the use of previously collected data, readily available to illustrate and demonstrate the concerns of the school and the need for the conference. Data to be sufficient should include a history of objective and specific information about the student's behaviors and the actions taken by the teacher and the school to manage them. Anecdotal records are an excellent source for this data (see Chapter Nine). These data provide a record, which (1) reduces the likelihood of the conference turning into a debate, (2) illustrates that the problem is not exaggerated, and (3) defuses any attempt by the parent to suggest that the school did not take appropriate and necessary actions.

Throughout the conference the parents' and student's feelings, viewpoint, and suggestions continually are actively solicited. The outcome of the conference, it is hoped, is an agreed-upon course of action or the decision that in the near future the counselor will contact the parents with a suggested course of action. The meeting ends on an optimistic note with a summary, a show of appreciation, and an encouraging statement that with both the home and school working as a team, a successful outcome is likely.

With some students, the decision will be made to try additional school and/or classroom strategies with little additional parental involvement. This decision is usually a result of revealing information that allows the school to design additional appropriate strategies in working with the student or because the parents clearly demonstrate their disinterest in any additional involvement, as does Sharon's mother in Case 42.

Case 42: "I Can't Be of Any Help"

Sharon is in eighth grade. Her behavior is perfect. She is of average intelligence, rarely absent, well dressed, and has some friends. She seems like the typical, happy eighth-grader. However, she never leaves for home at three o'clock. Instead she always asks one of her teachers if she can stay to help with anything. If there is nothing for her to do, she just sits and talks. As the end of the first report period approaches, it appears that Sharon will receive all D's and F's.

Most of her teachers have spoken with her and she has also been referred to the counselor. Throughout all of these sessions she maintains that she is happy and nothing is wrong. Extra academic help is given but results in no improvement.

Before the issuing of report cards, a conference is scheduled at which Sharon, her mother, the counselor, and teachers are present. Sharon's mother arrives; she is well dressed, well spoken, and seems somewhat concerned. She listens attentively to each teacher explain Sharon's poor academic performance. Afterwards she states, "Sharon's Dad left five years ago. I'm busy. I need to look after myself and get my life moving in the right direction. I have a career and I date a lot. Truthfully, besides buying her clothes and making sure she eats properly, I haven't much time for Sharon. I would truly appreciate anything any of you can do to help Sharon because I know I won't be much help. Is there anything else?"

Sharon's mother is atypical, not because she is so disinterested but because she so openly and honestly stated so. In such situations, there is sometimes a tendency on the part of the school personnel to give up and adopt an attitude that "if they don't care, then we've done what we can." However, children should never be denied access to potentially effective school intervention programs because parents are disinterested, uncooperative, or unsupportive (Walker, 1979).

With other students, increased parental involvement will be requested. This occurs when it is apparent that parental involvement will probably improve the child's behavior significantly or there is evidence of a deficiency in parenting skills. Many school districts now provide classes or employ parent educators to work with parents of children experiencing behavior problems in school.

Typically there are four levels of parent involvement: (1) informing parents of the intervention and keeping them informed of progress, (2) developing a parent praise program at home based on feedback from the school, (3) developing a structured home reward system based on specific school performance criteria, and (4) changing parenting style through parenting education programs. More detailed discussion of parental involvement as well as a discussion of parent education programs is found in Jones

(1980) and Walker (1979). A thorough examination of specialized education and intervention strategies for the chronically disruptive adolescent is
covered by Sabatino and Mauser (1978a, 1978b).

SYMPTOMS OF SERIOUS PROBLEMS

Whether or not accompanied by disruptive and/or academic difficulties,
some students display symptoms that indicate serious problems. These
problems may be related to physical or emotional health or associated with
an abusive home or with substance abuse. All of these areas may fall outside
the expertise and domain of the school. An aware teacher often recognizes
these telltale signs and notifies the appropriate school official, usually the
counselor, who then decides the proper next step.

Some of the signs that may be significant include the following:

1. *Changes in physical appearance.* Often students reveal their underlying problems
   through sudden changes in their overall physical appearance. Posture, dress,
   and grooming habits are reflections of underlying mood and self-image, and a
   student's deterioration in these habits should be noted with concern. More
   striking changes such as rapid weight loss or gain, particularly in light of the
   dramatic increase in eating disorders among high school students, should be
   investigated. Unusual soreness, bruises, cuts, or scarring are not only signs of
   possible neglect or abuse but may also represent self-mutilative or other self-
   destructive tendencies.

2. *Changes in activity level.* Teachers need to be aware of the significance of
   changes in activity level. Excessive tardiness, lethargy, absenteeism, and a
   tendency to fall asleep in class may result from a variety of problems including
   depression and substance abuse. Hyperactivity, impulsivity, reduced frustration, tolerance, and overaggressiveness also may represent the student's effort
   to deal with emotional unrest and discomfort.

3. *Changes in personality.* Emotional disturbances in children and adolescents are
   sometimes reflected in very direct forms of expression and behavior. The
   seemingly well-adjusted child who is suddenly sad, easily agitated, or has angry
   outbursts not characteristic of his prior behavior should be closely observed
   and monitored.

4. *Changes in achievement status.* A decline in a student's ability to focus on his
   work, persist at his studies, or produce or complete work successfully is often
   an indication of the interfering and draining effects of emotional turmoil or
   significant changes in the home environment.

5. *Changes in health or physical abilities.* Complaints of not being able to see or hear,
   when it appears the student is paying attention, should be referred to the
   nurse for follow-up. Complaints of frequent headaches, stomach aches, diz-
   ziness, unhealing sores, and skin rashes and frequent bathroom use lead to
   concern for the student's health.

6. *Changes in socialization.* Children who spend most of the time by themselves,
   seem to have no friends, and are socially withdrawn are not often identified as
   problem students because their symptoms do not have a disturbing impact on

Changes in personality and socialization are sometimes symptoms of serious problems needing referrals to specialized professionals. (Ken Karp)

the classroom. These students are described as quiet or strange and drift from one grade to another without appropriate attention and concern. However, they often leave a trail of signs of their underlying misery in their behavior, artwork, and creative writing samples.

In most cases of serious problems, schools are able to arrange for or make referrals to a host of specialized professionals, including psychologists, psychiatrists, nutritionists, medical doctors, social workers, and legal authorities. However appropriate intervention rests with the aware and concerned teacher who must make the initial observations and referral.

LEGAL ASPECTS OF SEEKING OUTSIDE ASSISTANCE

There are some legal issues that must be considered to protect children's and parents' rights when seeking outside assistance. Most school districts are aware of these laws and have developed appropriate procedures to abide by them.

P.L. 94-142 requires that parental consent must be obtained before conducting any evaluation that might change the educational classification, evaluation, or placement of a child. Evaluation is defined as any selective procedure not used with all children in a school, class, or grade.

The release of student files is regulated by the Buckley Amendment (P.L. 93-380, as amended by P.L. 93-568). Briefly, schools may not release a student's records to outside sources without written consent from the parents. This release must state the reasons for the release, the specific records to be released, and who will receive the records.

Many states also have laws that require teachers to report any signs of child abuse. Many of these have provisions that impose fines on school personnel who fail to meet this responsibility.

There are many areas such as freedom of expression, dress and grooming, corporal punishment, and student activities in which students have specific rights. Unfortunately many of these rights are infringed upon by certain disciplinary actions taken by teachers and school administrators. These infringements usually go unnoticed or unchallenged.

However, "when the infraction is of a very serious nature involving possible suspension or expulsion of the student, the legal rights of the student become of paramount importance" (Melnick and Grosse, 1984 p. 147). School officials must be aware of these rights and ensure that they are protected.

SUMMARY

Under certain circumstances, some type of specialized or out-of-school assistance is required for students. Some students simply do not experience the degree of success in the classroom that supports the development and maintenance of appropriate behavior. Their conduct problems remain unremitting despite the application of appropriate hierarchical strategies or they show other signs and symptoms indicative of serious underlying disturbances.

A team approach, which may include the student, parents, teacher, counselor, administrator, and outside specialists, is an effective means for expanded evaluation and for the development of specialized interventions that may extend beyond the normal classroom. The counselor typically plays the crucial role of team coordinator in communicating with and integrating the efforts of parents and in-school and out-of-school consultants. The support and cooperation of parents is critical to increase the likelihood of successful intervention. Any negative parental attitudes must be defused. This is best accomplished through careful planning and the skilled use of conferencing techniques when working with parents. Protecting students' rights throughout any process focused on managing misbehavior is paramount.

REFERENCES

AYLLON, T., GARBER, S., and PISOR, K. (1975). The elimination of discipline problems through a combined school-home motivation system. *Behavior Therapy, 6,* 616–626.

CANTER, L. (1989). Assertive discipline—More than names on the board and marbles in a jar. *Phi Delta Kappan, 71,* 1, 57–61.

Champaign Co., Ohio, Graham Local Schools, *Intervention Assistance Team Models.* Rosewood, OH.

GLASSER, W. (1969). *Schools Without Failure.* New York: Harper & Row.

Holmes Co., Holmes Local Schools. *Intervention Assistance Team Models.* Belin, OH.

JOHNSON, S. M., BOLSTAD, O. D., and LOBITZ, G. K. (1976). Generalization and contrast phenomena in behavior modification with children. In E. J. Marsh, L. A. Hamerlynck, and L. C. Handy (Eds.), *Behavior Modification and Families.* New York: Brunner/Mazell.

JONES, V. F. (1980). *Adolescents with Behavior Problems.* Boston: Allyn & Bacon.

JONES, V. F., AND JONES, L. S. (1981). *Responsible Classroom Discipline.* Boston: Allyn & Bacon.

MELNICK, N., and GROSSE, W. J. (1984). Rights of students: A review. *Educational Horizons,* Summer, pp. 145–149.

PATTERSON, G. R. (1974). Intervention for boys with conduct problems: Multiple settings, treatments and criteria. *Journal of Consulting and Clinical Psychology, 42,* 471–481.

SABATINO, D. A., and MAUSER, A. J. (1978a). *Intervention Strategies for Specialized Secondary Education.* Boston: Allyn & Bacon.

SABATINO, D. A., and MAUSER, A. J. (1978b). *Specialized Education in Today's Secondary Schools.* Boston: Allyn & Bacon.

WALKER, H. M. (1979). *The Acting-Out-Child: Coping with Classroom Disruption.* Boston: Allyn & Bacon.

WOLFGANG, G. H., and CLICKMAN, C. D. (1980). *Solving Discipline Problems: Strategies for Classroom Teachers.* Boston: Allyn & Bacon.

EXERCISES

1. An extremely important variable that influences student behavior is the student's success-failure ratio. There are many areas in which students experience success and failure, such as the academic, social, and extracurricular. List several specific areas in a school setting in which students can experience success or failure.

2. The importance of success in specific areas differs depending on the students' age. Using the list of specific areas for success developed in question 1, rate each area's importance for students in elementary, middle, junior high, and senior high school.

3. Some students do not experience much academic success. What can a teacher do to provide successful school experiences for such students?

4. Develop a list of symptoms that could be added to the list in the chapter of potentially serious problems that may warrant outside assistance. Be able to justify why each symptom should be included on the list.

5. Are there any dangers associated with using a list similar to the one developed in question 4? Consider such areas as contextual setting,

duration and severity of behavior, and so on. If so, what can a teacher do to minimize such dangers?

6. Even when students are not exhibiting behavioral problems it is important for teachers to gain the support of parents. In what ways can teachers develop such support?

7. Sometimes teachers may decide to contact the parents before consulting a student's counselor. When should parents be contacted before the counselor?

8. In consultation with your instructor, contact a school (use your own school if you are presently teaching) and identify all the resources available to assist teachers with seriously misbehaving students.

APPENDIX

The Discipline Problem Analysis Inventory (DPAI)

The discipline problem analysis inventory is a tool that the classroom teacher can use to reflect on inappropriate student behavior and its prevention, causes, and solutions. The inventory presents questions teachers can ask themselves regarding the development of hierarchial management plans or a particular student misbehavior. Part I of the inventory contains questions regarding the prevention of misbehavior. Part II contains questions regarding the resolution of misbehavior.

PART I: HAVE I DONE ALL I CAN TO PREVENT MISBEHAVIOR?

Chapter One: *The Basics*

1. Do I consider how my behavior affects student behavior?
2. Am I familiar with the principles of classroom management as presented in this book?
3. Do I employ a hierarchical approach to classroom management?

Chapter Two: *Nature of the Discipline Problem*

1. Do the behaviors I am trying to correct constitute discipline problems as defined in the text? Do they interfere with teaching or the rights of others to

learn? Are they psychologically or physically unsafe? Do they destroy property?

2. Do my behaviors contribute to any discipline problems?
3. Do my behaviors maximize the time students spend on learning?
4. Do I deal with motivational behavior problems after the rest of the class is involved in the learning activities?

Chapter Three: *Understanding Why Children Misbehave*

1. Is the misbehavior a result of unmet physiological needs (for example, nourishment, rest, temperature, ventilation, noise, lighting)?
2. Is the misbehavior a result of unmet safety and security needs (for example, fear of other students, teachers, staff members, parents, other adults; insecurity about rules and expectations)?
3. Is the misbehavior a result of unmet needs for belonging and affection?
4. Do I provide opportunities for students to feel significant, competent, and powerful?
5. Is the misbehavior a result of a mismatch between the student's cognitive developmental level and instructional goals, tasks, or methods?
6. Is the misbehavior a result of a mismatch between the student's moral developmental level and my treatment of the student?
7. Is the misbehavior a result of striving to meet the faulty goals of attention, power, revenge, or inadequacy.

Chapter Four: *Philosophical Approaches to Classroom Management*

1. Have I analyzed which power base(s) I employ to manage classroom behavior?
2. Have I asked myself the seven basic questions to analyze which theory of classroom management is consistent with my beliefs about teaching and learning?
3. Do I employ the power base(s) that is consistent with my beliefs about teaching and learning?
4. Are my management behaviors consistent with the power base(s) and theory of management I want to employ?

Chapter Five: *The Professional Teacher*

1. Do I plan my lessons to include findings from effective teaching research by
     Including an introduction
     Clearly presenting the content
     Checking for student understanding
     Providing for coached and solitary practice
     Providing for closure and summarization
     Conducting periodic reviews
2. Do I increase student motivation to learn by considering student interests, student needs, instruction novelty and variety, student success, student attributions, tension, feeling tone, feedback, and encouragement?

3. Do I communicate high expectations for learning and behavior by equalizing response opportunities, providing prompt and constructive feedback, and treating each student with personal regard?

4. Do I use questioning to involve students actively in the learning process by asking questions at different cognitive levels and using probing questions, wait time, a variety of techniques to elicit response, and a variety of positive reinforcements?

5. Do I maximize both allocated and engagement time in learning?

6. Do I use criterion-referenced evaluation?

7. Is the content at the appropriate level of difficulty for the student?

Chapter Six: *Structuring the Environment*

1. Do I make my room physically comfortable by considering lighting, ventilation, and noise reduction?

2. Do I design seating arrangements to accommodate the various learning activities?

3. Does the seating arrangement ensure that each student can see the instructional activities, the teacher has close proximity to each student, and seats are not placed in high traffic areas or close to distractions?

4. Do I use my bulletin boards to recognize students and provide students with active participation?

5. Do I develop and teach procedures for everyday routines?

6. Do I analyze the classroom environment to determine the rules needed to protect teaching, learning, safety, and property?

7. Do I clearly communicate the rules and their rationales to students?

8. Do I attempt to obtain student commitments to abide by the rules?

9. Do I teach and evaluate student understanding of the rules?

10. Do I develop and enforce each rule with a natural or logical consequence?

11. Do I analyze student characteristics, teacher characteristics, learning activities, and environmental factors by using the vulnerability index to reduce the occurrence of classroom management problems?

PART II: AM I EFFECTIVELY RESOLVING MISBEHAVIOR?

Chapter Seven: *Managing Common Misbehavior Problems: Nonverbal Intervention*

1. Do I meet the five prerequisites to appropriate student behavior?

    Am I well prepared to teach?

    Do I provide clear directions and expectations?

    Do I ensure student understanding of evaluation criteria?

    Do I clearly communicate, rationalize, and consistently enforce behavioral expectations?

    Do I demonstrate enthusiasm and encouragement and model expected behavior?

2. Do I effectively employ preventative coping skills by changing the pace of

instructions, removing seductive objects, boosting interest, redirecting behavior through nonpunitive time out, reinforcing appropriate behavior, and providing cues?

3. Do I effectively use the remedial coping skills (planned ignoring, signal interference, proximity control, and touch control) in a hierarchical order?

Chapter Eight: *Managing Common Behavior Problems: Verbal Intervention and Application of Logical Consequences*

1. Do I follow the guidelines for using verbal interventions?
    Do I keep them as private as possible?
    Do I make them brief?
    Do I speak to the situation, not the person?
    Do I set limits on behaviors, not feelings?
    Do I avoid sarcasm and belittlement?
2. Do I employ verbal interventions in a hierarchical manner (adjacent reinforcement, call on student, humor, awareness questioning, direct appeal, "I message," positive phrasing, "are not fors," rule reminders, triplets, explicit redirection, "broken record")?
3. Do I use natural and/or logical consequences?
4. When I use consequences do I consistently follow through or use them as threats?

Chapter Nine: *Classroom Interventions for Chronic Problems*

1. Do I effectively use appropriate receiving skills during private conferences with students?
    Do I use nonverbal attending cues?
    Do I use probing questions?
    Do I check perceptions?
    Do I check feelings?
2. Do I effectively use appropriate sending skills during private conferences with students?
    Do I deal in the present?
    Do I make eye contact?
    Do I make statements rather then ask questions?
    Do I use "I" to relate my feelings?
    Am I brief?
    Do I talk directly to the student?
    Do I give the student directions on how to correct the problem?
    Do I check for understanding?
3. Have I reviewed the Behavior Contract Checklist to ensure that I have effectively developed and employed the behavior contract?
    Do I specify the behavior, time period, reward, and evaluation?

Do I provide a motivating reward?

Do I ensure that the student understood, agreed to, and signed the contract?

Do I sign the contract?

Do I, the student, and the student's parents get copies?

4. Have I reviewed the guidelines for initiating and employing anecdotal record keeping to ensure that I have effectively implemented the procedure?

Am I positive?

Do I help the student recognize the past behavior and its negative impact?

Do I explain that the behavior is unacceptable?

Do I explain the anecdotal record procedure?

Do I communicate an expectation for improvement?

Do I attempt to obtain the student's commitment for improved behavior?

Do I record the conference and obtain the student's signature?

5. Do I exclude the student from the classroom and require a written statement of better behavior before allowing the student to return to class?

Chapter Ten: *Seeking Outside Assistance*

1. Do I provide many opportunities for the student to be successful in the classroom?

2. Does the behavior warrant outside consultation?

3. Do I consult with a counselor or an administrator about the chronically misbehaving student?

4. Should parents be contacted?

Does the student display unremitting misbehavior?

Has the consultative team decided that the student needs a change of schedule or teacher; should be removed from class or school for a period of time; should be tested for learning, emotional, or physical difficulties; should be referred to outside specialists?

5. Do I employ the behaviors that allow me to work positively with parents and gain their support and cooperation?

6. Does the student show any behaviors or signs that may be symptomatic of other serious problems?

Has the student undergone changes in physical appearance, activity level, personality, achievement states, health or physical abilities, or socialization?

7. Do I protect student rights?

Index